GENESIS:
A New Teacher's Guide

THE MELTON GRADED CURRICULUM SERIES

| BIBLE | LEVEL ד | בראשית |

GENESIS:
A New Teacher's Guide

by Ruth Zielenziger

Third Edition

Edited by Barry W. Holtz and Miles B. Cohen
Seymour Fox, *Curriculum Supervisor*

The Melton Research Center for Jewish Education
of The Jewish Theological Seminary of America

Copyright © 1991 by The Melton Research Center for Jewish Education
of The Jewish Theoogical Seminary of America, 3080 Broadway,
New York, NY 10027.

All rights reserved.

First edition, 1979
Second edition, 1982

5 4 3 2 1

Manufactured in the United States of America
Design and composition by Bet Sha'ar Press, Inc.

CONTENTS

INTRODUCTION
Teaching Bible …………………………………………………… vii

UNIT I
The First Creation Story ………………………………………… 1
Genesis 1–2:4a

UNIT II
The Second Creation Story ……………………………………… 59
Genesis 2 and 3

UNIT III
After the Garden ………………………………………………… 81
Gen. 4:1–6:4

UNIT IV
The Flood ………………………………………………………… 99
Gen. 6:5–11:32

UNIT V
Stories about Abraham ………………………………………… 135
Genesis 12–24

UNIT VI
The Jacob Stories ……………………………………………… 207
Gen. 25:19–36:43

UNIT VII
The Joseph Story ……………………………………………… 265
Genesis 37–50

APPENDIX A
Supplemental Classroom Activities …………………………… 307
Miriam Brunn Ruberg and Susan Wall

APPENDIX B
Truth and Metaphor in the Bible:
An Essay on Interpretation …………………………………… 333
Fritz A. Rothschild

APPENDIX C
The Concept of God in Jewish Education …………………… 357
Fritz A. Rothschild

INTRODUCTION

Teaching Bible

Genesis: A New Teacher's Guide has been prepared specifically for teaching a class of twelve-year-olds in an afternoon school (the Dalet level). The Melton Research Center's approach to the teaching of Bible can, however, be used for students of all ages, including adults. (With modification it can also be used for students too young to analyze a text. For such children we recommend Shirley Newman's *A Child's Introduction to Torah*, and its accompanying workbook, published by Behrman House.)

Two considerations underlie our approach to teaching Bible. These must be mentioned at the outset:

(a) Do not teach your students anything that they will eventually have to *unlearn*. Do not teach false information which will have to be discarded at some later date.

(b) Do not give your students information if they can discover it for themselves when directed to the proper texts. Information which is discovered firsthand by the student will be more meaningful and better remembered than information presented by the teacher.

In our experience, the most effective way of learning Bible is through a careful analysis of a text, taught by means of a guided discussion, or *inquiry*.

◻ Biblical Inquiry: A Methodology

Students attending a Jewish religious school must, of course, be able to read and know the biblical narrative. Superficial knowledge of the biblical stories, however, is only the first step in teaching a biblical passage. The teacher must next determine what *ideas* can be learned by studying that passage and then decide which of those ideas will be discussed in class.

Biblical inquiry is a method of studying Bible which uses the biblical text itself as data. In conducting an inquiry, one directs questions to specific places in the biblical text, drawing the reader's attention to significant aspects of the text. This inquiry takes place on three different levels: (A) What does the text say? (B) What does the text mean? and (C) What do these ideas mean to me?

(A) What does the text say?

At this point we are only interested in *objective statements*. Opinions or underlying meanings do not belong at this stage. You may want to ask your students to restate the story, explaining difficult words and clarifying possible confusions and misunderstandings. For example, when teaching the first verses of Genesis 3 (about the woman and the serpent in the Garden of Eden), the teacher might want to ask:

— Who are the parties involved?
   (The woman and the serpent.)
— Where does the scene take place?
   (In the garden, in front of the tree.)
— What information does the text give about the serpent?
   (God made him. He is sly.)

The teacher would, however, not ask at this point: "What feelings does the word "sly" evoke in you?" This kind of question belongs to the next stage—it addresses the *meaning* of the text.

You will realize, however, that one cannot always be a "purist." Whenever students restate a given text in their own words some "interpretative" reading is unavoidable. In the biblical passage mentioned above, for example, a student might say that the "serpent tempted the woman." Since the term "tempted" is defensible within the context of the story we would not want to reject the student's answer.

However, should the restatement of the facts be misleading (for example, "The serpent *made* the woman eat"), the teacher will have to direct the student's attention to the text and ask him to defend his statement.

A word of warning: Many teachers consider this first level of text analysis too "simple" or "obvious" and thus skip it altogether. Remember, not all of your students are careful readers.

Have your students use the *Student's Guide for Genesis* in preparation for a lesson or as as a testing device.

(B) What does the text mean?

This level of inquiry is much more difficult than the first. Progress initially may be slow. Textual analysis is a skill which must be learned; once learned, the skill can be applied to other

Introduction ix

texts as well. At first your students may feel that there is little difference between one word or expression and the next. You will have to sensitize them to the different shadings and nuances of words and expressions. For example, what is the impact of Esau saying, "Give me some of that red stuff to *gulp down*" (Gen. 25:30)? It should be relatively easy to teach your students that the text intends to describe Esau here as a boor.

You yourself, as well as your students, will have to defend your answers with textual evidence, by citing the words or verses that substantiate your opinion. It is a good habit to ask: "Where does the text say this?"

Many facts are stated explicitly in the text (e.g., "God made the sky" [Gen. 1:6]). Some facts, however, can only be understood indirectly. Although not *stated*, they are *implied*. A fact can be true (or false) by implication. The statements: "An apple tree cannot grow grapes" is implied by Gen. 1:11–12. Your students should eventually be able to justify an answer by saying that it is either stated in or implied by the text.

Another one of your tasks is to teach your students to distinguish between what a text says and what others have said about it. What Rashi or other commentators have said about a text is not admissible at this stage of our study. By quoting Rashi we rely on authority rather than understanding; thus, we deprive the students of their own struggle with the text.

In a meaningful discussion, a question posed by the teacher should trigger a number of responses from the students. Students should have the opportunity to argue for the plausibility of their replies. All attempts at explanation must be taken seriously. Obviously, many of the questions you may want to ask of the text have been asked of the text before (the same is true of the science teacher who conducts with his students experiments with magnetism or electricity). The fact that the class may reach conclusions that others have reached before does not invalidate the experience of discovery that the students have shared.

Not every interpretation of the text is admissible or valid. An interpretation is not acceptable if it violates either the content of the text or the reality of the biblical cultural milieu. For example, one may not interpret that Abraham failed the test in Genesis 22 (the binding of Isaac) since the text contradicts this statement in Gen. 22:16.

Although the teacher must know in advance what ideas are conveyed by a text and upon which the class will focus its attention, the *process* of inquiry should be open and flexible. The student may give an answer which the teacher had not anticipated. If the answer is defensible based on the *textual* evidence, it deserves due credit. Incorrect answers should be rejected on the basis of *textual* evidence.

Although a teacher must prepare a list of questions to be asked in class, the list should not be followed blindly. The teacher must listen carefully to the students' answers and form the next question accordingly. "Leading questions" should be avoided since they limit the scope of the student's answer. For example, "How do we know Abraham was a man of great faith?" is a leading question because the teacher has told the students in advance in what light they are supposed to regard Abraham. "What do we learn about Abraham in this chapter?" is a better question, since it is open to a variety of responses.

Students should have their copies of the biblical text open throughout the inquiry. You are teaching for understanding, not memorization.

(C) What do these ideas mean to me?

"What meaning does this text have for my life?" This kind of discussion generally takes place at the end of a guided inquiry. For example, in Genesis 3 the man and the woman have acquired the ability to feel shame. You may want to ask your class: "Have you ever felt shame? Why? Did your ability to feel shame in any way influence your future behavior?" This kind of discussion is "freewheeling." Since it is not based on text, no evidence from the text is required.

Fleshing out the text. In general the biblical narrative is skeletal. It concentrates on *actions*. We are not told *why* people act in a certain way, or what they *think* or *feel*. For example, we do not know how Abraham felt on his way to perform the sacrifice of his son Isaac, how Reuben felt when Rachel's son Joseph was born, or if Rachel was involved in the deception of Jacob. These details are left for us to flesh out, ponder, question and speculate about. We are assuming that although the cultural milieu has changed since biblical times, the way in which people act and react in general, has not.

Your students may volunteer many feelings and opinions. By all means, encourage them to do so. At times you may have to direct the discussion since students may lack the life experience to know how people may behave in certain situations. Have your students discuss human nature and the possibilities for change in conduct and actions. Encourage them to identify with the feelings and motivations of the characters. This in itself may prove to be a rewarding educational experience.

Introduction

❐ The Use of Commentaries

As we view the wealth of commentaries past generations have left us, it becomes obvious that throughout the ages different commentators found it necessary to interpret the texts in light of whatever they themselves held true, applying the methods of inquiry that were available to them.

For instance, Abraham Ibn Ezra (1089–1164) was acquainted with Arabic philology and linguistics and therefore could utilize these tools in compiling his commentary. Knowledge of these subjects was not available to Rashi (1040–1105), who lived within the same century but in a different locale. In making the text meaningful, each had his own approach to textual interpretation.

There has never been a single, timeless and authoritative understanding of the biblical texts. It is an *affirmation of our tradition* that we, too, interpret the Bible in light of current knowledge and contemporary science, and in accordance with our needs.

❐ *Peshat* and *Derash*

Traditionally Jews have interpreted the Bible according to one of two modes of interpretation (or a combination of the two). One mode is called *peshat* (פְּשָׁט); the other *derash* (דְּרָשׁ).

Peshat

We use the term *peshat* to refer to the meaning of a particular text *within its original historical and contextual framework*.

In terms of understanding language this means that we study the language of the Bible as it was used in biblical times and not as it may have been used In later or modern Hebrew. For example, although we today use the word *Torah* to describe the Five Books of Moses (the חֻמָּשׁ, or Pentateuch), in the Bible the word means "instruction" (Lev. 14:54: זֹאת הַתּוֹרָה לְכָל־נֶגַע הַצָּרַעַת; Num. 19:14: זֹאת הַתּוֹרָה אָדָם כִּי יָמוּת בְּאֹהֶל). In the above examples we are given the *torah*—the "instruction" of how to behave when *Tzara'at* or death strike home. The word *torah* here could not refer to the Five Books of Moses.

In terms of understanding events, this means that we use the *historical approach*, setting the text in its original cultural environment or milieu. Frequently this is done by comparing the biblical world with other cultures that existed at the same time. We may have to explain to our students, for example, that Sarah's giving her maid Hagar to Abraham as a concubine was within the tradition of the Ancient Near East.

Throughout this *Teacher's Guide* comparisons are made between the cultural milieu of the Bible and that of Mesopotamian societies. For example, we compare the biblical creation story to *Enuma Elish* (the Babylonian creation epic) and the Noah story to the Epic of Gilgamesh (the Bablylonian Flood story). We use these myths and not some other—say, Greek—myths because, according to the Bible, the Hebrews originally came from Mesopotamia. It is the culture of that civilization—both its similarities and its contrasts to the biblical world—which will be the most relevant for understanding the *peshat* of the biblical text. For this purpose we recommend Nahum Sarna's *Understanding Genesis* (Schocken Books), which studies the Bible within its Ancient Near Eastern setting.

Derash

The second traditional mode of interpretation is *derash*. By *derash* we mean interpretation of the text that *disregards* the historical and contextual limits of the text. Gen. 24:1 וַיי בֵּרַךְ אֶת־אַבְרָהָם בַּכֹּל is translated in the New Jewish Publication Society translation as: ". . . and the Lord had blessed Abraham in all things." However, the Rabbis of talmudic times, disregarding all rules of context and grammar, said in a *midrash* (an interpretation resulting from the use of *derash*) that בַּכֹּל was the name of Abraham's daughter! For the Rabbis' value system stated that a man must have at least a son and a daughter. How then could Abraham, the symbol of righteousness, not have had a daughter?

Also consider Genesis 12:5: "Abraham took . . . the persons that they had acquired. . . ." The Midrash (classical collections of *mishrashim*) explains that "Abraham had been converting the men and Sarah had been converting the women," thereby disregarding the text's historical framework and the fact that conversion as such was not known or practiced in early Israelite times. Similarly, the story of Abraham's breaking his father's idols, which is not in the Bible, was told by the Rabbis to explain why God chose Abraham from all other people (Gen. 12:1–4).

If you choose to teach these or other examples of *derash*, your students must know that these stories are not *peshat*. These are not biblical stories, nor do they fit within the historical, contextual limits of text. In addition, students should be able to understand what motivated the Rabbis to tell each *midrash*.

Our first concern is with the *peshat* meaning of the text. However, when we ask ourselves, "What does this text mean to us today?" we are not any longer dealing with the *historical* meaning of a text. We are in effect engaged in the making of a new *midrash*!

Introduction xiii

For example, if we explain Gen. 1:26 ("Let us make man in our image . . . they shall rule . . . the whole earth") as relating to issues of environmental protection, we can assume that this was not the original meaning of the text. Nonetheless, it may be an explanation of significance to us today.

❐ Language and Meaning

It must be emphasized that when we say *peshat* we do not mean the *literal* meaning of the text. The medium of the Torah is language, and language is not always self-explanatory; it often requires interpretation. Words function on many different levels of meaning. Throughout the generations, our Rabbis were aware of the difference between the obvious, literal meaning, and the underlying or metaphorical meanings of a text.

Metaphor

There are at least two ways of talking about ideas. One is abstract, the other metaphorical. Some texts use philosophical abstract language to deal with ideas, but the Bible belongs to the style of literature that uses metaphorical means to express abstract ideas. The word *metaphor* is derived from the Greek *meta-* ("beyond") *phore* ("carry"). *Metaphor* means "carry beyond." A metaphor transfers expressions from one area of experience to another. Hence, when we say that God took us out of Egypt "with a strong hand and an outstretched arm" (Deut. 4:23) or that God brought us to Him "on eagles' wings" (Exod. 19:4) we do not conceive of God actually having a hand, arm, or eagles' wings.

"My love is a red rose" or "My anger is a burning fire" are obvious metaphors. As we use them, we know that we are borrowing the imagery of the rose and the fire from the physical world in order to express our feelings more concretely. Often, however, we are not even aware of the fact that we are using a metaphor. When I ask, "Do you see my point?" and you answer, "Yes," in a literal sense, you are wrong. You do not "see my point" at all, since in reality there is no tangible "point" that you can perceive with your eyes. However, inasmuch as I have been using a metaphor, your answer is correct. A metaphor has a true and real meaning, although not a *literal* meaning, in the Bible. The more abstract the ideas, the more metaphorical the language used to depict them. For example, when we refer to God by calling him *Adonay* (my Lord) or *melekh* (King), we are borrowing terms from the area of human relationships. A metaphor serves to describe the unfamiliar, ineffable and indescribable—in this instance, God—in terms of a known model (a lord, master or king). It thus becomes easier for us to deal with something as complex and overwhelming as God. For example, we read: "God said: 'Let there be light!'" (Gen. 1:3). Instead of saying in abstract terms that the light came into being through the will of God, the text borrows the expression "God said" from the area of human behavior. Just as a king would declare his will through speaking, God's abstract "willing" the light to be is depicted in terms of human speech. For speech is the most natural means for a person to let his thoughts be known.

A word of warning: Metaphors serve as tools for dealing with the abstract, but they are never *identical* to the idea they help to convey. We can never assume that everything that is true of the metaphor can be transferred to the abstract idea. Thus, taking our example of God saying, "Let there be light," we are not to understand that God really spoke in a human voice. Students' questions as to whether God used Sephardic or Ashkenazic pronunciation of the Hebrew language reflect an overly literal reading of the text. The metaphor has to be taken seriously as being true to a limited degree, but *it must not be taken literally.*

Parable

The Bible also uses parables (from the Greek *paraballein,* "to throw beside," "to compare"). A parable is a short fictional story or narrative from which moral or spiritual truth is drawn.

The parable operates on at least two levels of meaning. One level is "within" the text—the story itself, which can be understood in its own terms. Another level is the meaning "beyond" the text. Other meanings are alluded to by the first. For example, the book of Jonah is a parable. It can stand on its own as a story about a man and a big fish. But the story has other levels of meaning at which certain morals or lessons can be learned.

Myth

The Bible also contains myths. A *myth* in the technical sense that we use it is an extended metaphor. It is a narrative or story that uses subjects and actions from known experience to express the ideas, relationships and values which are essential to a particular culture or community. (We are not using the term *myth* in its popular sense of "that which is not true," "a fable" or "illusion.")

In the same way that the metaphor says something true about the object being described (love is like a rose in *some* respects) so a myth reflects some truth about God, mankind, and the world. For example, whether the Flood did or did not take place in history is irrelevant to us. The Noah story is a myth that teaches us about the ways in which God reacts to human conduct.

Beginning myths

Some myths deal with the beginnings of a people—how that people came to be. These myths are called *beginning myths*. Different peoples have different beginning myths. The particular beginning myth of a people has a great deal of influence on their way of life, ethics and observances. Such myths actually express the concerns and values of the people who tell the story.

In *Enuma Elish,* the Babylonian creation myth, beginning is conceived as struggle and discord. Men and women are created to serve the needs of the gods. They have no value in their own right. According to this myth, the gods made the world out of the dead body of the goddess Tiamat, and they made mankind out of the blood of the god Kingu. In the Babylonian myths, gods, man and world are all made out of the same raw material. This reflects the Babylonian view that it is possible for human to become semi-divine or even divine.

The opening story of Genesis also deals with the relationships between God, mankind and the world. However, the story begins with the pre-existence of God and a mass of primordial raw material which God shapes and forms into an orderly world, much as a builder would use raw materials to build a house. The analogy is that of a craftsman and his creation. To continue this analogy: a building may tell a great deal about its architect's ability and genius, but the building can never *become* an architect. In this way, the metaphors of the creation account in Genesis teach us that humans can never become divine.

Studying the beginning myth of a people can tell us much about how that people understood themselves, their world, and their God.

❐ What is the Bible?

Sacred Literature

The Bible is a collection of many *books* (in Greek, *biblia*) which were considered holy by the people of Israel. They were therefore preserved and recopied by hand countless times, and passed from one generation to the next. Biblical scholars differ over the question of when the Bible was finally assembled in the form we know today. Most scholars believe that the first five books, the Torah, achieved its present form after the Babylonian exile, (6th century B.C.E.).

We also know that many other books must have existed, but were not preserved. Some of them, such as the Book of Jashar (referred to in Josh. 10:13, 2 Sam. 1:18) and the Book of the Wars of the Lord (Num. 21:14) are mentioned within the Bible itself. In ancient Israel, books were generally written on papyrus or parchment scrolls (as is the Torah in the synagogue today). Parchment is much less durable than the clay tablets that were used for writing in Babylonia. Considering the humid climate of the land of Israel, which is corrosive to parchment, and considering the large number of wars that took place in the area, it is surprising that so many books *were* preserved. These books were preserved because people of Israel fervently believed that these books were the inspired words of God, a sacred literature. Accordingly, they took great pains in keeping and preserving them.

Organization of the Bible

The Bible, or תנ״ך, is divided into three major sections. The Hebrew word תנ״ך is made up of the first letter of each of the sections: (1) תּוֹרָה, (2) נְבִיאִים, and (3) כְּתוּבִים.

(1) תּוֹרָה—The Torah, the Five Books of Moses, חֻמָּשׁ, Pentateuch (from the Greek words meaning "five books"). (See below.)

(2) נְבִיאִים—The Prophets. This section has two subdivisions: (a) Early Prophets: Joshua, Judges, 1 Samuel (called "First Samuel"), 2 Samuel (called "Second Samuel"), 1 Kings (called "First Kings"), and 2 Kings (called "Second Kings"). (b) Late Prophets: the so-called Major Prophets (Isaiah, Jeremiah, and Ezekiel) and twelve so-called Minor Prophets.

(3) כְּתוּבִים—The Writings. This sections contain: Psalms, Proverbs, Job, the Five Scrolls (Song of Songs, Ruth, Lamentations, Ecclesiastes, Esther), Daniel, Ezra, Nehemiah, 1 Chronicles (called "First Chronicles") and 2 Chronicles (called "Second Chronicles).

The Torah is divided into five books:

(1) בְּרֵאשִׁית—Genesis (Greek, meaning "beginnings")
(2) שְׁמוֹת—Exodus (Greek, meaning "going out")
(3) וַיִּקְרָא—Leviticus (Greek, meaning: "concerning the Levites")

Introduction

(4) בְּמִדְבַּר—Numbers (in part having to do with the census of the Israelites)

(5) דְּבָרִים—Deuteronomy (Greek: "second law")

The Hebrew name of each book is derived from the first verse of the Hebrew text. When the Torah is read in the synagogue, it is read according to a traditional schedule of weekly *parashiyot* ("sections"). However, when we *study* the Bible, it is customary to refer to chapters (a later division of the text into smaller subdivisions by non-Jewish scholars, which has become standard). To identify a particular text, we shall refer to chapter and verse (never to page number, since pages numbers differ from edition to edition and translation to translation).

As in some other Hebrew books your students may have read, the number of the chapter appears in large Hebrew letters at the beginning of the chapter of the Hebrew text. The first letter of the Hebrew alphabet, א, stands for 1, the second, ב, for 2, and so on, up to 9. י stands for 10, כ for 20, and so on, up to 90. ק stands for 100. Letters are combined to represent other values (e.g., קי״ט stands for 119).

The numbers of the verses appear in small numerals throughout the text. When we want to write chapter 4, verse 20, we write 4:20. A verse is generally composed of one or more sentences; however, there are verses that contain only part of a sentence, such as lists of names.

❐ Suggestions for the Classroom

Leading an inquiry is much harder than lecturing since the teacher is less in control. Your students may swamp you with questions or alternate answers. This may be the first time that they will have been encouraged to probe and doubt. You will find, however, that problems come in categories (e.g., "Bible versus science," "Bible versus historical fact"). Once you have dealt with one problem in a category, the next problem in that category will go much faster.

Not every lesson will take the form on an inquiry. You may occasionally, for the sake of variety or saving time, present the narrative of an inquiry yourself, as long as it is based on evidence from the text and not presented as arbitrary opinion.

If you don't know all the answers, be honest. Do not panic and do not pretend. Ask some students to look up the needed information, or offer to do it yourself. The spirit of inquiry is for the teacher as well as for the student.

From past experience, we have found it is possible to finish the

Jacob story (or most of it) in the first year of study, and to conclude the book of Genesis in December of the second year. In schools where the Melton Biblical Hebrew Program is used for the first three grades, students should be able to use the Hebrew text as a basis for the inquiry (although teachers may choose to use only some Hebrew chapters and teach the rest in English).

In some classes teachers will be able to teach the biblical text in Hebrew; other classes will study the Torah in English translation. It is recommended that classes studying the text in Hebrew spend at least three hours a week on the study of Bible, while two hours are considered a minimum in classes where the text is studied in English. We strongly recommend that you use the new Jewish Publication Society (JPS) translation of the Torah (all translations in this *Guide* are from that translation).

Before you start teaching a chapter, it will be necessary for you to read the chapter in the Bible as well as all the material pertaining to it. The lesson plans in this *Guide* are designed to help the teacher lead a guided discussion in class. Some provide questions and suggested answers. A teacher to whom this kind of teaching is new may welcome these suggestions, while more experienced teachers who know their students can integrate these questions into their own teaching styles. Other lesson plans do not provide specific discussion questions, but offer instead a guide, framework or sense of direction so that teachers can construct their own questions for the discussion. Although the *Guide* is divided into "lessons," you may find that you need more or sometimes less than one class session to deal with the given material.

This *Guide* also attempts to help the teacher with problems that may arise in the classroom. These problems may be linguistic, or they may be of a moral or theological nature. You may be selective. Not all lessons have to be taught, neither do you have to teach every chapter in depth.

We recommend using a tape recorder to record your lessons. Listen to your own tapes. Check the quality of your questions: Are they direct? Are they simple or ambiguous? Do they expand or limit students' thinking? Do you answer your students' questions? Or do you veer off the subject? We have found that a tape recorder is an excellent self-teaching device.

Make sure that each lesson is summarized at the end. Each student should keep a copy of ideas discussed in a loose-leaf book. You may want to collect students' ideas and distribute copies to the class.

UNIT I
The First Creation Story
Genesis 1–2:4a

UNIT I

The First Creation Story
Genesis 1–2:4a

❐ Overview

The book of Genesis begins with the story of the creation of the world. The understanding of the first story in Genesis is essential to an understanding of the biblical view of the world. It introduces the reader to the Torah's understanding of the relationship between God, man, and the world. God is *the Creator.* Man, woman and the world are creatures which God has created. It also introduces us to the role man and woman are to play as caretakers and nurturers of the world.

Some of your students may profess an inability to deal with the biblical text since they "do not believe in God." Do not at this point deal with God as a theological issue. Simply draw the analogy of the Bible to a story with God as the main character. We have the ability to read and enjoy stories about characters both real and imaginary without having to believe in their historicity or reality.

Although your long-term goal includes the religious education of Jews, that goal may have to wait. Concentrate for the time being on your short-term goal: teaching the text, the ideas and values of the book of Genesis.

LESSON 1

The Structure of the Story
Genesis 1–2:4a

☐ **In Preparation for Teaching**

The basic structure of the creation narrative can be divided into three parts:

1) Pre-creation (1:1–2)
2) The creation process (1:3–31)
3) Post-creation (2:1–4a)

We shall for convenience sake deal first with the second part, the creation process, and proceed from there to parts 1 and 3.

The creation story is a myth (we are using the term as explained in the Introduction; see above, p. xiv) that expressed the biblical idea that the parts of the world are arranged according to God's plan. The creation process is a sequence of events which takes place over a period of six days. The creation of day and night (and, as we shall see, the element "time") make up the events of the first day of creation. The sky is created on the second day (as is the element "place"). On the third day, dry land, seas and vegetation are created (as is the element "species" or "kinds"). The sun, moon and stars are created on the fourth day. On the fifth day God created all living things that creep or swim in the waters and fly in the air, as well as the great sea monsters. On the sixth day God created all creatures that live on dry land, from creeping animals to cattle, to wild beasts—and man and woman.

God blessed all living things by bidding them to "be fruitful and multiply." He gave man and woman an additional blessing, setting them above all animals to "master and rule." God gave all living creatures the vegetation of the earth for their food. The seventh day stands out as a celebration of the completeness, the perfection and the harmony of creation. The creation process is one of bringing order and fulfillment. *Order* stands in opposition to תֹהוּ וָבֹהוּ ("unformed and void"), a chaotic mass of raw material. According to this story, as we shall see, *creation is accomplished by God imposing order on this raw material.*

Lesson 1: The Structure of the Story

Creation begins on the first day with the establishment of *time:* day and night. This is the first step from תֹהוּ וָבֹהוּ to *order*. This process continues with the creation of *place*—sky, dry land and seas (on the second and third days); the creation of *different kinds* of creatures—vegetable and animal (on the third, fifth, and sixth days); and, the creation of the markers of extended time—months, seasons, and years (on the fourth day).

In order to study the text we must first identify the units of which it is composed. Determining these units is made difficult by the fact that the text as it has come down to us has not been divided into units. There is not always enough time to identify these units in class; therefore they have been presented to you. In Lesson One you may want your students to attempt the division (you can best judge if your class can do this without too much difficulty).

The story is bracketed between 1:1, "When God began to create the heaven and the earth," and the first part of 2:4 (referred to as 2:4a), "This is the story of heaven and earth as they were created." The seventh day obviously belongs with the six preceding days. 2:4b (the second part of verse 4) is the first line of the next story because it serves as an introduction to 2:5. Ancient texts, like Torah scrolls today, had no punctuation and no division of the text into verses. Here we begin a new sentence in the middle of what the tradition later defined as a verse.

The fact that 2:4b begins a new unit is also indicated by the language of the text. For example, all throughout 1–2:4a God is referred to as אֱלֹהִים (God). From 2:4b on the text uses the name יי אֱלֹהִים (The Lord God).

☐ Teaching Procedure

A) *Defining the story.* You may decide to let your students attempt to define the limits of this story. This is a mini-inquiry that should not take more than six minutes. Ask them to read the first creation story (this can be done at home or in class, preferably silently) and to stop wherever they think the story ends. Since you do not want them to read *too much,* tell them that if they reach the description of a garden, they have read too far! Some of your students will suggest that the story ends with the last verse of Genesis 1. If so, ask how the story "came out" or concluded. There is, of course, no proper ending at this point.

Others may suggest that the story ends with 2:4. Some students may consider the whole verse as part of the first creation story, while others may see it as part of the next story.

Let students make suggestions and ask them to defend their answers. They may need some help in identifying 2:4a as the last verse of the story.

After the framework has been agreed upon, ask your students to restate the content of the story: What does the text say? Invite your students to contribute bits and pieces (with their books open). The aim is for a rather loose discussion, so do not insist on details or even on the correct order. However, do not accept incorrect contributions—for example, "God created Adam and Eve" is not part of *this* story. When some agreement has been reached about the content of the story, you may want to ask the class to suggest an appropriate title. "The Story of Creation" or "God Creates the World" are some suggestions your class may come up with. There are, of course, many acceptable possibilities.

B) *Discovering the Structure.* You are now ready to teach the section on the creation process (1:3–31), which begins with the creation of light. Before you do so, however, you will have to divide the story into its three parts (see p. 4 above). It may be easiest to define the content of Gen. 2:1–4a. You may want to ask:

a) What do 2:1–4a deal with?
b) Why did God cease from work?
c) When did God conclude His work of creation?

Gen. 2:2 could be understood to mean that God concluded His work on the seventh day. The New J.P.S. translation, however, translates the verse "And on the seventh day God finished the work which He *had been doing*," indicating work had been concluded before the seventh day. In the Septuagint and the Samaritan translations of the Bible, Gen. 2:2 refers to "the sixth day," indicating that our Masoretic text may be in error.

Your students should be able to recognize that these verses deal with a time *after creation*, or "post-creation." Tell your students that verses 1:1–2 deal with a time before creation, "pre-creation," and that creation begins with 1:3. List on the board:

1:1–2	Pre-creation (*or:* before creation)
1:3–31	Creation
2:1–4a	Post-creation (*or:* after creation)

Should your students question this division, you can do one of two things:

a) Ask them to accept your division for the time being; a discussion is to follow.

b) Skip to "Pre-creation" (p. 15, below), and teach that section first. Although we have chosen to teach "Creation" before "Pre-creation," there is, of course, no one correct way to approach the teaching of this chapter.

LESSON 2

The Sequence of Creation
Genesis 1

◻ **Teaching Procedure**

Your students will probably discern that creation takes place in six different steps, on six separate days. You may want to ask your students to list the "creations" for each day. This can be done at home in preparation for the lesson, or in class. A chart of the sequence of creation is available in the *Student's Guide*.

Sequence of Creation

Day One:	light, day and night
Day Two:	sky
Day Three:	dry land, seas and vegetation
Day Four:	luminaries
Day Five:	fish (all water creatures), fowl and sea monsters
Day Six:	land animals and man

Ask your students if there seems to be any logic to the sequence. Some of your students may notice that the physical world was created before vegetation and living things, and may reason that the latter creations were dependent on the former. In some cases, you may have to help them by asking such questions as the following:

a) When were land animals created?
b) Why were they created on the sixth day?
c) What would have happened if they had been created on the second day? (The Bible implies that animals were originally vegetarians; thus one species of animal was not created to serve as food for another [1:29–30].)

Your class may wonder why vegetation was created before the luminaries. Leave this problem for later discussion.

Some of your students may have noticed a hierarchy of complexity among the *living* things created. Fish are more complex than vegetables, but less complex than mankind. There is no obvious hierarchy apparent among the non-living creations.

Lesson 2: The Sequence of Creation

Two facts should be noted on the board and in the students' notes. In the created world one can recognize:

a) A sequence based on *dependency*
b) A hierarchy of *complexity*.

The terms "sequence" and "hierarchy" are used, rather than "order" to avoid confusion. In this chapter, the act of creating means "imposing order on chaos."

(Supplementary activities related to the teaching of this lesson can be found in Appendix A, below, p. 314.)

LESSON 3

Recurring Phrases and Refrains
Genesis 1

☐ **In Preparation for Teaching**

Your students by now have many questions:

a) What is "a sky in the midst of the waters"?
b) What are "the great sea monsters"?
c) How does the biblical story of creation compare to or contrast with the theory of evolution?

List the questions as they are asked (appoint a secretary, or put the questions on a sheet of paper which you may want to keep on the wall). At some point, you will have to deal with these problems. Select the best time according to your own judgment. In general, it is best to answer questions when your students are most keenly aware of their *own need* for answers and most eager to listen to the teacher's explanations. Once your students have realized that their questions are treated with respect, they will learn to wait for answers.

This next section will probably have to be presented by you. Remember, however, that *none* of these lessons have been written to serve as *reading material* for the students. When you "lecture" or give the information to your students, it is important that you gear yourself to their level of maturity and understanding. You may want to leave out, shorten, simplify or add more or different examples.

☐ **Teaching Procedure**

Write on the board: "and there was evening and there was morning." Ask your students how many times this phrase repeats. Ask for other recurring phrases. Do not insist that the phrase occur on *each* day of creation. Your list on the board should include:

1) "God said"
2) "And it was so"

Lesson 3: Recurring Phrases and Refrains 11

    3) "God saw that it was good"
    4) "God called"

What is the purpose of a recurring phrase or refrain? Your students will probably tell you that it "sounds good." It gives a rhythm to the text. You may want to read aloud two or three days of creation in class to illustrate this point. Recurring phrases and refrains have other functions too. One important function of repetition is to give special emphasis (when your mother repeats a statement many times, you know she means it!).

Call your students' attention to the phrases that repeat. Notice that by their repetition they underline certain ideas in the text. For example, the repetition of the words "God said" underscores the idea that God created by fiat (command).

1) "God said."

You may want to ask: Who was there to hear God say, "Let there be light"? According to the biblical story, obviously no one! Therefore we must understand the verb "to say" in a nonliteral way. The creation of light, dry land and seas is not part of human experience or memory—nobody was witness to creation. In this context it is important to explain what a metaphor is (see above, p. xiii). A metaphor transfers expressions from one area of experience to another. Often metaphors are taken from areas of experience we *know* in order to explain something which is abstract and hard to understand. The phrase "my beloved is a precious jewel" is a metaphorical expression comparing a person to an object. We can infer from the metaphor that the person speaking believes his beloved to be beautiful, rare, highly valued and esteemed, etc. "The Lord is my shepherd" is a way to express ideas about God and the way God cares for people.

In this text, the biblical phrase "God said" is a metaphor—God is compared to a human being.

In human experience, the way to exhibit "willing something to be" is by *speaking*. What do we do when we want something? We demand or command it verbally! A baby demands by crying. A king or other people in power will state a command or order if they want something. The Bible is telling us that God *wanted* the world to be. God existed before creation (1:1); thus He did not *need* the world. But since the world exists, the Bible tells us that God must have *wanted* it to be. *He created it by willing it to be.* This concept is rendered easier to understand through use of the human metaphor of a king—God, like a king, created by speaking. God, of course, is not *exactly* like a king. When a king gives an order, there has to be someone to hear the words of the king and to carry it out. It also takes time to carry out the order. God creates by fiat, by word of mouth and His order is immediately fulfilled.

2) "And it was so!"

Ask your students to locate this recurring phrase. Where is it placed in the chapter? (1:9, 11, 15, etc.) Your students will note that it is placed immediately after God's command: "Let there be. . . ." Remind your class of the purpose of repetitions: aside from giving rhythm to a piece of literature, they emphasize a point and indicate a principle.

What is the Torah trying to emphasize by placing the statement "And it was so" directly after the command "Let there be"? Your class will probably provide a number of answers: it indicates God's power, it teaches that God can create whatever He wants to create, etc. All these answers are, of course, valid. You may want to ask how man differs from God in this respect. Again there are a number of good possible responses: man has limited ability, time is needed before a man's will can be executed, etc. A central point is that God has no opposition. Man's ability to act is limited by other people and circumstances that may oppose his will. God, however, is free! Whatever He creates will stay created and unchanged, since He is one and unrivaled.

In contrast, the Babylonian creation epic, *Enuma elish*, relates the birth of numerous gods in successive generations. It describes the struggle and final victory of order over chaos. The battle is won by the young god Marduk, who by defeating the primeval mother, the water deity Tiamat, set the stage for the creation of heaven, earth, the luminaries, man, etc.

Marduk, upon being elected as head of the assembly of the gods and setting out to vanquish Tiamat, addresses the gods saying:

> If I indeed, as your avenger, am to vanquish Tiamat and save your lives, set up the Assembly, proclaim supreme my destiny! Let my words instead of you determine the fates. Unalterable shall be what I bring into being. Neither recalled or changed shall be the command of my lips.

Marduk's statement indicates that in general a god's command could be altered, recalled or changed. This is in sharp contrast with the biblical "God said," "and it was so."

(The translation of *Enuma elish* can be found in *Ancient Near Eastern Texts*, edited by James B. Pritchard, Princeton University Press, 1969.)

Lesson 3: Recurring Phrases and Refrains

3) *"God saw that it was good."*

How does the Torah depict God's attitude toward His creation? What does the Torah visualize God doing each day after the day's creation has been completed? Use an example from the world of the craftsman to illustrate this point. After each brushstroke, a painter in the midst of creating a masterpiece steps back to view his work and evaluates it. If he concludes that His work is *good,* surely there is joy, elation, and satisfaction. When the last dab of paint has been put to the canvas, he evaluates it and declares it to be "very good."

The fact that God evaluates His work and finds it good indicates that God creates according to a plan. Had an artist stretched a canvas over a frame and then stopped painting, would the canvas still be considered "good"? If a builder excavated a site but never built upon it, would his project still be "good?" Each part of creation is "good" in view of the overall plan. Each is an intermediate stage in a project yet to be completed. Only at the end of the six days when all parts of the creation come together does God consider it "very good."

We see that this chapter does not depict the world as we know it. This is an *ideal world* which is not part of our experience. This story does not deal at all with *moral* good and evil. Evil came to be part of our lives at a later stage (Genesis 2 and 3).

4) *"God called."*

God completes His creations by conferring a name on each thing He created. You may want to start this discussion by asking your students if they like their given names. Why? If not, why not? Do they have nicknames? Do they prefer them to their real names? Why? Are there some names they particularly like? Why? The answers will be varied. Your students will mention the sounds of different names and the fact that names carry associations (e.g., they may dislike a name because it reminds them of a person they disliked). A name evokes a feeling, a picture, an identity.

Ancient people considered names very important. The Babylonian creation myth describes the pre-creation stage as a time when neither earth nor the seas had been "called by name." Having no name means *they did not exist.*

Ask if any of your students were named after relatives. What does this custom tell us? We want our parents and relatives to be remembered. On the other hand, we want to forget the names of those we hate. יִמַּח שְׁמוֹ ("may his name be wiped out") is a strong Hebrew curse meaning, "May it be as if he never existed."

As people change their names, they expect also to change their identity. Some of your students may tell you that parents or grandparents changed their names upon arrival to the United States. Obviously, they also changed their images: their clothes, language, habits and jobs. In short, by changing their names, they indicated a change of identity: they became "Americanized."

Giving of names in the Bible has many aspects, not all of which apply to the present discussion. One is the relationship between the giver and the receiver of a name. Who gives a child a name? Who names a pet? Obviously, the "creator" or "owner." The giver of a name has some power over the receiver of a name. This is why some black people (e.g., Muhammed Ali, formerly Cassius Clay) reject the names given to their families by their former white masters. Also, some women today prefer to maintain their maiden names at marriage, rather than taking their husbands' names.

LESSON 4A

Pre-creation
Gen. 1:1–2

❐ Teaching Procedure

Although your class is using the New Jewish Publication Society (JPS) translation of the Torah, some of your students may insist that on Day One, God created "the heaven and the earth." Ask your class to find the verses actually describing the creation of heaven (or sky) on the second day of creation (1:6–8) and the emergence of the dry land from beneath the waters on the third day (1:9–10). Note that in the translation of the first verse, the words "heaven" and "earth" are not capitalized, whereas in 1:8 and 1:10 "sky" and "earth" are capitalized.

In both 1:1 and 2:4a the term "heaven and earth" means "heaven and all that it contains" (such as stars, sun, and moon) and "earth and everything upon it" (such as trees, grasses, fish, birds, animals and man). In short, "heaven and earth" means everything we today refer to as the "world."

A Note on Different Translations

Some of your students may be aware of other translations, which lead to different understandings of these opening verses of Genesis. Should any of your students introduce the Old JPS translation or the King James translation, you may have to use the following information.

The first three Hebrew verses of Genesis present some difficulty because of their grammatical structure. According to these earlier translations, God first creates a mass of "stuff," or raw material, and then proceeds to impose order upon this raw material. Some scholars, both medieval and modern, disagree with this translation for grammatical reasons. They interpret the Hebrew verses to be saying that when God began to create, He used a *pre-existing* mass of raw material. Let us therefore compare the New JPS translation which we are using with earlier translations of the same verses.

Old JPS translation, 1917	*New JPS translation, 1962*
1 In the beginning God created the heaven and the earth.	1 When God began to create the heaven and the earth—
2 Now the earth was unformed and void, and darkness was upon the face of the deep; and the spirit of God hovered over the face of the waters.	2 the earth being unformed and void, with darkness over the surface of the deep and a wind from God sweeping over the water—
3 And God said, "Let there be light." And there was light.	3 God said, "Let there be light"; and there was light.

In the old translation, the creation is described in what seems to be two stages. In the first stage, God creates from nothing (*ex nihili*—יֵשׁ מֵאַיִן) a world which is *Tohu Vavohu*, with darkness over the face of the deep and the "spirit of God" hovering over the waters. Then, in the second stage of creation, He imposes order over chaos: He creates light, followed by sky, land, seas, etc. The new translation, on the other hand, describes the creation beginning with light. The raw materials are water, wind, darkness and, as we shall learn from 1:9, "pre-existing" earth (יֵשׁ מִיֵּשׁ). According to this translation, where the raw materials came from does not seem of particular interest. Creation equals: *forming, filling, ordering and fitting.* It is God who makes form and creates fulfillment. Man is the only creature who can comprehend God's creation, the ordering and fulfillment.

LESSON 4B

Tohu Vavohu
Gen. 1:1–2

☐ In Preparation for Teaching

The term *Tohu Vavohu* is untranslatable (the French Bible uses the term *Tohu Vavohu* and does not attempt to translate it). Here, as elsewhere in the Bible (e.g., Isaiah 34:11, 24:10, 45:18,19, 59:4; Jeremiah 4:23; and I Samuel 12:21), the word evokes a sense of having no form, being without purpose or use, empty of life. Gen. 1:2 describes the mass of raw material "when God began to create."

Tohu Vavohu is the *condition* in which the raw materials (water, darkness, wind and—as seen from 1:9—earth) were. The JPS version translates this term as "unformed and void." Nothing in our world is unformed. Liquids take the form of their containers. Borders and outlines give form and shape. In the world of *Tohu Vavohu*, however, there are no borders to give form, to separate one thing from another so that we can comprehend them as distinct entities. The world of *Tohu Vavohu* is incomprehensible. Yet the world of pre-creation is not empty of material. The *void* can only refer to the absence of life, meaning, and purpose.

☐ Teaching Procedure

Tell your class that the words *Tohu Vavohu* (or, if necessary, "unformed and void") refer to a situation or condition. Ask them what materials were to be found in this "condition." (Heaven and earth" means everything we know today as the "world.") The pre-existing world consisted of: (list on the board)

> water
> darkness
> wind from God
> earth

Some of your students may also question the term "a wind from God." In the creation stories of other peoples (e.g., the Babylonians), the winds were considered *gods*. Here the wind is *from* God: God controls the wind.

You may have to help your class with the image of the earth submerged until the third day when it emerged from beneath the waters (1:9).

Since the New JPS translation uses the word "unformed," you may want to ask your class if they know of anything from their experience which is "unformed." Show them a container of water; ask what shape a puddle or lake has and what gives it shape. Even air has shape—the shape of the "container" or the atmosphere. It is suggested, however, that you use the term *Tohu Vavohu* in Hebrew, even if your language of instruction is English. Translating from one language to another is difficult because words evoke associations and feelings that are not always translatable.

The words *Tohu Vavohu* and *Tehom* evoke feelings. Imagine you are in the middle of *Tohu Vavohu*. Listen carefully to the vowel sounds:

T–O–H–U V–A–V–O–H–U
T–E–H–O–M

How do you feel? What do you want to do? If you were producing a *Tohu Vavohu* movie, what kind of music would you play? What kind of lighting would you use?

Ask your students to finish the following sentence: "Being in the world of *Tohu Vavohu* is like. . . ." Some children may compare it to losing their way in their own bedrooms at night, touching a known object in the room but not being able to identify it in the dark. Others may imagine themselves walking in space and breaking the cord to the spaceship, catapulting head over heels forever in space with no "up" or "down," without time or end. Any image your students come up with is, of course, acceptable.

We may also understand *Tohu Vavohu* through the process of elimination. After we finish learning about the creation, ask your students to imagine the world *without* the elements of *time, place, different kinds* of vegetation and animal life. In doing so, we may achieve some understanding of what the Torah means by *Tohu Vavohu*.

LESSON 5A

The Three Steps of Creating
Gen. 1:9–13

☐ **Teaching Procedure**

Have your students read "Day Three" (1:9–13). What does God do first? What does He do next? When does He declare His creation "good"? Your students, with some help, should recognize that God's declaration comes after three steps: (1) fiat, (2) separation, and (3) naming. You have already discussed the meaning and implications of "fiat" and "naming." "Separation" is the third important factor in creation.

Lines, borders and outlines separate, thereby giving form to the "unformed and void." Show your students any map. What defines the form or shape of an ocean, a state, a country? Your students will recognize "natural borders" and man-made or artificial ones. In either case, borders give shape.

Direct your students' attention to Day Two of creation. The sky is also created in three steps: fiat, separation, and naming.

Your students may notice that the repeating phrase "God saw that it was good" is omitted on Day Two. Just like repetitions, omissions also can serve a purpose. For example, the refrain "and it was evening and it was morning" is missing on the seventh day. Obviously, the seventh day is different from the preceding six. Not all omissions, however, can be easily understood.

On Day Two, God does not declare "it was good"; on the third day, however, He declares it twice. There does not seem to be any simple explanation for this fact. The Midrash says that God had started to separate the waters on Day Two, but did not conclude this act of separating until Day Three when the seas were actually formed. That is why "good" was omitted on Day Two but used twice on Day Three. Tell your class that this explanation comes from the Midrash of the Rabbis, not from the book of Genesis itself.

LESSON 5B

The Creation of Time
Gen. 1:3–5

☐ In Preparation for Teaching

Light was created first. It was separated from darkness and called "day." Light, as it interchanges in regularity with darkness, becomes the element of time. Actually, any regular, recognizable, recurring event creates time.

God saw that the light was good. In connection with this, it would be helpful to teach, during the time allotted for prayer, the blessings הַמַּעֲרִיב עֲרָבִים from the Arvit (evening) service and יוֹצֵר אוֹר from the Shaḥarit (morning) service.

☐ Teaching Procedure

Your students have already listed all "creatures" created on the six days of creation. Let them turn once again to this list. You may want to copy parts of the list again on your blackboard.

Sequence of Creation

Day One   light, day and night

We listed "darkness" as one of the pre-existing elements in the realm of *Tohu Vavohu*. How does "darkness" differ from "night"? Your students may tell you that "night" is a span of time limited by "day." If they have difficulty, ask them: If you went into a deep cave, would it be night?

The notion of time is based on measurable intervals between regular, recurring events. You can tell time, for example, by watching the tides or counting your pulse. There is an expression that "you can set your watch" by some people. (When you see Mr. Green leave for work in the morning, you know it is 7:30!)

Add the word "time" to your list of creations on the first day. Time is the first element of order in the world. *The creation of time is the first step in bringing forth order from chaos.*

Sequence of Creation

Day One   light, day and night, time

Lesson 5B: The Creation of Time 21

Yours students may ask how light without luminaries is possible, for light was created on Day One but luminaries not until Day Four. Ask them to hold this question until you deal with the creation of the luminaries.

LESSON 6

The Creation of Place
Gen. 1:6–8

☐ **In Preparation for Teaching**

Day Two: "Let there be an expanse in the middles of the water" (1:6–8). Your class may find this concept difficult. What is meant by a sky in the midst of the waters? Is there water *above* the sky?

Day Three: "Let the waters below the sky . . ." (1:9). On the third day, the Torah tells us, God gathered the waters to one area, allowing land which had been covered by the water to appear.

In this lesson you are attempting to give your students some insight into our ancestors' view of the world. Scientifically, they envisioned the world differently from the way we do today. Some students may tell you that because the knowledge of the ancients was faulty, the Bible is irrelevant to us modern Jews. We have therefore placed the lesson "Is the Bible True?" directly after this lesson. You should teach that lesson, however, whenever the need for it arises.

☐ **Teaching Procedure**

Sky

Your students will probably ask some "practical" questions about the creation of the sky. Ask them: What is "sky," scientifically speaking? How do you know that the sky is gases, vapors, moisture, chemistry, etc.? "It says so in books" is not a satisfactory answer—how do the writers of those books know?

List the tools by which we acquire knowledge of the world: chemistry, geology, physics, airplanes, spaceships, telescopes, cameras, mathematics, etc. How complete is our knowledge of the universe? There is, of course, a great deal we do not yet know. Our knowledge of space has grown in the past few years as never before in the history of mankind. You may want to discuss moon landings, unmanned spaceships to faraway planets, or anything currently in the news.

Lesson 6: The Creation of Place

Ancient man had none of our scientific tools, yet he was by no means ignorant. Remind your class of the pyramids built by ancient peoples whose building techniques remain a mystery to us. Students may know of intricate ancient calendars. How could ancient man have made them? Your class will readily grasp the idea that people living in ancient times experienced the world through their five senses. They observed the positions of the sun, moon and other planets. Then they used intellectual insight—the ability to recognize recurrent patterns and decipher principles—and expressed their conclusions in calendars. But lacking technology, ancient man could not acquire information about many other things. He had no notion of a "universe" beyond that of "heaven and earth"; he did not know that the earth was a globe turning on its own axis; he did not know that the moon generates no light of its own but reflects the light of the sun, nor that the sun is the source of daylight and that without it no daylight would exist.

According to the Bible, the Hebrews came from Mesopotamia. Israelites left no pictures or maps. The Babylonians, however, left us a "picture" of the world" (see Nahum Sarna, *Understanding Genesis*, p. 5).

According to *Enuma Elish* ancient man perceived the sky as a solid membrane in the shape of a *kippah* stretching over the face of a flat earth. The word רָקִיעַ (from the root רקע) refers to something that was "hammered out," or "stamped flat."

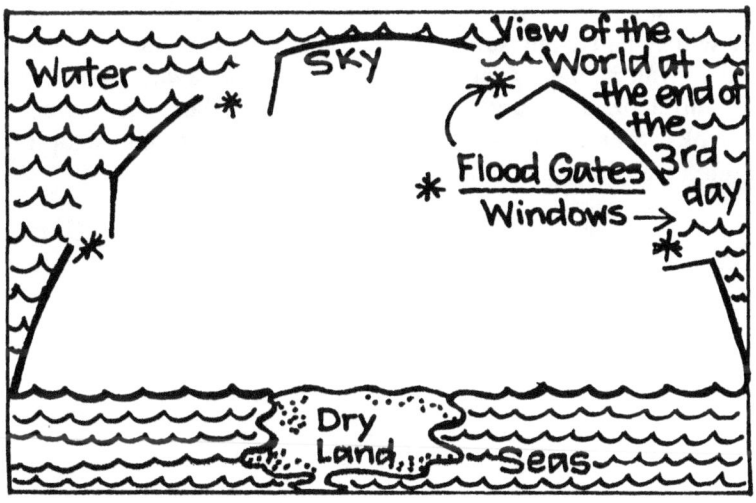

According to Genesis 1:6-8, the purpose of the sky is to separate the waters below the sky from the waters above the sky. Your students should have no difficulty understanding why the belief in "water above the sky" prevailed. How rain or snow could penetrate the membrane of the sky is explained in the Noah story (Genesis 7:11): there were אֲרֻבֹּת הַשָּׁמַיִם ("windows" or "flood gates") which God opened and closed at will.

Words like "above" and "below" are spatial. They answer the question *where*. Thus on Day Two, the idea of *place* is created. Add "place" to the sequence of creation list on Day Two. *The creation of place is the second step in bringing forth order from chaos.*

Land and Seas

Day Three: Let the waters below the sky . . ." (1:9).

On the third day, the Torah tells us, God gathered the waters to one area, allowing land which had been covered by the water to appear. How did people in biblical times visualize the world? Remember, they did not know the world was a globe, they imagined it flat and round, like a coin.

Let us imagine that we have no scientific knowledge except that which our experience and senses teach us. If we walked to the east coast of America, we would reach the Atlantic Ocean. Far away, at the horizon, the sea and sky seem to meet. If we turned around and walked all the way to the Pacific Ocean we would see the same. Man's experience taught him that the land he lived upon was surrounded by water, like an island or several islands, in the midst of water. It was natural for him to conclude that the land, which had been submerged, appeared as a result of the receding waters. If you were ever on a boat, far away from the coast and looked around you, the horizon—where sky meets sea—looks round like a circle. That is what ancient people imagined was the shape of the world.

LESSON 7

Is the Bible True?
Genesis 1–2:4a

☐ In Preparation for Teaching

This *Guide* has presented background material for myths and poetic readings (above, pp. xiv–xv). It is suggested that you reread these pages. Your students must have asked you a great many questions by now. You may be able to divide these questions into categories, so that you can deal with them in terms of principles instead of individual questions. Many of these questions will deal with the seeming conflict between the Bible and scientific or historical data. The value of the biblical story for us is not in its *scientific* information—which often does not agree with our own scientific observations—but in its *religious* aspects.

We do not read the Bible to discover scientific or historical truths. For scientific information we would turn to science books, the more recent the better, since our scientific knowledge is expanding daily and scientific data becomes "dated" very rapidly.

We do not read the Bible for historic knowledge either, although many events recorded in the Bible did actually take place. "History," however, aims for objectivity. The Bible, on the other hand, presents a *subjective* "point of view"—the world view of the people of Israel.

☐ Teaching Procedure

On the poetic versus literal reading of the Bible

We do not read the Bible literally. The Bible uses many different literary styles. Much of the Bible is poetic or metaphorical and is not *to be read literally*. Metaphor (the borrowing of images from one area of experience and using them in another) has been discussed earlier (see above, pp. xiv–xv). You may want to give some more examples of metaphors. "Howling wind" or "roaring oceans" are a few random suggestions. The teacher must also explain what a *parable* is. You may want to use the story of "The Little Boy Who Cried Wolf" as an illustration.

A little shepherd boy watching sheep on a hill not far from his native village cried out: "Wolves! Wolves!" The villagers, armed with sticks, rushed to his aid only to find out that the little boy had fooled them. He repeated this performance the next day. The villagers were a little suspicious, but turned out in full force; again they found that the boy had fooled them. On the third day, the wolves did indeed attack the flocks. The little boy repeatedly called for help, but no one came.

Ask your class some questions about this little boy: Where did he live? How old was he? What was his name? What were his parents' names? Eventually someone will say: "This little boy never existed; your questions are irrelevant." Some of your students will probably tell you that the story is only a vehicle for another hidden meaning, namely that people who habitually lie will not be trusted even when they speak the truth. A story that can be taken at face value but that also serves as a vehicle for ideas is called a *parable*. The story of the little boy may or may not be rooted in reality; the idea it conveys, however, is what is important!

Whether or not creation as depicted in Genesis 1–2:4a is rooted in reality is not important. What is important are the ideas the Bible attempts to teach us by means of this story. Although, strictly speaking, Genesis 1–2:4a is not a parable, we will read it like a parable in the sense that we will not take it to have actually happened.

On myth

The Bible contains the *myths* of the people of Israel. Your students may have heard the term *myth* before and may equate it with fairy tales which are not to be taken seriously. You may have to emphasize that we use this term differently (see above, pp. xiv–xv). Furthermore, many psychiatrists, such as Erich Fromm (in *The Forgotten Language*) and Bruno Bettleheim (in *The Uses of Enchantment*), stress that even fairy tales should be taken very seriously!

A myth is a way of telling in story form how a people views itself. For example, the people of Mesopotamia saw themselves living at the whim of capricious gods who were often in conflict with one another. However, the people of Mesopotamia did not come out and declare or "spell out" this view of themselves and their gods. Instead, they expressed this idea in their story, or myth, about the war between the gods. This myth is contained in *Enuma Elish*, the Babylonian creation epic.

Lesson 7: Is the Bible True?

Although the people of Mesopotamia did not witness the events described in *Enuma Elish*, the story had immense effect on the way the people of Mesopotamia thought of themselves and of the world in which they lived.

The story of George Washington chopping down the cherry tree is an American myth that tells us something about the "father of the nation." What does this story tell us about the American self-image? Another American myth is the story that America was built by people who came to these shores seeking religious freedom. (Some did, others came for economic or other reasons.)

The story of Remus and Romulus who were abandoned by humans and nursed by a she-wolf is a Roman myth explaining why the Romans are fierce and strong.

The existence of a myth as well as its particular content has proven to be of extreme importance to the life of a people. In order to survive, a people must have a sense of their own identity, spelled out in terms of their relationship to nature, to others, and to God. Without this form of self-awareness, a group lacks the stamina, tenaciousness and courage necessary for survival. Consider Genesis 15:19: you will find a list of nations, containing but a fraction of the nations mentioned in Genesis. The Kenites, Kenizzites, Kadmonites, and Hittites—what happened to these peoples? No trace of them remains today. Their descendants intermarried, merged with other peoples and lost their own identities, as did the ten "lost" tribes of Israel. On the other hand, the myth of Israel has survived, as has the people of Israel. For example, the myth of the Exodus from Egypt (יְצִיאַת מִצְרַיִם) is alive because the event of liberation that occurred in ancient times is used by the Jewish people still today as a model for their own experiences and hopes. It is expressed in the ritual of the *seder* and in the celebration of the Pesaḥ holiday. The Exodus is also mentioned in many of our daily prayers such as *Birkat Hamazon*, the *Sh'ma*, *Alenu*, and others.

LESSON 8

The Creation of Different Species
Gen. 1:11–22

☐ **In Preparation for Teaching**

Day Three

Your class will notice that vegetation, like the physical world, was created by fiat. The earth is commanded to "sprout" or "bring forth" vegetation. Vegetation is thus brought forth from its environment. God did not name the vegetables. He did, however, give each species its own seed with which to procreate and multiply, thus giving them permanence.

You may want to ask your students if the above steps are unique to vegetation. Direct their attention to the fifth and sixth days of creation. Swarms of living things were "brought forth" by their environment and separated into those that swim, those that fly, and those that creep. In naming these different categories, the Bible introduces us to the third "ordering principle," the principle of *kind*. This is made even more emphatic by the fact that each kind is to reproduce itself. The reproduction of the species, each according to its kind, is another principle of order. (We expect a cow to give birth to a calf, not to a wolf cub, and a sunflower to produce another sunflower, not a rose.)

The three principles of order—*time, place* and *kind*—are the laws which all things follow, the laws of nature. The story tells us that these laws were *created by God*. He rules them; they do not rule Him. You will be able to elicit some of the above information from your students. The rest you may have to tell them.

Your class may note that God blessed the fish and fowl, but not the animals of Day Five, nor the vegetation. The reason may be that vegetation is passive in its propagation (the wind and insects transfer their pollen and seed). The omission of a blessing for the animals, however, may be a device to highlight the blessing of God to man and woman. You may be able to illustrate this by writing a sentence on the board and underlining every word. Then write the same sentence again, underlining one word only. Your students will notice that when every word is emphasized, the effect is lost. (1) "The meeting *will* take place today" indicates that there had been some doubt about whether the meeting will or will not take place. (2) *"The meeting will take place today"* conveys nothing more than the same sentence without *any* emphasis would have conveyed.

Day Four

We have noted that light was created on Day One. Luminaries, however, were created on the Day Four. This presents a problem for us, since we know that there is no daylight without the sun. Biblical man, however, was able to conceive of light without a source. What, then, is the purpose of the sun and the moon? "They shall serve as signs for the set times—the days and the years" (1:14). Although the sun and the moon are to shine upon the earth, they do not "make" day and night but serve as "signs" for them. They are to serve us as a calendar.

Your class may wonder why the sun and the moon are called "the two great lights, a greater one and a lesser one" and not "the sun" and "the moon."

The sun and moon were revered as deities by other ancient peoples. Although the Bible recognizes their power, it regards them as God's creations. They were ordered by God to rule day and night, to shine on earth and to "serve as signs for the set times." Leaving out their names, the Bible undercuts their importance. Luminaries are not gods. As a matter of fact, light was created before the luminaries. *The Bible does not consider the luminaries to be the source of the light. God is the source!*

Some of your students may bring up the idea that days at the time of creation were much longer than they are today. This explanation was probably given to them by some teacher in the past. It attempts to reconcile the idea of creation in seven days with the later scientific theory that the world and its species have evolved over millions of years by explaining that days in biblical times each lasted millions of years.

However, the Torah uses the word "day," and there is no reason to assume that that word means anything other than its standard meaning. The Torah is, of course, "incorrect" according to our scientific knowledge. However, our aim in reading Bible is not to acquire scientific knowledge. The significant fact is the idea that God created the cycle of time: days, months, seasons and years.

Day Five

On the fifth day God commanded the waters to bring forth fish and fowl and God *created* the "great sea monsters" (1:21). The Babylonian creation story, *Enuma Elish,* tells of Tiamat and Apsu, as two sea monsters who are also the gods, out of whose bodies Marduk created the heavens and the earth.

We have seen that the word "create" (ברא) is used very sparingly in this chapter. Yet here it appears in connection with the sea monsters. The Bible does not deny the existence of sea monsters but emphasizes that they are *creatures,* not gods, *created* by God.

☐ Teaching Procedure

Have your students reread Day Four (1:14–19). What is the function of the luminaries? Aside from the fact that they are to shine on the earth and determine day and night, they are also to serve as "signs for the set times." In what ways do the luminaries serve as a calendar? Your students, with your help, will tell you that the sun enables us to know what season it is and when seasons are about to change. It also tells us what part of the day it is. The position of the moon indicates the days of the lunar month. The stars, too, indicate seasons. The constellations are in different places in the sky at different times of the year.

Why did the Bible choose to have God start the creation process with light? Your students already know that with the interchange of day and night (once light has been separated from darkness and named), the element of time is created. Without this creation we could not have a first day, or for that matter a seventh day. Time is the first step of bringing order into *Tohu Vavohu.* Some of your students may suggest that the Bible is *anthropomorphic.* Man conceives of God in his own terms. Since man needs light to carry out his work, man imagines God also needs light.

Why then did not God create the luminaries on Day One? List all creations, in order of their creation, in two columns (leaving out Days One and Seven in the following way:

A	B
Sky	Vegetation
Earth	Luminaries
Seas	Birds
	Animals
	Man

How do the two columns relate to one another? (Every item in Column B depends on one in Column A.)

Lesson 8: The Creation of Different Species

Now give each column a name. Your class may be able to come up with names like "places," "homes," "habitats," or "dwellings," for column A, and "inhabitants" or "things that need a place" for column B. To biblical man, the luminaries were creatures needing a place, as a fish needs water, or like a star in the planetarium needs a dome.

The Torah could, of course, have placed the luminaries before vegetation. Why did it not do so? We can only guess at a reason. If the items in column B were created in order of complexity, man might have conceived of luminaries as more complex than vegetation. Luminaries share with animals the power to move, something vegetation lacks.

LESSON 9A

The Creation of Humans

☐ In Preparation for Teaching

"Let us make man in our image" (1:26)

Here we meet the plural form "Let us." Your students have probably asked you on their first reading: Who is God talking to? Ask them for suggestions. They may say: To the angels! Some commentators (Rashi among them) have considered this a plausible answer, although "angels" are not referred to directly in this story. It may also be the plural of majesty. That is, the Torah has God refer to Himself in the plural (see also Gen. 11:7), much as the Queen of England and the President of the United States often refer to themselves as "we."

"In our image after our likeness"

Created in God's image and after His likeness, man's life is more valuable than the lives of other living beings (see also Gen. 9:5–6).

Today's Judaism, of course, views God as invisible, lacking any form or shape. Has this view always prevailed in the past or has it developed over time? Bible scholars believe that it developed. Man, of all creatures, is like God. On the first level there is physical likeness. The physical comparison is *metaphorical*. Language compels us to be anthropomorphic. People in biblical times may or may not have believed that in a physical way man is like God.

The story in Genesis contains no allusion to God's "history" or his physical attributes. By contrast, *Enuma Elish* (the Babylonian creation epic) describes Marduk in the following manner:

> Greatly exalted was he above them, exceeding throughout. Perfect were his members, beyond comprehension, unsuited for understanding, difficult to perceive. Four were his eyes, four were his ears. When he moved his lips, fire blazed forth. Large were all four hearing organs. And the eyes in like number scanned all things. He was the loftiest of the gods, surpassing was his stature. His members were enormous. He was exceeding tall.

Lesson 9A: The Creation of Humans

Now, it is possible that at some time in the past readers of the biblical story may have understood man's being in God's image literally. But for the story to have any meaning for us, *we must read it metaphorically*. The text says, "God said: Let there be light." We do not read this literally, but as a metaphor for "God willed the light to be." The text says that God *saw*. Again, we do not read this literally, as though God has physical eyes. The text says that God has a physical appearance similar to that of humans. We do not take this literally either, but read it as a metaphor.

A metaphor represents *partial* similarity. When we say "my beloved is a precious jewel" (see above, p. xiii) we are implying certain things about the person. In some ways, however, the beloved is *not* exactly like a jewel (you can't sell her, cut glass with her, mount her in a ring!).

Just as the beloved is *in some ways* like a jewel, man is *in some ways* like God. The text makes explicit one of the ways in which humans are like God: just as God rules the world, so are humans granted the power to "rule" that which God has created on earth.

"To master and rule"

This is a metaphor borrowed from the world of rulers in human society. We know from elsewhere in the Bible that the Hebrew roots רדה and כבש are harsh; they are used to describe domination. Obviously, man viewed his conquest and subjugation of nature as a struggle. Bear in mind as well that human rulers have been known to run the gamut from ruthless masters to thoughtful nurturers and protectors.

(The Torah conceives of mankind as having been created for a purpose: mastering and ruling God's world. This belief had, and still has, an impact on the way we live our lives: we have a task to fulfill. By comparison, the *Enuma Elish* epic conceives of the creation of mankind solely for the purpose of feeding of the gods by means of sacrifice. Mankind are slaves to the gods. After having created the heaven and the earth, Marduk announces that he is about to create mankind. He declares:

> Blood I will mass and cause bones to be. I will establish a savage, 'man' shall be his name. Verily savageman I will create. He shall be charged with the service of the gods that they might be at ease!

Marduk then kills one god and uses his blood to create mankind who are to be slaves of gods. The sole purpose of mankind is to be the feeding of the gods by means of sacrifices. The moral lives of people are of no interest to the gods. The Bible, in contrast, depicts mankind as partners of God.

❐ Teaching Procedure

Direct your students' attention to the text (1:26). They will notice that, unlike all other creations, man was not created instantaneously; instead, his creation is a gradual process. It begins with a stated plan and an articulated purpose: to master and rule. Students will realize that the things which we plan ahead in great detail are usually the projects to which we attach great importance: the building of a home, the planning of a meeting, or the choosing of our courses for the semester.

The word "created" (ברא) is used sparingly in the Bible and describes only acts by God. Your students may notice that the word "created" is used three times in connection with the creation of man. Let your students discover that throughout the story the word is mentioned only three more times: twice with the phrase "heaven and earth" (1:1, 2:4a) and once in connection with the great sea monsters (1:21), in order to emphasize their "creatureliness."

Ask your students what the words "image" and "likeness" bring to mind (in any context, not necessarily here). Some possible answers include:

having a strong resemblance to
being like something else
a copy
a mirror image
a picture or photograph

Your class will probably perceive that being in the image or likeness of something does not mean being *exactly* like it. Usually a copy is somewhat lacking in comparison with the original. It is likely that most examples of "image" or "likeness" brought by your students will be examples of physical resemblance. You may want your class to understand "image" also in metaphorical terms, a lesser but equitable replica. Pictures and sculptures are ony one kind of image, one which reflects physical resemblance. Other kinds of images might reflect resemblances in qualities, abilities, and actions. Thus, in this story God is portrayed as the active creator. And just as God is an active creator in His way, God gives to mankind, created in His image, the powers to be active creators in a human way.

What do we know so far about God from this story?

1) God brings order out of chaos.
2) He creates according to a plan.
3) He delegates authority.

4) He is concerned about His world being good (that is, it functioning properly).

What does being created in God's image mean to man?

1) God creates; man and woman can nurture and maintain.
2) God imposes order that man can comprehend.
3) Man can *act* with the aid of this order, which he comprehends.

Thus, in a limited way, humans can emulate God.

LESSON 9B

Humans and the World
Gen. 1:26–28

▢ In Preparation for Teaching

At this stage we know very little about God. Consequently, our understanding of "man in the image of God" is still limited. One way to enrich our understanding of "man in the image of God" is to discuss how mankind differs from God's other creatures. Mankind was given the task to "master and rule" the world and all its other creatures. Let us examine what qualities man has that enable him to fulfill this task.

As you proceed to teach this lesson, you must be aware of the fact that you are moving away from what the text says in order to discuss a contemporary understanding of man's role in the world. The text does not tell us how man and woman are different from animals or how they will master and rule the world. Thus, the following discussion will take us far afield of the text.

You may want to tell your class some of the following and you may be able to elicit many of the facts from them.

Language and Communication

Most living species communicate with one another in some fashion: dogs bark to attract attention; bees "dance" to indicate the location of nectar. Humans communicate with one another for some of the same reasons animals do. In addition, however, humans also need to share ideas and plans, express themselves artistically, etc. Only humans can preserve abstract knowledge, *orally or in writing,* from one generation to the next. Although some animals teach their young many practical skills, they cannot accumulate knowledge the way humans can. Animals today live more or less the way they did in biblical times.

Humans Can Understand the Laws of Nature

We have talked a great deal about order. Creation is the act of bringing order, giving form and substance to the primordial *Tohu*

Vavohu. Order depends on the existence of laws which all things must follow, i.e., *the laws of nature*.

The fact that different kinds of plants bring forth more of their own kind is an example of a "law of nature." Other laws of nature account for regular or expected changes, like the change of the seasons: the changing of summer into fall and fall into winter is based on the angle at which the earth tilts toward the sun. The changes that take place in a seed when planted in the earth also follow a fixed and predictable course.

Since God created the world, He is also the creator of the laws of nature. Man alone, among all living beings, possesses the intellect, the will and the means to investigate nature and discover its laws. Understanding the laws of nature has enabled man to use the laws of nature to improve his life and satisfy his curiosity. It gives man the capacity to farm land, tend cattle, delve into the depths of the sea and explore outer space. Although man cannot change the laws of nature, he is the only one of God's creatures who can understand them and thus use them for his benefit.

Instinct versus Free Will

Animals do most things by instinct. Squirrels store food for the winter, birds migrate south and build nests, and beavers build dams. Certain animals such as ants, termites and bees build intricate social structures. Some animals teach their young how to hunt or fly. Others abandon their young, who must fend for themselves instinctively (e.g., turtles). Humans too do many things by instinct (e.g., babies know at birth how to nurse). However, humans have also the ability to choose their own actions. Humans can conceive of ways to improve their society (although they may encounter difficulties in realizing their plans). Within their external circumstances people can choose occupations and marriage partners.

Man and woman, unlike other animals, can also choose to postpone the gratification of their appetites and wants. The more "civilized" humans are, the more they are able to conquer their basic instincts (e.g., hunger, anger, fear).

Conscience and Feelings of Shame

There are other ways in which man differs from all other animals: he can be sorry, regret past deeds and feel ashamed. It is, of course, possible that animals also experience some of these feelings. But we know that there is difference in degree.

☐ Teaching Procedure

Language and Communications

Ask: How do wolves, birds, or bees communicate among themselves? For what purposes do they communicate? For what purposes do humans communicate? In what way is the knowledge of a six-year-old child today different from the knowledge of a six-year-old in biblical times? (The child in biblical times did not know the world is a sphere or that the sun does not "go away" at night.) What about the human species made this progress in knowledge possible? (Writing, reading, storytelling.)

Humans Can Understand the Laws of Nature

What are some ways in which humans can understand and use the laws of nature. Man understands that fire melts metals and cooks eggs, that a ball can break a window, and that by the proper use of perspective an object on a canvas only inches away can seem far in the distance.

There are a great many ways to teach the fact that man can understand the laws of nature and its implications. Pick any example with which you are familiar and which your students can readily handle. Here are some suggestions:

What do you have to know before you attempt to grow a vegetable garden? Your students will no doubt be able to raise some of the following questions (do not devote class time to discussing the answers): (1) Which vegetable should be planted when? (2) What pests do we have to watch out for? (3) Should we use chemical sprays? etc.

Man can succeed at growing vegetables because he is able to perceive *regularity* in nature. He is able to discover the best way to grow each species of vegetation he needs. Animals forage the woods for sustenance. Some are able to store food for the winter, but none has man's ability to utilize knowledge of the laws of nature, say, to till the soil and grow its own food.

Discuss example (d) above, travel into space. Pick up a piece of chalk. Let go of it and then catch it before it drops to the floor. Why did the chalk fall? The fact that things fall when dropped is a law of nature—the law of gravity. What enabled you to catch the chalk before it fell? You have learned how the law of gravity works and can predict its effects. What would have happened to the object if you hadn't caught it? Which would fall faster, a piece of paper or a coin? We are able to answers these questions because we understand the law of gravity.

Lesson 9B: Humans and the World

We used to understand the law of gravity as, "Anything that goes up must come down." Yet space capsules have circled the earth and even gone off to the planets, never to return. Have we defied the laws of nature? Of course not! It means that we have learned enough about the laws of nature to overcome the obstacles they place in our way. We have learned that if we accelerate an object fast enough and with enough force, it is possible for the object to go into orbit. We can counter the force of gravity with centrifugal force (another law of nature!), or we can even escape the pull of earth's gravity completely. By understanding the laws of nature, man has been able to conquer space.

The first American space travelers, upon re-entry into the earth's atmosphere, read aloud the first chapter of Genesis. What did these men have in mind when they chose this reading? That day represented a tremendous accomplishment for mankind. But what struck the astronauts at that moment, as they viewed planet Earth, the moon and the stars from their spaceship, was the grandeur of the world God created and the stability of the structured and comprehensible laws of nature. God gave man the ability to use and understand these laws, in order to "master and rule." Without the stability of nature, the accomplishements of science would not be possible.

Instinct versus Free Will

Ask: Did you ever see birds congregate in the fall before they fly south? Describe what you saw. We do not know how a particular species of birds knows where to assemble. We assume that they know by inborn genetic instinct what to do in order to survive the winter.

Humans too do some things by instinct. We search for food or ask for it when we are hungry; we need other humans and look for love and friendship. However, civilized people have some control over their instincts. They are able to postpone the gratification of their needs. We may be hungry, but we do not tear into our food. What do we do first? (Set the table, wash hands, say a blessing, cut the food.) What happens when we see something in the store we want? We do not grab it. What do we do instead? (We have to buy it. If we do not have the money we have to wait until we can earn or save enough money.) When we are angry at friends, we do not hit or kill them.

Ants and bees cannot change their societies. People can! People can decide, for example, that a communist society does not work for them, or that they do not want a dictatorship.

LESSON 10A

Blessings and What They Mean
Gen. 1:22, 28

☐ **In Preparation for Teaching**

The creation story contains several references to blessings. A blessing in this context is an outright gift, flowing from God to man. "The Lord has greatly blessed my master," Abraham's servant tells Laban (Gen. 24:35). "He has become rich. The Lord has given him sheep and cattle, silver and gold." God's blessing referred to in that passage is the gift of material goods. God also blessed our ancestors with the gifts of land, peoplehood, His protection, and His teachings. These were outright gifts to the people, given by God out of charity, regardless of whether they were deserved.

In this lesson we are concerned with blessings that come from God. Students, however, may ask about blessings in another context—blessings offered by a person to God. Can such a blessing be regarded as a gift as well? According to Abraham Joshua Heschel, when a person blesses God he provides God with the only thing God may be lacking: namely, the freely offered expression of man's gratitude, love, and recognition that all things stem from God. Others think that a blessing given by man to God must be regarded as an expression of awe, gratitude and praise, but not necessarily as a gift.

In either case, your students should understand clearly that when we utter the traditional blessing over, say, wine or bread, we are not blessing the wine or the bread, we are blessing *God*. We are praising and thanking Him who has provided us with His bounty. The act of partaking of the wine or the bread offer us the *occasion* for blessing, the opportunity to express our gratitude to God.

In the creation story, God blesses the fish, the fowl and mankind by giving them the ability to reproduce. God also gives man the ability to understand and thereby to "master and rule" the earth. In addition, God gives the seventh day the gift of holiness. The theme of holiness will be dealt with in the next lesson.

☐ Teaching Procedure

Ask your students to find how many times the text mentions that "God blessed" His creatures. He blessed fish, fowl, and man by giving them the ability to multiply. God blessed man and woman with the power to master and to rule. He blessed the seventh day with the gift of holiness.

Up to this point, all acts of creation had come from God. How are things going to differ now that the creation has been completed? Your students will note that vegetation will bring forth new vegetation, each according to its kind. Humans and animals will procreate. Man will master the earth, which up to now has been God's prerogative. God is giving His creatures powers which were originally His—as a gift.

If your class is sufficiently mature, you may want to discuss these two gifts God has given mankind: human sexuality and human dominion over the earth. Both gifts come with a responsibility—the need to be handled wisely by mankind. It may be compared to "a gift with a string attached," such as a father's gift of a car to his teenage child. What might the father say as he hands over the keys to the car?

What might God have said to mankind as He gave them the power of reproduction? Your students may be able to enumerate the joys of parenthood versus the responsibilities (e.g., the right of a baby to grow up in a stable family, etc.). They may bring up birth control and abortion.

What might He have said when He gave man and woman dominion over the earth? Your students should be able to discuss conservation versus ecological misuse.

A word of warning: Do not start this discussion unless you are prepared to handle it. Also, do not allow the discussion to consume a great deal of class time.

LESSON 10B

Holiness
Gen. 2:1–4a

▢ In Preparation for Teaching

The term "holy" (קָדוֹשׁ) describes that which is "set apart," "made separate," "earmarked for the divine," "dedicated to God and His worship." God blessed the seventh day by making it holy—by giving it the distinction of being a span of time dedicated to study and worship.

A blessing is a gift. Some blessings are gifts of wealth, land, or children. This blessing was the gift of holiness. It is important for students to understand the distinction between "blessing" and "holiness."

▢ Teaching Procedure

What is holiness? Do not expect your class to know. They may, however, know what things are traditionally considered "holy."

1) The land of Israel
2) The people of Israel
3) The Torah
4) The seventh day

Other responses may be *mezuzah* and *tefillin* (which contain parts of the Torah) or Ḥanukkah candles.

1) *The Land of Israel.* Holiness was concentrated in the Holy Temple, particularly in the Holy of Holies (site of the ark and the cherubim, i.e., God's throne). It extended from there over the city of Jerusalem, and to a lesser degree, over the whole land of Israel. All religious rituals took place in the Temple: sacrifices, prayers, the singing of Psalms, the playing of musical instruments, the congregating of people on the festival days. The area was separate and dedicated to God.

Inform your students that everything that took place in the Temple had to do with the religious observances of the people of Israel. The Temple was not used for games, circus performances, drinking parties or secular events. Moreover, since holiness emanated from the Temple over all of the land of Israel, the

Israelites believed that they were expected to live a life dedicated to God or else the land would "spew them out."

2) *The People of Israel.* On Mount Sinai, the people of Israel were commanded to be a holy people (Exod. 19:6). Following this command, they were given the Ten Commandments. Obviously there is a connection between these two events. (You may want to read that chapter aloud to point out this connection.) The people of Israel attain holiness through the fulfillment of God's commandments, living a life dedicated to God and dealing justly with their fellowmen.

3) *The Torah.* What is the Torah dedicated to? To teaching the worship of God and the observance of His commandments.

4) *The seventh day.* Your students will probably initially say that the seventh day is dedicated to rest. Establish that the word "holy" means dedicated to God and to His worship. The seventh day is the *span of time* dedicated to the worship of God through the observances at the Holy Temple (or modern synagogue), the study of Torah and the sense of belonging within the fellowship of Israel.

LESSON 11

The Seventh Day
Gen. 2:1–4a

☐ In Preparation for Teaching

Observance of the Sabbath is a frequent theme in the Bible. You may want to tell your students the story of the manna (Exod. 16:22–27) and the story of the man who was gathering wood on the Sabbath (Numbers 15:32–36). We know that the day was celebrated with festive family meals (2 Kings 4:23; Isaiah 1:13, 66:23). On the other hand, there were times when the Sabbath was often desecrated, as we learn from the admonitions of the prophets (e.g., Jeremiah 17:21–24).

Although in the text of the creation story we do not find a commandment for people to cease from work on the seventh day, later generations saw in Genesis 2:1–4a the beginning of the institution of the Sabbath.

Following this lesson you will find additional material dealing with the Sabbath to use with your class.

☐ Teaching Procedure

You may want to start this lesson by telling your class about the *shapattu*, a day that was known in Babylonia, and sounds like Sabbath (*Shabbat*), but was quite different in essence (see below, pp. 47–49). Discuss the differences between the two as a way to clarify the nature of the Sabbath.

You may also want to discuss the fourth of the Ten Commandments, which ordains the observance of the seventh day as a day of rest. The Torah contains two versions of the commandment concerning the Sabbath day (Exod. 20:8–11 and Deut. 5:12–15). The Exodus passage tells us that on the Sabbath we commemorate the peace and harmony of the seventh day of creation. According to the Deuteronomy passage, however, by celebrating the seventh day we commemorate our delivery from Egyptian slave labor. A day dedicated to God and His commandments is part of what makes the difference between a beast of burden or a slave, and a free person, created in God's image.

Lesson 11: The Seventh Day

Now, return to the creation story. God created the land, animals, and man, all on the sixth day. He did not reserve a separate day for the creation of man. What does the Torah seems to be teaching us by this fact? Your students should readily perceive that man is an animal. He is born, grows up and procreates, and he needs food, drink and air like any other animal. He also is a mortal like the other animals. Yet man is much more than any other animal because he was created in the image of God.

Draw two circles on the board. Circle "A" symbolizes God, while circle "B" stands for the world. We have already compared the relationship between God and the world to that of a craftsman and his work, a builder and his building. The two can never merge; they are intrinsically different. No matter how much the architect cares about his building, he cannot become a building, and vice versa.

Man lives *within nature;* he is part of the world. Yet, in some ways, he also resembles God. Let us add circle "C" to represent man. Man's position is, to a certain degree, flexible in that it can move between these two realms. It is within his power to become more like God and less like an animal. He can, on the other hand, choose to live like a beast and ignore his God-like aspects.

The seventh day may be one way by which man can elevate himself to become more in the image of God. The Bible presents us with two reasons for keeping the Sabbath day. One, in Exodus 20:8–11, is a religious one: God created the world in six days and ceased from work on the seventh. The second reason, in Deuteronomy 5:12–15, is a social reason: "Remember that you were a slave in the Land of Egypt." Slaves do not have a day of rest and contemplation. Only by having one day of rest can humans raise themselves above the level of an animal or a slave and get closer to God, in whose image they were created.

Proceed to teach whatever you consider necessary from the supplement dealing with the Sabbath (below, pp. 47–57).

Today we live in a society where most people only work five days a week. But even in our society, the seventh day maintains its unique identity among the Jewish people. For the seventh day is not just a day refraining from physical labor. It is a day dedicated to our worship of God, our study of God's commandments, and our seeking out of God, in whose image we were created.

SUPPLEMENT

The Sabbath
Beyond the Text

☐ *Shabbat* and *Shapattu*

> And God blessed the seventh day and declared it holy, because of it God ceased from all the work of creation which He had done. (Gen. 2:3)

These verses tells us that the holiness of the seventh day originated at the time of creation—it was not Israel's observance of the Sabbath that made it holy. Although one of the Ten Commandments commands the Israelites to observe the Sabbath, the book of Exodus tells us that the Israelites observed this day even before the Commandments were given. When God supplied them with food from heaven ("manna") they were instructed to gather a double supply on the sixth day, so that they would not have to gather any on the seventh day (Exod. 16:5, 22–30). In fact, even the language of the Sabbath commandment, "Remember [in Deuteronomy: 'Observe'] the Sabbath day," takes it for granted that the Israelites already knew what the Sabbath was.

Since the Torah indicates that the Sabbath was known even before Israel received her laws from God, the possibility arises that the Sabbath day, or something like it, was known even before the people of Israel existed.

Has the ancient Near East supplied us with examples of Sabbath observance by other peoples, peoples before the time of Israel? The Babylonians lived in Mesopotamia, the region between the Tigris and the Euphrates Rivers. Among the Babylonians two different Sabbath-like observances have been discovered.

The solar calendar that we use is based on the earth's revolution about the sun. A *lunar calendar*, however, is based on the moon's revolutions about the earth. According to a lunar calendar, a month does not have a fixed number of days. Rather, it lasts from new moon to new moon.

Archaeologists have found that in the lunar calendar used in Babylonia, the seventh, fourteenth, twenty-first, and twenty-eighth days of certain months were all regarded as unlucky days (like Friday the thirteenth, but worse!). In most months, the nineteenth day was called a "day of anger." The nineteenth day of a month is the *forty-ninth* day after the new moon of the previous month. The number forty-nine was important because it is the product of seven times seven. These days were thought to be controlled by evil spirits, and so people fasted on them. One of the ancient Babylonian texts records laws that forbid the king to eat cooked meat, change his clothes, offer a sacrifice, ride in a chariot, or make legal decisions on these days. A priest was forbidden to deliver a message from the gods, nor might a physician care for the sick. Curses uttered against enemies were thought ineffective.

From all this we learn that the seventh, fourteenth, twenty-first, and twenty-eighth days of certain lunar months were days of a very special kind. To the Babylonians they were unlucky.

By contrast to these unlucky days, the day of the full moon, which usually occurred on the fifteenth day of the month, was described by the Babylonians as the "day of the quieting of the heart [of the god]." The meaning of this phrase is not completely understood, but it seems to indicate a day which was considered especially good for soothing the gods with certain ceremonies. This day was called *shapattu*, a word which looks as if it might have the same origin as the Hebrew word *shabbat*.

Some scholars have thought that Israel's idea of the Sabbath came from these Babylonian observances. They point out the importance of the seven-day units of time and the limited activities on the seventh day, as well as the similarity between the words *shapattu* and *shabbat*. But the two institutions are quite distince, and there is not as yet have enough evidence to conclude that there is a connection between the biblical and Babylonian observances. It is true that the names *shapattu* and *shabbat* may be related, but other factors seem to show that there was not a direct influence of the Babylonian day on the Israelite day.

First of all, the *shapattu* is not, as far as we know, a day of limited activity—the Babylonians limited their activity on the unlucky seventh, fourteenth, twenty-first and twenty-eighth days, which are not related to *shapattu*.

Second, sometimes one of the Babylonian unlucky days does not come at an interval of seven days from the previous one. After a thirty-day month, the seventh day of the next month is actually *nine* days after the unlucky twenty-eighth day.

All of these Babylonian days—the unlucky days and the *shapattu*—are based on phases of the moon. The phases are its changes in appearance from new moon to full moon and back again. On the other hand, the Hebrew Sabbath has nothing to do with the moon. It is based on a count—*every* seventh day.

If the Israelites did borrow the Sabbath from Babylonian practice, they would seem to have borrowed the name of one day and the practices of another, and to have ignored the one thing that both of the others depended on, the moon.

Also, the work that was forbidden on the days of limited activity in Babylonia was not forbidden to the entire population, but only to certain classes of people (king, doctor, seer, etc.).

Finally, the limitations were imposed in Babylonia because the Babylonians feared the evil character of the day. In contrast, the biblical Sabbath is considered a holy and blessed day. Man ceases from labor because he wishes to imitate God's actions.

It is true that the similar names, the number seven, and the limitation on normal daily activity tempt us to find a connection between the biblical Sabbath and these Babylonian days. But the discussion above seems to show that in any case, even if Babylonia played a part in the development of the biblical day of rest, it must have been a small one. The biblical Sabbath is a totally different kind of day; in many respects it is the very opposite of the Babylonian days. Perhaps the one characteristic that the biblical Sabbath did receive from the rest of the ancient Near Eastern culture, was the idea of a seven-day unit of time.

In adopting the seven-day unit, however, the Bible freed the Sabbath from its dependence on the moon. The Sabbath recurs every seven days, and the period from Sabbath to Sabbath is never longer than seven days. The Torah proclaims that the seventh day received its special character from God alone—not from the moon, one of God's creations. *The seventh day is the Sabbath because God chose to bless it by declaring it holy.*

What, then, is the answer to our original question? Have we discovered any examples of Sabbath observance in the Ancient Near East before the time of Israel? No, at least not the kind of observance which the Torah demands. Although the Babylonians had observances which may have been similar to Israel's Sabbath, the observances had entirely different meanings in the two different civilizations.

The Torah was unique in establishing the Sabbath and connecting it with the creation of the world. Since the Sabbath did not originate with the nation Israel but rather with the creation of the world, its benefits must apply not to Israel alone. This idea was expressed in the Ten Commandments: the Sabbath rest was extended equally to the slave and to the foreigner, to the beast of burden and the cattle in the field (Exod. 20:10; Deut. 5:14).

❐ The Sabbath to Be Kept

Genesis Is the Origin of the Sabbath

In the *Amidah* of the Friday evening service, we find the following selection:

וַיְכֻלּוּ הַשָּׁמַיִם וְהָאָרֶץ וְכָל־צְבָאָם. וַיְכַל אֱלֹהִים בַּיּוֹם הַשְּׁבִיעִי מְלַאכְתּוֹ אֲשֶׁר עָשָׂה, וַיִּשְׁבֹּת בַּיּוֹם הַשְּׁבִיעִי מִכָּל־מְלַאכְתּוֹ אֲשֶׁר עָשָׂה. וַיְבָרֶךְ אֱלֹהִים אֶת־יוֹם הַשְּׁבִיעִי וַיְקַדֵּשׁ אֹתוֹ, כִּי בוֹ שָׁבַת מִכָּל־מְלַאכְתּוֹ, אֲשֶׁר בָּרָא אֱלֹהִים לַעֲשׂוֹת.

The heaven and the earth were finished, and all their array. On the seventh day God finished the work which He had been doing, and He ceased on the seventh day from all the work which He had done. And God blessed the seventh day and declared it holy, because on it God ceased from all the work of creation which He had done. (Gen. 2:1–3)

In the Friday night *Kiddush*, we find the same selection, this time preceded by the verse:

וַיְהִי עֶרֶב וַיְהִי בֹקֶר יוֹם הַשִּׁשִּׁי.

And there was evening, and there was morning, the sixth day. (Gen. 1:31b)

The inclusion of these selections in the Sabbath prayers makes it clear that the Sabbath which we observe has its roots in the verses that appear in Genesis, at the end of chapter 1 and the beginning of chapter 2. These verses describe God's actions on the seventh day—He ceased from His creating, and He blessed the seventh day by declaring it holy.

Resting Because God Rested

But where in these verses are we told that man should do the same with the seventh day? For instructions about man's setting aside the seventh day, we must turn to one of the Ten Commandments:

זָכוֹר אֶת־יוֹם הַשַּׁבָּת לְקַדְּשׁוֹ. שֵׁשֶׁת יָמִים תַּעֲבֹד וְעָשִׂיתָ כָּל־מְלַאכְתֶּךָ. וְיוֹם הַשְּׁבִיעִי שַׁבָּת לַיי אֱלֹהֶיךָ, לֹא תַעֲשֶׂה כָל־מְלָאכָה אַתָּה וּבִנְךָ וּבִתֶּךָ עַבְדְּךָ וַאֲמָתְךָ וּבְהֶמְתֶּךָ וְגֵרְךָ אֲשֶׁר בִּשְׁעָרֶיךָ. כִּי שֵׁשֶׁת יָמִים עָשָׂה יי אֶת־הַשָּׁמַיִם וְאֶת־הָאָרֶץ אֶת־הַיָּם וְאֶת־כָּל־אֲשֶׁר בָּם וַיָּנַח בַּיּוֹם הַשְּׁבִיעִי עַל כֵּן בֵּרַךְ יי אֶת־יוֹם הַשַּׁבָּת וַיְקַדְּשֵׁהוּ.

> Remember the Sabbath day and keep it holy. Six days you shall labor and do all your work, but the seventh day is a sabbath of the Lord your God: you shall not do any work—you, your son or daughter, your male or female slave, or your cattle, or the stranger who is within your settlements. For in six days the Lord made heaven and earth and sea, and all that is in them, and He rested on the seventh day; therefore the Lord blessed the sabbath day and hallowed it. (Exod. 20:8–11)

Here we see that the commandment instructs the Jews to remember to keep the Sabbath day holy because God rested from the work of creation on the seventh day. The commandment further states that because God rested on the seventh day, He blessed it and made it holy. (In our previous discussions, we explained the words וַיְקַדֵּשׁ אֹתוֹ "made it holy" to mean "set it aside for a divine purpose.")

It is worth noting that in instructing Israel to use the seventh day of creation as a model for its own Sabbath, the Torah uses the word וַיָּנַח "He rested" to describe what God did on the seventh day. This word does not appear in the Genesis account of creation. Surely the commandment does not mean to teach that God became physically tired from the work of creation and therefore rested, as man does. Why then, does the commandment use the word וַיָּנַח? The Rabbis of long ago struggled with this question, and offered the following answer:

> Has it not been said: "The Creator of the ends of the earth neither tires, nor is weary"? And it says: "He gives power to the weak." And it also says: "By the *word* of the Lord were the heavens made." How then can Scripture say: "And He *rested* on the seventh day"? Now . . . you must reason: If He, who cannot become weary, allowed it to be written that He created His world in six days and *rested on the seventh*, how much more should man, of whom it is written: "but man is born to toil," rest on the seventh day. (*Mekhilta de-Rabbi Ishmael*)

In this passage the Rabbis explain to us that the Torah cannot mean that God was tired after having worked hard, because God neither works nor tires the way human beings do. However, the Torah knew that when human beings work they do get tired. Therefore, it commanded the people to use the seven days of the creation week as a model for their own behavior—to do all their work in six days and stop on the seventh.

What are we to learn from this? It is as if the Torah said the following: You are now being commanded to take God's activity as a model for yourselves. As God created for six days, so you create (or work) for six days. As God stopped on the seventh day, so you stop on the seventh day. In this way, you are like God. However, in one important way you are different from Him. Whereas God never tires, you do tire, and after six days of work, your bodies will be very weary. Therefore, when you stop you must, first of all, give your bodies a chance to rest.

Reliving the Perfection of the First Sabbath

In Deuteronomy, the commandment about the keeping of the Sabbath is repeated. This time physical rest is stressed even more than it is in the commandment that appears in Exodus.

> Observe the sabbath day and keep it holy, as the Lord your God has commanded you. Six days you shall labor and do all your work, but the seventh day is a sabbath of the Lord your God: you shall not do any work—you, your son or your daughter, your male or female slave, your ox or your ass, or any of your cattle, or the stranger in your settlements, so that your male and female slave may rest as you do. Remember that you were a slave in the land of Egypt and the Lord your God freed you from there with a mighty hand and an outstretched arm; therefore the Lord your God has commanded you to observe the sabbath day. (Deut. 5:12–15)

But had the Torah meant to instruct Israel *merely to rest* on the seventh day of each week, it need not have referred to the seventh day of creation as a model for the Sabbath which people were to observe. It could have said: "You must set aside the seventh day of each week as a day of rest for your work-weary bodies." But, by means of the Exodus and Deuteronomy versions of this commandment, the Torah does more than this. First, it instructs the people to "Remember the Sabbath day and keep it holy." Through these words, the Torah seems to be asking that we remember (and try to understand) what the first sabbath day was like, and the purpose for which God set it aside, and that we then try to make of our own Sabbath a day which is similar to that seventh day and is set aside for a similar purpose.

Let us stop for a moment to recall the seventh day. The world was in a state of perfection, harmony and peace. Everything was in its proper place and performing its proper function. Nothing was in conflict with anything else. Both man and animals ate only plant food. There was neither strain nor pain. This was the world which God found to be "very good" on the sixth day (Gen. 1:31). This was the world that greeted the seventh day, and on the seventh day God neither added to His creation nor changed any part of it. He merely blessed the seventh day and declared it holy (i.e., set it aside for a divine purpose—a purpose which the Torah does not make clear to us).

Now, how can man "Remember the Sabbath day and keep it holy"? Obviously he cannot do this in a God-like way. He can only do it in a human way. We have already said that one human way of setting the Sabbath aside and making it holy is by resting physically from the work of the week.

How else can we set the Sabbath aside? There are several other ways:

(1) Since the seventh day of the creation week was a day of perfect peace and harmony we can try to make it such a day in our lives. Human beings find some measure of peace and harmony when they feel no tension, worry or anger. Therefore, we must aim to make the Sabbath a day in which we are free of these troublesome feelings.

(2) The seventh day of the creation week came after God saw all that He had made in the first six days, "and found it very good." Similarly, we may say that the human Sabbath should follow a week in which people work to keep the world "very good." Then, when the Sabbath approaches, they too, will be able to look upon all they have done with a feeling of satisfaction.

Refreshing the Spirit

Jewish tradition developed many laws and rules of behavior for the Sabbath. The purpose of these laws was to remind the people of the meaning of the Sabbath and to help them live according to its spirit. Their aim was to encourage the people to create a personal world of "holiness" for one day each week.

The laws enforce physical rest. They also separate the Jews from things or activities that are associated with strain and worry. For example, Jews are not permitted to use money on the Sabbath—or even to touch it. In this way, people could free themselves for a single day each week from the thing which most occupies and worries them during all the other days. The Sabbath is to be a day of relaxation and pleasure.

Not all kinds of relaxation and pleasure, however, are considered proper for the Sabbath. Not everything that is "fun" expresses the spirit and the idea of the Sabbath. For instance, the Rabbis taught that just as God had created nothing new on the Sabbath, so people should refrain from making new things (like painting a picture) or even changing things from one condition to another (like mowing the lawn) on the Sabbath. This kind of activity is prohibited even if it is considered pleasurable or relaxing. The Sabbath is to be a day in which people find satisfaction in that which already exists and do not try to make anything new.

Jewish tradition also teaches that the Sabbath is to be a day of study—especially of those things which might help us to understand better how we should behave towards God and man. In keeping with this thought, many Jews set aside some time each Sabbath for the study of the Torah and other books that deal with Jewish law and life.

So important a role did the Sabbath play in the education and life of the Jews throughout their long and often difficult history that Ahad Ha-am, a modern Hebrew writer, was moved to say:

יוֹתֵר מִשֶּׁיִּשְׂרָאֵל שָׁמְרוּ אֶת הַשַּׁבָּת, שָׁמְרָה הַשַּׁבָּת אוֹתָם.

More than Israel guarded the Sabbath—the Sabbath guarded Israel.

Stated less poetically, this means that the Sabbath—that day which the Jews set aside each week as a day of holiness, a day of rest from the work and the worry of the week, and a day of refreshment for spirits as well as for bodies—helped make it possible for the Jews as a people to continue to live through good times and bad.

How, specifically, does the Sabbath serve as guardian of Israel? It does this by providing the time each week in which all Jews can share a common spiritual experience. All Jews can devote themselves to God and to things of the spirit. This can give Jews strength to live on despite hostility or temptation.

Laws of the Sabbath

We shall now direct our attention to some of the laws and rules of behavior that are part of authoritative Jewish tradition. These laws continue in our own day to guide the behavior of the large numbers of Jews who strive to obey Jewish law and tradition. Some of them come from the Torah itself, and some were formulated and developed by our Rabbis.

(1) It is forbidden to cook and bake on the Sabbath. Therefore, all Sabbath food is prepared before sunset on Friday.
(2) It is forbidden to wash clothes on the Sabbath.
(3) It is forbidden to build on the Sabbath. This includes making things out of clay, wood, and other materials that are often used for artistic purposes.

(4) It is forbidden to write on the Sabbath. This includes drawing, painting, and related activities.
(5) It is forbidden to cut and tear on the Sabbath. This includes cutting cloth, picking flowers, cutting hair and nails.
(6) It is forbidden to light a fire or put out a fire on the Sabbath. Therefore, the oven is lit before the Sabbath begins and remains lit throughout the Sabbath day. This enables the Jew to warm the Sabbath food (which was cooked before the Sabbath began) without lighting a fire on the Sabbath.
(7) It is forbidden to use money or even handle it on the Sabbath.
(8) It is forbidden to ride on an animal, such as a horse, on the Sabbath. (This carries out that part of the Sabbath commandment which instructs Israel to provide rest for its animals as well as for its people on the Sabbath.)

Welcoming the Sabbath

In our own day, Jews who observe the Sabbath refrain from traveling in automobiles or other vehicles on the Sabbath. (Some authorities permit the use of automobiles for traveling to the synagogue for Sabbath services.) Avoiding travel has become an important way of assuring that the peace and calm of the Sabbath will not be destroyed by intrusions from the restlessness and turmoil of the "non-Sabbath world." It isolates Jews for one day a week in a "holy" atmosphere which each family creates in its own home by not traveling on the Sabbath. Jews are guaranteed an opportunity to spend the day enjoying the company of family and like-minded friends, reading, resting, studying and relaxing.

Many beautiful ceremonies have developed over the centuries as Jews have tried to find ways of setting the Sabbath apart from the weekdays and making it "holy." Let us imagine a modern Jewish home in which the Sabbath laws and customs are kept. What are we likely to find there?

Before the Sabbath begins, the house is cleaned, the family is bathed and dressed in fresh clothes, and the table is beautifully set. On the table stand a decorative wine bottle and a silver wine cup. Nearby lie two uncut loaves of *hallah*, a tasty and attractive-looking bread, covered with a colorful hand-embroidered cloth. In the center of the table is a vase filled with flowers.

Everything is in readiness—but one more thing needs to be done before the Sabbath can be welcomed into the home. Each member of the family drops a coin into a charity box, in this way sharing with others what the family has earned from the work of the week.

Now the home is ready to receive the Sabbath. It is a little before sunset. The mother approaches the table where two white candles are waiting to be lit. (In some families, the mother adds one candle for each child so that the number of Sabbath candles lit will vary with the size of each family.) She lights the candles, covers her eyes with her hands and recites a blessing:

בָּרוּךְ אַתָּה יי אֱלֹהֵינוּ מֶלֶךְ הָעוֹלָם אֲשֶׁר קִדְּשָׁנוּ בְּמִצְוֹתָיו וְצִוָּנוּ לְהַדְלִיק נֵר שֶׁל שַׁבָּת.

Thus, the Sabbath is welcomed into the home with a soft, glowing light. Members of the family might now leave for the synagogue. There too the Sabbath is welcomed—this time in the words of the *Kabbalat Shabbat* service. *Kabbalat Shabbat* literally means "The Welcoming of the Sabbath."

After the family returns from the synagogue they are ready for the Sabbath meal. First we hear the singing of *Shalom Aleichem* "Welcome"), a song in which the angels of harmony are asked to enter the home and bless its occupants. This, of course, is a poetic way of expressing the family's hope that the Sabbath day will be one of harmony and rest. Now the members of the family rise, lift their wine cups and chant the *Kiddush*, which begins with the Torah's description of the end of the creation week:

וַיְהִי עֶרֶב וַיְהִי בֹקֶר יוֹם הַשִּׁשִּׁי. וַיְכֻלּוּ הַשָּׁמַיִם וְהָאָרֶץ וְכָל־צְבָאָם. וַיְכַל אֱלֹהִים בַּיּוֹם הַשְּׁבִיעִי מְלַאכְתּוֹ אֲשֶׁר עָשָׂה, וַיִּשְׁבֹּת בַּיּוֹם הַשְּׁבִיעִי מִכָּל־מְלַאכְתּוֹ אֲשֶׁר עָשָׂה. וַיְבָרֶךְ אֱלֹהִים אֶת־יוֹם הַשְּׁבִיעִי וַיְקַדֵּשׁ אוֹתוֹ כִּי בוֹ שָׁבַת מִכָּל־מְלַאכְתּוֹ אֲשֶׁר בָּרָא אֱלֹהִים לַעֲשׂוֹת.

The *Kiddush* ends with a recitation of thankfulness for God's having given us the holy Sabbath day.

After reciting the *Kiddush*, the members of the family sip the wine and prepare for the meal. We drink wine on most happy Jewish occasions. Here it is the symbol of the joy that Jews find in the celebration of the Sabbath.

Celebrating the Sabbath Day

On Saturday morning the family attends another Sabbath service in the synagogue. At this service a portion of the Torah is read aloud. Each week a different portion is read.

During the day our family separates itself from the confusion, rush, and strain of the world. They rest, read, study, walk, and visit friends, things which encourage relaxation for their minds as well as their bodies. Even the greeting they use as they come and go and as they meet their friends on this day is different from what they use during the rest of the week. Rather than *hello* and *good-bye,* they say "*Shabbat Shalom*" ("a Sabbath of harmony") or "*Good Shabbos*" ("a good Sabbath").

The Sabbath is brought to a close with a ceremony known as *Havdalah.* This means "separation," and its purpose is to mark the point that separates the Sabbath from the rest of the week. A special candle is lit, a cup of wine is poured, and a beautiful spice container made of silver or carved wood, is placed on the table. A prayer that declares our faith in God is chanted. It is as if the Jew who recites the *Havdalah* prayer were saying, "The Sabbath day is over, the work week must begin. I trust that God will help me through this week. I pray that it will be a week of brightness and joy for all."

And then the work days begin.

UNIT II

The Second Creation Story
Genesis 2 and 3

UNIT II

The Second Creation Story

Genesis 2 and 3

UNIT II

The Second Creation Story
Genesis 2 and 3

☐ Overview

Although the creation of man, woman, and all living things has been described in Genesis 1, we find yet another description of their creation in Genesis 2. The creation story commencing with Genesis 2:4b makes no reference to the previous narrative. The earth, seas and luminaries have already been created; the earth, however, is barren, lacking both rain and the care of man (the "flow" described in 2:6 does not seem to substitute for rain).

God creates a man out of dust (or clay) and breathes into his nostrils the breath of life. He plants a beautiful garden in which He places man, "to till and tend it." The man is given only one prohibition: he must not eat from the "tree of knowledge, good and bad."

The Bible locates the garden in Eden, between the Tigris and the Euphrates rivers, in Mesopotamia. The Pishon and Gihon rivers have not been identified and may be imaginary. Oddly enough, the text veers off here to tell us about a land of precious stones and gold. A Babylonian myth tells of a garden of the gods where precious stones and gold grow on the trees. This creation story may be a subtle polemic against this Babylonian myth. This is a garden meant for man; its trees grow fruit, not gold or jewels.

God decides to create a fitting companion for man. He creates all the animals of the world and brings them to the man, who gives them each a name, but is unable to find a "fitting helper" amongst them. God creates woman out of one of the man's ribs. The man finds her to be a fitting helper. The man and the woman are naked, yet they feel no shame. The serpent tempts the woman to eat of the forbidden fruit. She eats and in turn gives some to the man who eats with her. As a result, they perceive that they are naked and make loin cloths for themselves.

God discovers that the man and the woman have disobeyed Him. He sentences them to a life of hard labor. He also expels them from the garden, thereby depriving them forever of the chance to eat from the "tree of life" and become immortal.

Do not be surprised if your students find it hard, as they read this story, to disregard the first creation story. They may be wondering: If there are *two* creation stories which one is true? Neither story, of course, depicts a historical event, and neither was written at the time of creation. The message of Genesis 1, by itself, leaves the reader with a "very good" world, but when complemented by Genesis 2 and 3 we gain a more complete view of the world as we know it (which is not always "very good") and the human beings in it. Some ideas which we will find in this story did not appear in the first story (e.g., that evil is a human product). Also, each story may teach the same idea by different means. For example, although man was created *last* in Genesis 1 and *first* in Genesis 2, in both cases the text teaches us that man is the pinnacle of creation.

This story is obviously a parable (see above, p. xiv).

LESSON 1

Finding a Name for the Chapter
Gen. 2:4b–3:24

◻ **Teaching Procedure**

Ask your students to read part or all of Gen. 2:4b–3:24. What elements in the story indicate that it is not a historical event? Your class should come up with some of the following responses:

1) The Tree of knowledge, good and bad
2) The Tree of life
3) A man made out of dust
4) A woman made out of a rib
5) The talking serpent

It is evident that the story is a parable. How does reading a parable differ from reading, say, a detective story? In a detective story, we expect every question to be answered and each "loose end" to be accounted for and "tied" into the plot by the end of the story. A parable, on the other hand, has *one main thrust*, one dominant idea. Side issues may or may not be picked up again elsewhere in the Bible (e.g., why do *we* have to suffer for the disobedience of the man and the woman?).

Review the structure of the first creation story (Gen. 1:1–2:4a; see above, pp. 4–5). Ask them to find the first verse of the second story (2:4b). Ask for possible reasons why the order of "heaven and earth" in the first story appears reversed in the second story, "earth and heaven." Your students may realize that the first story deals with the creation of the physical world—earth, sky and luminaries (as well as living creatures), while the second story focuses on the events transpiring on earth. Remind your class of the name they had chosen for the first story, and ask them to choose a name for the second one. Emphasize the following point: In the first story, everything happens because God makes it so. In this story, however, both God and man are responsible for the development of events. God is the Creator, but it is man who names the animals, disobeys God and ultimately is responsible for his expulsion from the garden. Your students may sugestion names such as "Man in God's World" or "Man as God's Partner."

LESSON 2A

The Prohibition
Gen. 2:4b–17

☐ Teaching Procedure

This story lends itself to dramatization. Discussing the story as a possible play is a helpful device. You may want to delineate the plot first and save discussion for later. In the following lessons, however, ideas are discussed as they come up within the unfolding story. In using either approach, it is essential that the teacher read all the material pertaining to Genesis 2 and 3 before attempting to teach it.

Present the idea of a play to your class. Ask how many actors would be needed. List them on the board:

1. God
2. Man
3. Woman
4. Serpent

God and man are the main characters for the first scene. Ask for suggestions about scenery. What colors would we need to paint the scenery for the first scene? (Do not be surprised if your students at first reject the notion of a barren earth, since vegetation had already been created in the first story.) As your class refers to the text and makes suggestions, you may want to outline the drama on the board:

ACT ONE, SCENE ONE

Place	Actors	Action
Barren Earth	God, man	1) God creates a man.
		2) God gives the man breath of life.

The Bible says that man was made out of dust. What is the Torah trying to teach us by this detail? (Remind your class that this story is a parable.) As your students may be aware, "the dust of the earth" is an expression denoting the lowliest of the low—it is what we step on. Also, man is dependent on the earth for his sustenance. Finally, after death, his body will turn to dust. Ask

Lesson 2A: The Prohibition

your students for the meaning of the sound-alike words *adama* and *adam* in Hebrew. They may know that *adama* means earth and *adam* means "man" or "mankind." Remind your students that in the first story, man and animals were created on the same day, indicating that man, too, is an animal; yet we are told that he was created in God's image. Here the "breath of life" refers to the physical act of breathing—it does not mean "soul" or "spirit." Animals too breathe, but the Bible tells us that man alone gets his breath from God. Thus, here too we have a dual image: man is created from the lowly dust, but he receives his breath directly from God. Throughout the Bible and in the prayerbook liturgy, we find this recurring concept: the greatness of man coexists with the fact that he is no more durable than a blade of grass. (See Psalms 90:5–6, recited in the morning service on Sabbath and festivals; and Kohelet [Ecclesiastes] 3:19, recited every morning.)

Next, God plants a garden in Eden and places man there to "till and tend" it. Is this hard or easy work? If your students do not know, leave the answer to this question suspended until you come to Genesis 3:18, where it becomes clear that this was easy work. (The earth did not grow thorns and thistles.) Work is part of the perfect world.

What prohibition does God give man? What does the story seem to imply by the fact that there are no prohibitions regarding the tree of life? Your students may realize that had man not disobeyed, he may have been permitted to eat of the fruit of this tree. Ask: What is a "tree of life"? Your students may have some notion of a tree whose fruit would enable man to live forever or make him young again in old age, since this motif appears in the myths of other peoples and in many fairy tales.

What is a "tree of knowledge, good and bad"? (Note the unusual grammar in both English and Hebrew.) Your students' suggestions might center around the idea that eating the fruit of this tree would make the man aware of the difference between good and evil. Why, then, does God prohibit eating from this tree? Some students may suggest that man must have had *some* of this knowledge already: God could not have expected obedience from man had he not known that obedience to God is *good* and disobedience *bad*. You may want to discuss "blind obedience," the kind of obedience not based on understanding. An eighteen-month-old child knows not to cross the street or touch the stove because "mother says not to," not because he understands that it is dangerous. That is the kind of knowledge the man and the woman might have had before eating the fruit. At this point, the nature of the tree is not important (for the time being you may want to call this tree "brand X"). What is important is not the specifics of the prohibition, but that *God had given man a prohibition*. He could have said, "Don't drink of the Tigris," or "Don't ever step into the glade near the Pishon."

The question may be raised: If God does not want man to eat of the tree of knowledge, why does He place it in the middle of the garden? Unless there is a prohibition, man has no opportunity to control his appetites and prove his goodness! Unless there is a possibility for being *bad*, man cannot get credit for being good. Try using the following example:

Your mother told you not to use her car (bike, boat, or whatever is appropriate to the age and desires of your students). Situation A: Mother locked the car and took the keys to work with her. Situation B: She locked the car and left the keys on the hook in the garage. Which would you prefer your mother to do? Why?

Your students will, no doubt, voice different opinions. Situation A is easier because no choices have to be made. Situation B is more flattering. Mother trusts you and is treating you as a mature person. On the other hand, there are inherent difficulties: you may be tempted, your friends may dare you, you are responsible for your actions, etc. Situation B, in the long run, is an "educational" experience. Mother is trying to teach you something by leaving the keys on the garage hook. An ethical society can only survive by making individuals responsible for their own acts, leaving them unable to say, "I did it because my friends told me to."

Continue developing the play on the board, through the point where the prohibition is given.

LESSON 2B

A Fitting Helper
Gen. 2:18–24

☐ In Preparation for Teaching

According to the ethos of Israel, only woman is seen as a "fitting helper" for man. She alone, of all living creatures, is able to *talk*, to communicate with man and share his feelings. She can understand his thoughts and plans and help to carry them out. The union of man and woman also guarantees the continuation of the human race.

With young students you may want to downplay the sexual aspects of a "fitting helper," and deal with it on the level of friendship. In a more mature class, the subject of homosexuality may come up. Some societies (e.g., ancient Greece) glorified the attachment of one male to another. If you are willing and able, you may want to discuss the Israelite ethos versus the defensibility of homosexuality. While we may all agree today that homosexuals should not be harassed the Israelite ethos affirms that society at large is best served by the union of man and woman.

☐ Teaching Procedure

Pick up the train of the story. What happens after God gave the man the prohibition? The text tells us that God decided it was not good for the man to be alone (2:18).

What might have prompted this observation? The man may have been depressed, walking around aimlessly. Your students may observe that God seems to be more aware of man's needs than man himself, who never having had a "fitting helper," may not have recognized his need for one. How does the Bible have God try to solve man's problem of lonelinesss? He creates the animals to see if man would find a "fitting helper" among them. Direct your student's attention to 2:19–21.

What is a "fitting helper"? Whom would *you* consider a "fitting helper" for yourself? You may want to ask your students to respond to this quesiton in writing.

Students may list a variety of answers, ranging from "someone who is like me" to "someone who is good at things I am not good at" (a complementary companion). Their lists may include:

someone who likes to play ball (as I do)
someone who likes to read (as I do)
someone who can cook (which I cannot)
someone who has survival skills (which I do not)

The main point is that a person needs *someone he can talk to*, someone who can feel empathy and express sympathy. Although some animals (e.g., dogs and horses) can provide companionship for man, only with another human being can one discuss shared experiences and feelings. Only a being that can express itself in human terms can be a "fitting helper" for man.

In this story, the man is to name the animals, as God named the elements of the physical world in the first story. The purpose of this is (a) to give each animal its own identity, (b) to give the man mastery over them.

What happens as the man calls one animal "cat" or "donkey"? When we say "cat" we evoke a certain image. We have not all seen the same cat, yet we all are aware of the "catness" of the animal. Ask your class what they think of when they think "cat." Your students will come up with a long list:

soft, cuddly
furry, agile, has whiskers
eats mice and birds, a hunter

What comes to mind when you say "elephant"? What image does "butterfly" evoke? How do you suppose the man felt after he named all living things—frogs, apes and lions? Your class will readily see that the man felt superior, proud, etc. It may take longer to realize that he would also feel lonely, "different"; he is *man*—not lion, frog, or ox. He did not find a fitting helper among the animals. Did not God know this in advance? Yes, but He might have wanted the man to discover this for himself.

Next God puts man to sleep and creates a woman (she is not called Eve until the end of the next chapter) out of his rib. Find, in the text, how the man felt about the woman. He identifies with her. He recognizes that *she is like him*, though not identical with him and *he gives her a name* (אִשָּׁה) *that sounds like his own* (אִישׁ). He recognizes in her a "fitting helper."

Continuing the play, your board at this point should look something like this:

Lesson 2B: A Fitting Helper

ACT ONE, SCENE TWO

Place	Actors	Action
Garden	God, the man, the woman	1) God notices man is lonely. 2) God creates animals. 3) The man names the animals. 4) God creates woman. 5) Man likes her.

This may be a convenient place to lower the curtain!

LESSON 3A

The Temptation
Gen. 2:25–3:7

◻ In Preparation for Teaching

Every society is governed by certain rules and norms of behavior. As human beings, we are susceptible to feelings of shame and guilt when we violate the norms we grew up believing were just and good. We feel frightened and diminished by such violation. A society that fails to teach its members to feel shame and guilt has failed in its task.

In Genesis 3, we are told that the man and the woman are naked, yet they feel no shame. This story was obviously written in a society that regarded wearing clothes as the norm. In other societies, the norm may be that a woman covers her face but bares her breasts. Nudists feel no shame or guilt because in their subculture, nudity is the norm. This kind of shame is acquired, not "natural."

The man and the woman in Genesis 3 feel no shame—they are naive, one with nature, like babies or animals. The Hebrew text juxtaposes the word עֲרוּמִּים ("naked," 2:25), with the word עָרוּם ("sly," 3:1). In using these two like-sounding words, the text associates the animal-like naïveté of the man and the woman with the negative side of animalness—the snake!

Note that in today's language "naked" sometimes stands for "innocent." When the accused person says, "I stand *naked* before you," he does not mean "without clothes." We also use "*bare* the facts" and "*uncover* the truth." Conversely, we speak of a "coverup" when the truth is hidden.

There is irony here: a man and a woman who go around naked like the lower animals, and a lower animal (a snake) talks and deceives like a person. This point is lost in the English translation, where the similarity of words עֲרוּמִּים and עָרוּם cannot be appreciated.

Note that in 3:7–8 the man and the woman hide in spite of the fact that they are now wearing loin cloths and thus are not naked. They are aware of what they did and hide out of shame—not because they are naked.

☐ Teaching Procedure

Have your students read the first paragraph of Genesis 3. Where does the next act of the drama take place? How should the tree of knowledge be depicted? Obviously, it is a delightful tree, with beautiful fruit, etc. What type of fruit does it grow? (We do not know. We assume, however, that it is *not* an apple tree, as students are apt to say, since apples are not native to Mesopotamia. It may be a fig.)

How many actors will we need? Although only the woman and the serpent are on stage at first, the man and God have to stay in the background, ready to enter the play on cue.

Let your students provide you with the facts for Act Two of the play.

ACT TWO, SCENE ONE

Place	Actors	Action
In front of the Tree of Knowledge	Serpent, the woman, the man	1) The serpent entices the woman. 2) The woman eats. 3) The man eats with her.

Did the woman and the serpent know of the prohibition. Their conversation indicates that they did. Your students can probably tell you that the serpent is feigning confusion about the details. Does the woman have all the facts straight? Had God told the man not to *touch* the tree? Who is responsible for this embellishment? Did man add it? Did she herself add it? What does this addition teach us about the one who added it? Either the man did not trust the woman, or she herself did not trust her own ability to overcome temptation.

What takes place before she eats? Note the sensual words used by the text: "good," "a delight" "desirable" (3:6). All her senses seem to have been overwhelmed. What does she assume the tree will give her? Evidently she expects in some way to become "God-like." Your students may say that the serpent was right insofar as she did not die upon eating the fruit. The expression מוֹת תָּמוּת (2:17) is ambiguous. It means either "you shall die" (i.e., immediately) or "you are doomed to die" (i.e., you will not become immortal, you will never eat from the tree of life). From the continuation of the story we will learn which of the two interpretations is correct here.

The woman eats, and shares the fruit with the man, who has appeared on the scene. Their eyes are opened and they perceive their nakedness. They are ashamed and cover themselves with a garment made of fig leaves. Let your students complete the drama on the board.

Although you have already discussed the story as a parable, your students may ask if the serpent really talked, or whether he walked on two legs or four. Since this is a parable, the serpent need not have existed. Do not attempt a "scientific" explanation. We may interpret the snake to stand for temptation. Just as the characters of the man and the woman stand for *every* man and woman. Each of us has to withstand temptation.

Ask your students how they would depict the tempting of the woman by the serpent in a comic strip. What would the woman's "bubble" say? What about the serpent's? Can you imagine yourself in the woman's position? How would you describe the same events *without* a serpent? The woman is having an inner struggle, an internal conflict. It is possible to envision this in terms of two inner voices: one enticing her to do what she knows to be wrong, the other trying to stop her. The second voice is often called "conscience." What is the name of the first voice? Appetite, Challenge, Desire, "I dare you"—are all good suggestions.

What might the man and the woman expect would happen to them? What happens according to the story? How disappointing this must have been! What kind of music would you play here? How would the two actors indicate their sense of shame? Cringing and covering themselves with their hands are two plausible suggestions. Your class may suggest lowering the curtain now, or possibly after the making of the loincloths.

LESSON 3B

Shame and Guilt
Gen. 3:7

☐ **Teaching Procedure**

We have briefly discussed shame and guilt as feelings unique to human beings. "Conscience" is part of what makes us "in the image of God." We have, however, not discussed the emotions of shame and guilt in depth. You may want to begin by asking your students in what ways the man and the woman are different after the eating of the forbidden fruit. Who, in general, does not know shame or guilt? (Babies and animals.) What is there about babies and animals that makes them feel no shame or guilt? They are innocent, one with nature.

Did you ever experience shame or guilt? Let your students talk. Be careful not to moralize, since they are volunteering their experiences. Some of your students may claim feeling shame only when "found out"; others may say they felt shame or guilt even though no one ever discovered they had broken the rules. The ability to feel shame and guilt depends to a large degree on how well we have been "socialized" through our upbringing, i.e., by what our parents and teachers have taught us.

The fact that we can feel guilt and shame is a great "inhibitor." It stops us from doing what we know is wrong. There may be some people—very few—who are unable to feel shame and guilt. Such people are more likely to break the rules. This should be an open discussion.

LESSON 4A

Confrontation With God
Gen. 3:8–13

☐ Teaching Procedure

Where do we find the man and the woman as the curtain rises on the next act of the drama (3:8)? What are they doing? What do they hear? How do they feel?

Does God know where they are? Why does God ask a rhetorical question ("Where are you?" 3:9)? What chance does God give to man? He gives the man and the woman the chance to explain and apologize. Instead the man blames the woman for tempting him.

Some of your students may say that the man did not know that the fruit he was given was from the forbidden tree. Direct their attention to 3:12: "The woman you put at my side—she gave me of the tree." His excuse seems to be that she tempted him; he therefore disclaims responsibility for his act. He does *not* claim that he did not know what he was eating. This view is reinforced by verse 3:17, where God says to the man: "Because you heeded your wife and ate of the tree about which I commanded you saying, 'You shall not eat of it. . . .'"

Does the fact that the woman enticed him excuse him? Why not? Let your students find in the text that the woman too "passes the buck" (the serpent "duped" her, 3:13).

What might God have said to man and woman, as they claimed to be victims of seduction? Your students may come up with a variety of responses:

They did not *have* to eat.
They had a chance to choose.
They misused their freedom.
They were weak. Now they will have to pay the consequences!

On the board, outline the scene as your students supply the data.

ACT TWO, SCENE TWO

Place	Actors	Action
The garden	the man, the woman, God, the serpent	1) The man and the woman are in the garden. 2) They hear the sound of God. 3) They hide. 4) God calls out to man.

LESSON 4B

Consequences of Disobedience
Gen. 3:14–21

☐ In Preparation for Teaching

The story in Genesis 1 commences with the world in a state of *Tohu Vavohu*. Day by day the world improves until at the end of the sixth day, it is a very good world. If we were to draw a line graph of the story, we would get an ascending line.

What about this story? In Genesis 2 there too is an ascent: First the world is barren. Then a man is created. God plants a garden and creates animals. With the creation of woman, everything seems to be "very good." But then the graph of the story takes a "nose dive" as a result of the disobedience. All relationships are changed. Write "Before" on one side of the board and "After" on the other side. Fill in the details offered by your students as they review the punishments. On the following page is found a possible schema:

Lesson 4B: Consequences of Disobedience

Relationship	Before	After
God and the man	God protects the man. God gives him a garden, food, beauty, light work, partial helpers (animals) and a woman.	God punishes the man. God does not, however, turn away from him completely, as shown by the fact that God makes clothes for him.
The man and God	The man obeys God. He does not eat of the tree.	The man disobeys, then fears God. He blames God for giving him the woman.
The man and the woman	"Bone of my bones, flesh of my flesh"—he identifies with her. She is his fitting helper, an equal partner.	He accuses her. He now will be her master.
The man and the animals	The animals come to the man to receive a name. He is their master.	There is enmity forever between human and serpent.
The man and the earth	The man performs easy work. The earth provides him with ample fruit.	The earth grows thorns and thistles. The man will have to work hard in order to eat.
The man and life	The man might have been permitted to eat of the tree of life, and live forever. (There would, therefore, be no need to bear children.)	The man has to die. He can never eat of the tree of life. Women will bear children in pain.

LESSON 5

Tree of Knowledge, Good and Bad
Gen. 3:22–24

▢ In Preparation for Teaching

At this point your students may be angry with God. Why is the punishment so harsh? Can't God forgive, just this once? You may now want to discuss the nature of the tree. What kind of knowledge does it give the man? What does the expression טוֹב וָרָע ("good and bad") mean?

It is often helpful to ascertain how expressions are used in other parts of the Bible. In Deuteronomy 1:39, "Your children who do not yet know good from bad," the terms "good" and "bad" deal with moral discretion. The children are too young to know the difference. In 2 Samuel 19:36 Barzillai declares that he is too old to "know good and bad" This does not imply anything about the state of his moral judgment. The rest of his words indicate that he is too old to enjoy the pleasures of the world's temptations: wine, song, and probably women. The word "knowledge" often has a sexual connotation.

In 2 Samuel 14:17, the woman from Tekoa says to David, "For as an angel of God, so is my lord the king to *discern good and bad*." And later, in 14:20, she continues, "my lord is wise, according to the wisdom of an angel of God *to know all things that are in the earth.*" The knowledge of good and bad, which makes King David like an angel of God, is equated here with the "knowledge of all things." In this case, "good and bad" is a *merism*, an all-inclusive term. ("A to Z" is an example of a merism: it means *all* the letters from A to Z. Other examples of merisms are: "from the cradle to the grave," meaning all of one's life; or "from young to old" including *everybody*.) With the eating of the fruit, the man and the woman have acquired all the knowledge one needs to live in this world—knowledge, not only moral and sexual, but also manners and conventional behavior, knowledge which is indispensable for living in this world (when and how to wear clothes, grow food, etc.)

The man and the woman could either have lived forever (having eventually eaten of the Tree of Life), or else have eaten of

Lesson 5: *Tree of Knowledge, Good and Bad*

the Tree of Knowledge. They could not have both everlasting life and also the knowledge of all things. Had they obeyed, they would have remained forever "children," dependent on God. Now that they have acquired knowledge, they no longer belong in a protected environment.

☐ Teaching Procedure

Tell your students as much or as little of the above as you find necessary. It is unlikely that they will reach by themselves the conclusion that "good and bad" is a *merism.* You will have to explain why this use of the expression is most apt here, although you do not have to bring the sources.

Ask your students if they would want to live in the garden in Eden. Interestingly enough, while adults may long to "return to the womb," most young people look forward to growing up. They want to make money (and spend it), they want to drive a car, get married, be independent, make their own decisions. Many young people would regard living in the garden as dull and boring ("no television").

God's words to the serpent, the man and the woman are statements of punishments. However, in God's punishment of the man, one key word is repeated, the word "eat." The man will have to toil and work by the sweat of his brow, *but there will be bread for him to eat.* Similarly, the woman's punishment is severe, but not so severe as to dissuade her from having children. Many mothers willingly—eagerly—have second, third and more children, even after experiencing the pain during childbirth of the first. They consider the pain worthwhile. Children compensate for the pain.

You may want to compare the relationship of God to the man and the woman, to the relationship of parents to their children. Although parents love their grown-up children as much as they loved them when they were babies, relationships change. Children become less dependent on their parents, parents become less protective of their children. As a matter of fact, parents in their old age may become in one way or another dependent on their adult children.

This change in relationships is not always smooth and gradual. It often involves pain and friction. A child's maturity does not always go hand in hand with its wish for independence. Parents sometimes underestimate the maturity of their child. This stage of a child's rebellion against his or her parents often occurs as the child experiences puberty. The man and the woman's disobedience and revolt against God may be considered their puberty. This episode may be analogous to a young adult's breaking away from the parental home and its authority.

You may start this discussion by asking: What takes place in a household when a new baby is expected? Your class may know that everything is cleaned and made sterile by the parents in anticipation. Yet, when the time comes, the same parents who welcomed the child as a baby help that child pack his or her bags to go to college.

It is possible that the man and the woman—having gained the knowledge of "all things"—no longer belongs in the garden, just as after a while the child no longer belongs in the nursery.

It is only now that the man names his wife Eve. She acquires a new role in life, that of the mother of all mankind. God drives the man and the woman out of the garden and places the cherubim (mythological beings, part-man, part-lion, part-eagle) at the gate to keep the man and the woman from returning to the garden and from partaking of the fruit of the tree of life. Humans are mortal, and they must make their way in the harsh world of reality.

UNIT III
After the Garden
Gen. 4:1–6:4

UNIT III

After the Garden
Gen. 4:1–6:4

☐ Overview

These chapters can be broken up into four parts:

1) 4:1–16   The Story of Cain and Abel
2) 4:17–24   Cain's Generations
3) 4:25–5:32 Seth and His Descendants
4) 6:1–8   The Divine Beings and the Daughters of Men

It is important at this point to remind your class that the Bible is not a "history of civilization." We are not dealing with a linear history. There are gaps in the account which the Torah does not seem to be interested in (although we may be!). One story does not necessarily follow the previous one as would a sequel. These various stories about different personalities were passed down orally and separately, and eventually were collected and recorded. We are dealing with a patchwork of stories, rather than one continuous narrative.

For example, in the preceding story we read of Adam and Eve, the first man and the first woman in the world. In Genesis 4, we learn that Cain and Abel are their sons. Yet Genesis 4 also assumes that there are already more people populating the earth: Cain is afraid of being killed, he builds a city, he takes a wife. Where did all these people come from? The Torah does not tell us. We are reading from a collection of separate stories.

In Lessons 1 and 2, we will explore the story of Cain and Abel—the offering and the murder, respectively. We suggest that the teacher read both lessons before commencing to teach this story.

LESSON 1

The Story of Cain and Abel, I
Gen. 4:1–7

☐ In Preparation for Teaching

In Genesis 4, the births of Cain and Abel immediately follow the loss of access to the tree of life. We are not told anything about the childhood of the boys. Instead we are told in one and the same verse that they are born and that they have grown up.

Eve is delighted with the first human being created by her, with the help of God. Cain is a tiller of the soil; Abel is a keeper of sheep. We do not know anything about the relationship between them. We are told of only two events in the lives of the brothers: (1) Cain and Abel bring offerings to the Lord, and (2) Cain kills Abel.

Cain brought an offering to God from the fruit of the soil. Abel brought the choicest of the firstlings of his flocks (מִבְּכֹרוֹת צֹאנוֹ וּמֵחֶלְבֵהֶן). God accepted Abel's offering but rejected Cain's. Why? The only indication can be found in the words "firstling" (בְּכוֹר) and "choicest" (חֵלֶב). Later in the history of Israel, the firstling (בְּכוֹר) would be dedicated to God and the hard fat (חֵלֶב) would be burned to God on the altar. Thus by bringing the choicest (fattest) firstlings, Abel brought a proper, acceptable gift. The Bible views the stories prior to the formation of the Israelites according to later biblical values, stated at a later period.

Cain seems to be bringing a gift without being selective. In effect, he is keeping the best for himself. Cain is distressed at God's rejection of his offering. God is not angry! Like a father who turns to his upset son with words of encouragement, God says to Cain, "Why are you distressed? Surely if you do right, there is uplift (of face)." "This is not the end of the world! It is within your power to change the situation." However, the Lord cautions, "If you do not do right, sin is like a demon at the door whose urge is toward you." Sin, like a demon waiting to ensnare you, is always at the door—as you come and as you go—a constant threat! The Lord concludes with another verse of encouragement: "Yet you can be its master."

☐ **Teaching Procedure:**

Have your students read Gen. 4:1–17.

How does Genesis 3 end? The stationing of the cherubim at the gate of the Garden of Eden indicates that man can never attain eternal life. What is man's answer to death? It is giving birth—the continuation of the species.

Gen. 4:1 tells us that Eve gives birth to a son. How does Eve feel about the child? (Remind your class that "pangs of childbirth" were given as a punishment in the preceding chapter.)

Gen. 4:3–4 cover a lot of ground. Why did Cain and Abel bring sacrifices in the first place? They were not asked to do this. Your students may say that they feared God and wanted to pacify Him, or that they wanted to insure His help in the future. Do not be surprised if the motive of thanksgiving has to be broached by the teacher. Ask your students how we substitute for sacrifices today? We pray and say *berakhot*. Our motives for prayer could be thanksgiving, request or even apprehensive supplication. The familiar *Birkat Hamazon* (grace after meals) contains all of these motives.

How does man know whether his offering has been accepted or not? The text does not say. Your students may say that if Cain had brought his gift in the hope of obtaining a good future yield and instead had a crop failure, he may have assumed his gift was rejected. Others may say that Cain who had chosen his gift haphazardly knew in his heart that it was not an acceptable offering. Say, for example, I give my friend something I happen to have around the house (a white elephant) as a gift. Since I do not like the gift, I sense that my friend will not like it either. A good gift is something the giver himself would like to receive.

Your students may mention two different ways by which Cain could tell whether his gift was accepted or not: (1) external, i.e., God's reaction to the gift at some future date; and (2) internal, i.e., Cain's knowledge of his own *kavanna* (intention).

Some of your students may voice anger with God. Why did He refuse a gift offering? We have all been taught to accept a gift gracefully, acknowledge it and thank the giver, regardless of what the gift is. "One does not look a gift-horse in the mouth."

You may want to ask them how God as a recipient of gifts differs from man as a recipient. God *knows* man's intentions, while man can never quite be sure of another person's motivations. Moreover, God does not *use* gifts; God does not require food or drink. Man brings a gift (קָרְבָּן) to God because he seeks to be near (קָרוֹב) to God. Therefore to God the *intention* is more important than the gift itself. It is absurd to think that God might prefer meat to the fruit of the soil, or the expensive gifts offered by the rich to the meager ones of the poor.

Some students may say that Cain brought his gift first, and that Abel may have brought a better offering to "show Cain up." It is unlikely, however, that God would have accepted Abel's gift knowing of such intentions.

How does Cain feel? He is sad, dejected. The text says his "face fell." He seems ashamed to face the world. Are these the reactions of an evil man? Probably not. Cain does offer a gift to God. He is upset because God rejected him. He might have made an error in judgment. Still he wants to be acceptable to God.

Write Gen. 4:6–7 on the board and explain them.

(a) Why are you distressed?
(b) And why is your face fallen?

(c) Surely, if you do right,
(d) There is uplift [of face].

(e) But if you do not do right
(f) Sin couches [waits for you] at the door;
(g) Its urge is towards you [it wants to grab you],

(h) Yet you can be its master.

Phrases (c) and (d) are encouragement: God urges Cain, "If you do better, there is uplift of face," i.e., you will be able to face the world again.

Phrases (e)–(g), however, are a warning: God cautions Cain, "Once you fall into the clutches of evil, it is hard to extract yourself."

The passage ends with phrase (h), on a note of encouragement: "Yet you *can* master it."

You may want to discuss "falling in the clutches of evil" using the following analogies: A person borrows money from the till to pay a small bill. He is unable to return the money. What may happen next? Small indiscretions often lead to larger ones.

LESSON 2

The Story of Cain and Abel, II
Gen. 4:8–16

☐ **In Preparation for Teaching**

The two events—the offering and the murder—seem to be related: God said to Cain, "If you do better. . . ." We can infer some omission in connection with the offering. Immediately after this address by the Lord we find a mutilated sentence: "Cain said to his brother Abel. . . ." (The Septuagint, the Greek translation of the Bible which dates from the period of the Second Temple, seems to have been made from a copy of the biblical text slightly different from the one we know today, adds: "Let us go to the field.") When they are in the field, Cain attacks his brother Abel and kills him. God asks Cain where his brother is. As in the case of God's confronting Adam in the garden, God knows the answer but gives Cain a chance to explain, repent or justify himself. Instead Cain lies: "I do not know," and callously adds, "Am I my brother's keeper?"

Gen. 4:10, "Your brother's blood cries out to *Me* from the ground," may need some additional explanation. Ancient tribes believed that human blood, when spilled, had to be avenged. In some societies, it did not make any difference whether a death had resulted from a murder or an accident. In either case, the relatives of the dead person would try to kill the party responsible. If they killed him, *his* relatives would, in turn, try to kill the avenger. This was called a "blood feud"; sometimes a blood feud would take generations to settle.

In Israelite society, the spilling of blood was seen as a sin against God. Here too, at first, the family of the victim was responsible for obtaining revenge. But already in early times, a distinction was made between murder and manslaughter: the accidental killer was permitted to escape to a "city of refuge." Eventually, courts replaced the family as rightful avengers.

The blood of Abel, however, calls out to *God* for revenge. Cain is banned from the soil, which in a sense, cooperated with him by receiving his brother's blood. The image of the earth "opening its mouth" is a metaphor. It refers to the ground "soaking up" the blood or possibly opening its mouth for a grave. Adam, we learned, will have to work hard, but at least his labor produce bread for him to eat. But for Cain the earth will not yield its "strength" (or produce) even if he should till the soil.

Only now does Cain break down. His punishment (the word עָוֹן means both "crime" and "punishment") is too great to bear. Anyone who meets him may kill him (either because this was the fate of the homeless in ancient times, or because of the "blood feud"). God gives Cain a sign to protect him. We do not know what kind of sign this was. Anyone who kills Cain will be avenged "sevenfold" by God. Cain settles in the land of Nod. (The place name נוֹד from the root נדד ("wander") may indicate that he lived in the "land of wandering.") Cain's punishment ("You shall become a ceaseless wanderer") may not pertain to Cain himself but to his descendants. It may be the etiology (explanation) of why the Kenite people (in Hebrew the names Cain and Kenite are both spelled with a ק) were nomads, who lived in tents. (Later, in the time of the Judges, Yael, wife of Heber the Kenite, lived in a tent.)

◻ Teaching Procedures

The killing of Abel by Cain comes as a surprise. Ask: How would you feel if a parent or teacher addressed you as God addressed Cain (4:6–7)? Some students will say that they would try hard to please and win acceptance. Others will acknowledge feeling angry at the parent or teacher and at their brother. What actually happened in the field? We shall never know. Some of your students may claim that Cain had always been jealous of Abel and asked him to come to the field with the intention of killing him. This, of course, would make Cain an evil man and a brutal murderer. It is also possible that Cain asked Abel to join him in the field for some other harmless reason, to view the crops or even to select a better offering, when suddenly, perhaps after a careless remark or gesture, tempers flared up and Cain killed Abel. Your students might see Cain as an irresponsible "hothead," unable to control his instincts and his temper. Maybe Abel taunted him. In either case, murder can never be condoned!

Ask your students what God's questions ("Where is your brother Abel?" "What have you done?") remind them of. They will no doubt recall God's rhetorical question to Adam ("Where are you?" 3:9). You may want to ask: Why does the Bible have God ask, "Where is *your brother* Abel?" How many times is the word "brother" used? Your class may remember that repetitions create emphasis. What aspect of Cain's crime is God emphasizing?

Is Cain aware of the horror of his deed? His callous answer, "Am I my brother's keeper?" indicates that he is not.

Gen. 4:10, "Hark, *your brother's blood cries out to me from the ground*," and also 4:11, "Therefore, you shall be more cursed than the ground which *opened its mouth wide to receive your brother's blood from your hand*" are poetic. Your students may be sensitive to it and be able to describe the imagery as they read the verses.

Your class may wonder why Cain was not condemned to death. The answer probably is that although God expected man to know instinctively that he must not kill, He had not "spelled it out" for him. (The suggestion that Cain "did not know death" is a later, midrashic one. Cain must have been aware of death since Abel killed the sacrificial animals.) Some may consider Cain's punishment worse than death, while others may disagree. We tend to say, "As long as there is life, there is hope." On the other hand, we know of people who ask to be executed instead of sentenced to life imprisonment.

Why is Cain afraid of losing his life at the hands of others? You may want to discuss "blood feuds" here. Also discuss the hardships of the homeless man without a tribe in ancient times. God gives Cain a protective sign. He promises to avenge the death of Cain on his would-be killer.

A possible subject for discussion: Am I my brother's keeper? The fact that this rhetorical question is put into the mouth of the villain indicates that in actuality, the opposite is true—I *am* my brother's keeper! All of mankind, descending from Adam and Eve, are brothers. We can speak of a close family, and a more remote family. Our closer family is that of Israel, our more remote family is all of mankind. Where do our responsibilities lie? What are some of the duties I have toward Israel, Soviet Jews, accident victims, the poor of India? What would Cain say if asked to help in these situations?

LESSON 3

Cain's Generations
Gen. 4:17–24

◻ In Preparation for Teaching

The descendants of Cain are recounted in Gen. 4:17–24. In 4:17, Cain takes a wife and builds a city (we have to assume that there are enough people to populate the city).

There is a view in the Bible that the city and city life in general are associated with sin and corruption. Later on we will see that the building of Babylon (the biblical Tower of Babel) is viewed as a sin. Sodom and Gomorrah are hotbeds of sin. The prophet Amos first encounters corruption when he leaves his pastoral life as farmer and shepherd and comes to the city. Maybe this is why the Bible attributes the building of the first city to Cain.

In the following verses we are told of the generations of Cain. Time is passing. People are following diverse professions; there are now shepherds, metal workers, and musicians. According to the biblical view, it seems natural for people to acquire professions. In other traditions, it was the gods who gave these skills to mankind.

The story of Lamech is told in Gen. 4:23–24. Lamech triumphantly tells his wives that he slayed a man for wounding him. These verses are written in verse. Biblical verse consists of couplets in which the same idea, related ideas, or opposite ideas are worded in "parallel" lines. The second line often repeats the idea of the first line, using different words. For this reason it is probable that the man who wounded Lamech and the lad who bruised him are one and the same person. However, the number of people Lamech killed is immaterial. The idea is that proud and haughty Lamech has killed to avenge a minor infraction. The punishment does not fit the crime. Lamech compares himself to God, who had declared that He would avenge Cain sevenfold. Lamech declares that anyone who kills him will be avenged seventy-seven fold. There is a tendency, triggered by the Midrash, to read Lamech's song as a lament. The evidence, however, points to a song of triumph.

❏ Teaching Procedure

Verses concerning the descendants of Cain (4:17–22) and the story of Lamech (4:23–24) should be read and briefly discussed in class. Do not spend too much time on these verses. The goal is simply to ascertain what they are saying. Utilize as much of the above information as you deem necessary to illuminate the text.

You may want to ask which of the three people—Adam, Cain, and Lamech—is the best? Which one is the worst? Your students will probably select Lamech as the worst. He kills and then brags about it to his wives. Apparently he hopes that his actions will gain their approval!

Why is Cain better than Lamech? Cain too commits murder. Yet Cain shows fear of God, for he lies about his act in attempt to conceal it. Lamech, on the other hand, brags about his deed. What about Adam? He emerges as the best of the three: he disobeyed, but he did not spill blood.

How would you describe the worlds of these three men in terms of technological development? Adam lives in a garden. He eats whatever grows naturally (as the earliest homo sapiens had). Cain is a farmer. He needs tools, and some knowledge of agriculture. What about Lamech? He lives in a city. His society knows about building and possibly trade. They use fire to forge metal. People even know the luxury of music. The text is describing the process of the development of civilization in terms of arts, techniques or crafts. On the other hand it tells of the decline of morality: people were cruel to one another, human life was not considered important. Biblical stories are related to one another; they form a sequence. The trend of moral decline that started with Adam and continued with Cain and Lamech will eventually cause God to destroy the earth in a great flood.

LESSON 4A

Seth and His Descendants
Gen. 4:25–5:32

☐ **In Preparation for Teaching**

In Gen. 4:25–26 we learn that Eve had given birth to a son called Seth. This, of course, must have occurred before the Lamech story, but the writer did not want to interrupt the story of the descendants of Cain.

Genesis 5 records the line of Adam through his son Seth. Note that Noah is a descendant of Seth. We are not told whether Abel had any descendants. We are not told if Lamech was punished.

Your class will no doubt ask why the Bible claims people lived such long lives. Some students may have been told by previous teachers that years were much shorter or somehow counted differently. A careful reading, however, of Gen. 1:14–15 will reveal that years were determined by the same calendar "signs" we use today, namely, the position of the sun, moon, and stars in relation to earth. Days, months, and years of four seasons are part of the laws of nature (hours and seconds are units of measurement invented by people). Abraham at 100 and Sarah at 90, are indeed *old*.

How, then, can we explain the longevity of our ancestors? In these verses we are not dealing with a description of reality. Methuselah, if he ever existed, did not have a birth certificate (in this respect he was like some of our great-grandparents). Anthropologists, moreover, tell us that people thousands of years ago died *younger* than we do today.

Man's greatest desire is to live forever. Many stories tell of man's search for eternal life. The fact that some people request that their bodies be frozen after death, in the hopes of resurrection at some future date, clearly bespeaks this longing. Adam has forfeited his chance for immortality; the next best thing is a long, long life. A short life is regarded as a punishment.

The ancient Sumerians, whose civilization flourished in the third millenium B.C.E., attributed lifespans of 28,800 years, 64,800 years, and 36,000 years to the ancient kings who lived before the "Great Flood." According to the Sumerian myths, the earliest generations of man consisted of a line of kings, some of whom were semi-divine. Thus the biblical tradition shared to some extent the commonly held belief that before the flood people lived much longer lives than after it. In the Bible, however, the first ancestors of man are ordinary mortals. Biblical lifespans are much shorter than those attributed to Sumerian kings. By comparison, even Methuselah, the biblical character with the longest lifespan (969) lived only a short while.

Excerpt from the Sumerian King List

When kingship was lowered from heaven,
Kingship was first in Eridu;
In Eridu, A-lulim became king
and ruled 28,800 years.
Alalgar ruled 36,000 years.
Two kings
thus ruled it for 64,800 years.
I drop the topic Eridu
because its kingship to Bad-tibira was brought;
In Bad-tibira, En-man-lu-Anna
ruled 43,200 years,
En-men-gal-Anna ruled 28,800 years. . . .
These are five cities;
eight kings
ruled them for 241,000 years;
Then the Flood swept over the earth,
After the Flood had swept over the earth,
and when kingship was lowered
again from heaven
kingship was first in Kish.

◻ Teaching Procedures

Ask your students to glance over Genesis 5. Broach the question: Why does the Bible have people live so long? Is this man's secret desire? Does it replace the quest for immortality? If we cannot eat of the tree of life, a long life is the second best alternative.

You may want to show your class the segment of the Sumerian King list reproduced above. Ask them to compare their lifespans to those of our biblical ancestors. Draw their attention to Methuselah (5:27), the oldest on our list. None of our ancestors lived to be one thousand years old. They were old, but all of them mortal; none have the immortality of a deity.

Lesson 4A: Seth and His Descendants

Ask your students to find the most important words in the listing of Cain's generations in Genesis 5. They may choose the refrain, "then he died." The list of ten generations ends with Noah, the hero of our next story unit.

LESSON 4B

The Divine Beings and the Daughters of Men
Gen. 6:1–8

◻ In Preparation for Teaching

Gen. 6:1–4 are among the most difficult verses in the Bible. They tell us that the divine beings took the daughters of men to be their wives. God disapproves of this sort of union, and limits the lifespan of their descendants to one hundred and twenty years, because they are *flesh*—human, not divine. The children of such unions are called *nephilim*, the heroes of former ages, the men of renown.

This story is obviously a very ancient one and has many pagan elements in it. Who were the divine beings? The sons of God? Angels? We don't know. The word *nephilim* could have been derived from the root נפל ("fall"). Are these fallen angels? *Nephilim* appear in later biblical passages together with *Anakim* (giants).

The Bible views this obscure passage with disdain. If such a union were possible, God would regard it as the epitome of evil. Gen. 6:5a tells us: "The Lord saw how great was man's wickedness on earth and how *every* plan devised by his mind was *nothing but* evil *all* the time." God decides to destroy all that He created.

God limits the lifespan of the offspring of the divine beings and the daughters of men to one hundred and twenty years; they will not be divine. The Torah also tells us in 6:5–8 that God regretted having made mankind and that His heart was saddened. Your class may voice surprise; didn't God know how man would turn out? Why is He surprised?

We have two contradictory ideas: Man's freedom and God's omnipotence. On the one hand, man has the ability to choose. He is a free agent. On the other hand, if God *knows* how man will act, and can predict the outcome, does man still have free choice? Your students will have to learn that not all problems have answers. This is true for adults as well as for children. We all have to live with these problems. God created man expecting him to make the right choices. In a sense, God willingly limited his own power by giving man free choice. Yet when man proves to be weak or evil, God is disappointed. The Torah conceives of God in human (anthropomorphic) terms. God can be sorry, sad and angry. He can be influenced and is willing to change His mind. That is how the Israelites understood God to be. The opposite view of God is seen in the Greek tradition, whose gods are distant, remote and unreachable by mere mortals.

Most of the above ideas will have to be presented by the teacher.

UNIT IV
The Flood
Gen. 6:5–11:32

UNIT IV

The Flood
Gen. 6:5–11:32

▢ Overview

The bulk of these chapters contain the story of Noah and the Flood. Gen. 6:5–8 serve as a bridge between the previous story and the present one. God saw mankind's great wickedness on earth and His heart was saddened. He resolved to destroy all that He had created. Noah, however, found favor in His eyes.

Flood stories exist in many ancient traditions. The Noah story, like the story of creation, may be a version of an already well-known story. We read the story not to gain historical or scientific facts, but to establish a set of relationships between God, man, and the world.

This story must be seen as a parable. It is therefore immaterial whether or not the flood ever actually took place. Questions like, "How did all animals fit in the ark?" are irrelevant.

It is a story that serves to carry ideas. Some ideas in the first (pre-flood) part of the story are:

1) Human actions have consequences.
2) God is concerned with the state of man's morality.

Some ideas to be found in the latter (post-flood) part of the story are:

3) Human life is precious.
4) Mankind can have confidence in the stability of the physical world.
5) God will, in the future, treat mankind with mercy.

LESSON 1

The Story of the Flood
Gen. 6:5–8:22

☐ **Teaching Procedures**

The flood story is contained in Gen. 6:5–8:22. Assign smaller segments for reading, or read the story to your students, since the long reading may be tedious for some students. Elicit from your class an overview of what they have read or heard. List all contributions.

Your class will no doubt notice that there are contradictions and inconsistencies within the story. We are told, on the one hand, that Noah took two of each species—one male and one female–aboard the ark. On the other hand, we read that Noah took seven males and seven females of all the ritually "clean animals" (those species considered appropriate for sacrificing) into the ark. We are told that Noah entered the Ark on the day the flood began (7:13) and yet that the flood started seven days after Noah entered the ark (7:4, 10). The story wavers back and forth between two versions of the same narrative. This wavering is smooth, but contradictions are apparent.

The story begins with God's decision to destroy the earth and all its living creatures. Noah is the one righteous man in his "generations" (all men live in a society consisting of several generations). Noah finds favor with the Lord. God tells Noah to build an ark, to save his own life, the lives of his wife, three sons and daughters-in-law, and also representatives of all animal species. God commands Noah to take aboard the ark enough food to sustain all of the creatures aboard. Noah enters the ark, and God closes the door behind him. The storm rages. The fountains of the great deep burst open, as do the floodgates of the sky. Earth and vegetation are submerged; even high mountains are covered by the waters of the flood. All life is blotted out. Only Noah and those with him in the ark survive.

God "remembers" Noah. ("Remembering" in the Bible means "acting for the well-being of.") He causes a wind to blow across the earth; the fountains of the deep are stopped up; the sky once again retains its waters. Slowly the waters recede. The ark comes

Lesson 1: The Story of the Flood

to rest on Mount Ararat. On the fortieth day Noah sends out a raven, but the raven returns to the roof of the ark because it can find no resting place. After seven days, Noah sends out a dove. The dove too returns to the ark, having also failed to find a resting place. Noah takes the dove back into the ark, for a dove feeds on grain and would as yet find no food (in contrast to the raven, which lives on carrion and therefore could remain outside the ark.) After seven additional days, Noah again releases the dove. This time it returns with a fresh plucked olive branch in its bill. Noah now knows that the surface of the earth is drying. When God commands Noah to leave the ark, he goes out with his family and the entire entourage.

Noah brings a sacrifice to God. God, smelling the pleasing odor of the sacrifice, decides never to destroy the world again. God realizes that man is weak and vulnerable, and therefore likely to do evil again. "The devisings of man's mind tend to be evil from his youth." This does not mean that man has not also an inclination to be good. It is just easier to do evil. Now that God is aware of man's limitations, God is going to treat him with mercy. Never again will God destroy the world, even if man should deserve it.

LESSON 2

Pre-Flood Society
Gen. 6:5–12

☐ Teaching Procedure

Noah's Character

Begin a verse-by-verse study of this chapter, focusing on some of the following points:

What kind of conduct had God objected to before the flood? Your students may list disobedience, murder, etc. Ask your students to find in the text how Noah's own generation was found wanting. The list should include corruption, injustice, and wickedness (6:5, 11, 12). The earth is full of חָמָס ("lawlessness," referring to offensive acts of a person against a fellow human being).

What do we know about Noah? He was righteous and irreproachable: "Noah walked with God" (6:9). Noah is called צַדִּיק תָּמִים, a righteous man without blemish (6:9). Some of your students, influenced by the stories of the Midrash, may tell you that Noah was righteous in "his generations," but would not be considered righteous in a generation of good people. Which is easier—to be good in a good generation or in a bad one? Some of your students will say that it is easier to be good in a wicked generation since, in comparison to others, even an average man may seem good. Others will realize that in order to "walk with God" and to be considered blameless in a wicked generation, one would have to be exceptionally courageous. For the righteous man would likely be shunned, isolated, and even exposed to bodily harm.

The text does not tell us anything about Noah's life with his contemporaries. Since we are told that Noah was a blameless man, we must attribute to him moral strength and courage.

Some of your students may contrast Noah to Abraham, who pleads for the lives of the people of Sodom (Gen. 18:22–32). Noah does not protest God's plan (in fact he says nothing at all). All we are told is that he does what God commands him to do. In all fairness to Noah, however, we must note that God presents Noah with a final decision. In the case of Sodom, God invites Abraham to participate in the decision-making process. (See also below, pp. 115–121. Utnapishtim, Noah's counterpart in the non-biblical Babylonian flood story, actually deceives the people with regard to the upcoming destruction.)

Exercise in Ethical Reasoning

The Bible describes Noah as the only righteous man in his generations. Today it is difficult for us to conceive of a situation in which *one man* finds himself taking an ethical stand in opposition to the society in which he lives; however, we can think of parallel situations. Three such parallels are stated below:

   A. Five Palestinian leaders announce to the P.L.O. leadership willingness to negotiate peace with Israel.
   B. Three members from among twenty-five decide to resign from the board of the labor union and organize their own because they feel that the union has become corrupt, and the offices are using union funds for personal gain.
   C. Ten high school students out of a group of a hundred taking a final examination in chemistry refuse to cheat or share information, though there is no proctor in the room and everyone else in cheating.

1. What is especially difficult about the moral situation of Noah and of the people in the above situations?
2. Think of an instance in your own life in which you might observe someone about to take such a position and describe it.
3. Think of a situation at school or at play which might present *you* with the possibility of taking a moral stand such as the ones listed above.
4. Try to describe the mixed feelings that you would have if you did take this difficult moral position.

This exercise is an adaptation of Burton Cohen and Joseph J. Schwab, "Practical Logic: Problems of Ethical Decision," *Genesis: The Teacher's Guide*, (New York: Melton Research Center, 1967), pp. 493–497.

The Ark

If we were to generalize about the characteristic style in which most of the book of Genesis is written, we would note the extraordinary sparseness of detail. We are not told how people look, what they wear, or what they are feeling, Why then all the details about the vessel: what it is made of, its length, width, height, etc.?

Noah is told to build a תֵּבָה ("ark"). This word is found in only two places in the Bible—here, in the Noah story, and in Exodus 2:1–4, referring to the basket in which Moses was found floating in the Nile. Both vessels were constructed to save lives. Neither has sails, oars, or rudders. Both are entirely in the hands of God. The details of the ark may be more important because of what they *leave out* than for what they do mention. (See also below, pp. 116–117. Utnapishtim builds an actual boat.)

(Supplementary activities related to the building of the ark can be found in Appendix A, below, p. 317.)

LESSON 3A

The Undoing of Creation
Gen. 6:5–7:23

☐ In Preparation for Teaching

Gen. 6:5–7:23 narrates the destruction of the world, from God's decision to destroy it, through the actual flood. Verse 6:5 states: "God saw how great was man's wickedness on earth." Ask your class what the words "God saw" in this verse reminds them of. They may remember "God saw that it was very good," referring to the creation, in Gen. 1:31. How must God feel now, on the eve of the flood? He must be sad, disappointed, and disgusted. Show students that verse 6:5 "echoes" 1:31. Ask them if they can find other "echoes" of Genesis 1 in the Noah story. (For each "echo," give the students either the verse from Genesis or from the Noah story; do not make them find both verses.) This is a difficult exercise. It should be done in class.

Draw a diagram of the "created world" on the board, like the one we used in Unit I (see above, p. 23).

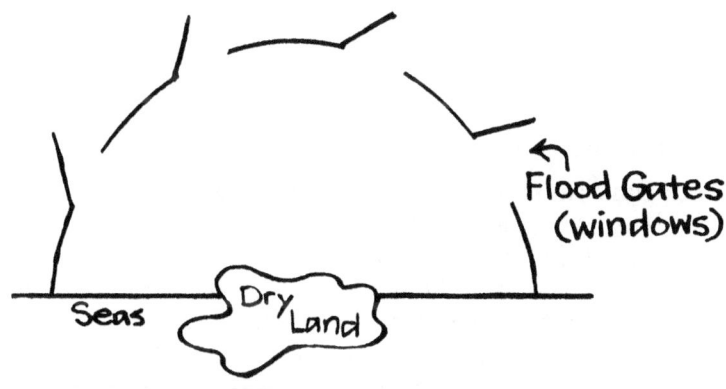

Read 7:11 to the class: "All the fountains of the great deep burst open and the floodgates of the sky broke open." 7:11 echoes 1:6, the creation of the sky. Start a list next to the diagram, beginning with the word "sky." This list, and the "echoes" of Gen. 1, will reveal that the destruction follows the order of the creation: it is a step-by-step undoing of the creation.

Remind your class of the purpose of the sky—namely, to hold back the upper waters. What has happened now? Although the sky is still there, it has lost its function.

The sky was created on Day Two. Let students re-read what happened on the third day—the separation of seas and dry land (1:9). Look for the echo in 7:19: "All the highest mountains everywhere were covered." The separation was undone. Write "seas" and "dry land" under the word "sky" on your list. What has happened to the vegetation? Vegetation was submerged, but it did not actually die (see 8:11, the dove finds an olive leaf). Write "vegetation" on the board.

What happened to the *creatures*? "And all flesh that stirred on earth perished—birds, cattle, beasts, and all the things that swarmed upon the earth, and all mankind (7:21-22).

Your students may wonder about the fish. Did they die too? Tell them the fish are not of specific interest to the text, and are therefore not mentioned. List "birds, animals, man" on the board. Students may also notice that the luminaries are not mentioned. They, too, are still in existence, but in a big storm, one does not see them. Your list on the board will now read:

Sky
Seas, dry land
Vegetation
Birds
Animals
Man
(Luminaries)

Your class can now see that the destruction follows the order of the creation; the world is almost returned to *tohu vavohu*—almost, but not quite. What saved it was the little ark, tossing on the waters. Within the ark remained the harmony which existed on the seventh day of creation: God protects man and animals and takes care of all their needs. Man, in turn, completely obeys and trusts God. Man takes care of the animals and they, presenting themselves to him to be taken aboard the ark, accept his lordship over them.

Lesson 3A: The Undoing of Creation 109

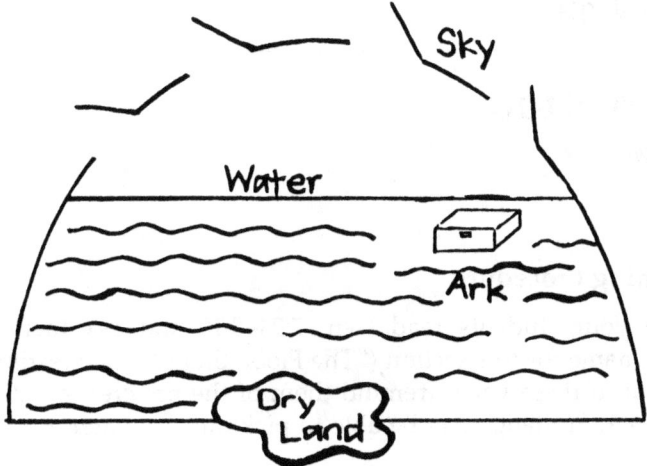

The "almost" return to *tohu vavohu*

LESSON 3B

Re-Creation
Gen. 7:24–8:19

◻ **Teaching Procedure**

Have your students read Gen. 7:24–8:19 and ask them to suggest a name for this section ("The Flood Stops," "Re-creation," etc.). What in these verses remind them of the pre-creation stage in Genesis 1. Students may be able to pick out the water and the wind.

Which verse does 8:2 echo? Your students may notice that the sky has regained its function: "the floodgates of the sky were stopped." Make a checkmark next to the word "sky" on the list on the board. In this way, students can see that the order of re-creation again parallels that of the original creation of the world.

Continue reading the text, verse by verse. Check off "dry land" and "seas" when you come to verses 8:4–5. The borders and coastlines that give shape and form to the continents and oceans are restored. At verse 8:9, check "vegetation," and at verse 17, "birds," "animals," and "man."

LESSON 4

The Promise
Gen. 8:20–22

◘ **Teaching Procedure**

Gen. 8:20–22 tell us of Noah's sacrifice. In 8:21 we read: "The Lord smelled the pleasing odor." Some may find this verse distasteful because it makes it seem as if God were "bribed" or was somehow in the need of food. (Note their remarks, but keep their questions suspended until you the material on p. 119 below, lines 156–163.)

Some of your students may raise an objection to this sacrifice. For if only two of each species had been saved, offering one as a sacrifice would mean the end of this species. This is apparently the motivation for the version of the story which records that *seven* pairs of each of the ritually "clean" (appropriate for sacrificing) species entered the ark.

Why does God vow to never again bring total destruction upon the earth? Let your students find the answer: "Since the devisings of man's mind are evil from his youth (8:21)." Make sure your students understand that man has also good instincts. Man is weak however; it is often harder to do good than to do evil. Ask your students whether they agree or disagree.

What element does God now add to the world in terms of His relationship with man? Your class may need some help to realize that God, knowing man's nature, now promises to treat him with *mercy*. In Genesis 1, God created the world. In Genesis 7, he almost returned the world to *tohu vavohu*. The circle almost closed. But now God promises that it never will close, that the continuous spiral of days, seasons, and years shall never cease. God will never again intervene to stop the physical world from functioning according to its set ways.

However, Noah, is not yet aware of God's decision. (He is not informed until Gen. 9:8–17.)

LESSON 5

The New Covenant
Gen. 9:1–17

☐ In Preparation for Teaching

In Genesis 9, God blesses Noah and bids him be fruitful, multiply, and once again fill the earth. He also gives man permission to eat meat. As a result, animals will be fearful of mankind. The blood of animals, however, may not be eaten, since blood represents life. (Later in the history of Israel, when sacrifices become a regular part of the cult worship, the blood was poured upon the altar, symbolically returned to the Creator of all life.) This symbolic gesture indicates respect for the animal's life. Lest we think, however, that life has become cheap, the text emphasizes that for taking a man's life (life-blood), a reckoning will be required from man or beast. Man is now responsible for punishing the murderer in his midst. "Whoever sheds the blood of man by man shall his blood be shed, for in His image did God make man" (9:6).

God makes a covenant with Noah. Interestingly enough, it is a one-sided covenant: God alone volunteers a promise. Noah is not required to pledge anything in return. We find that God makes one-sided promises when man is in need of support and encouragement. God promises never to flood the earth again, nor to destroy all living beings. The sign of this covenant is the rainbow, which will serve as a "visual aid," to remind God of His promise to mankind.

☐ Teaching Procedures

Have your class read Gen. 9:1–17, and re-state what the text says. Who else was told to be fruitful and multiply? (Gen. 1:28) Your students will also see the parallel between Noah and Adam. Both were "the father of mankind."

Which of the two—Abraham or Noah—would feel more secure in the position of a "father," who is required to be fruitful and have his children fill the earth? There may be conflicting opinions. Some of your students will consider Noah, the survivor of the flood, more secure. They may say that Noah would feel

Lesson 5: The New Covenant 113

special, proud, "great." Try to make them realize the tragedy of Noah—the terror of seeing all of mankind destroyed, the sense of futility and anguish he may have felt at God's command to increase and fill the earth. For what? For another destruction? You may want to bring in some examples from our own times. People may have different reactions to the same events. Some Jews who survived the Holocaust decided never to have children, to avoid exposing them to such a fate; others have had *several* children in an attempt to compensate for the losses of the Jewish people. The second alternative reflects a more optimistic way of thinking. Ask your class to look for other contrasts that can be made between the worlds of Adam and Noah. (Whenever you ask for comparisons or contrasts, make sure you supply *one* of the pair.)

Animals, we are told, will now fear people. Ask your students what relationships were like before the flood. The world depicted in the first creation story was a vegetarian world. In the second story, animals willingly came to Adam. Which kind of world is morally superior—one that is vegetarian or carnivorous? Why does God permit people to eat meat? Your students may suggest that people might have eaten meat anyway, considering the general corruption of mankind. Suggest the notion of permission as a compromise. God is saying, "I would rather have you be vegetarian—but since you are going to eat meat anyway, I give you permission to do so." You may want to discuss the necessity of making compromises in general.

Why must we *not* eat blood? The text does not say, but it uses the term "life-blood." What does that mean? Blood represents "life." By not eating blood, man acknowledges that the life of animals too is God-given and therefore is to be valued. The fact that we do not eat blood makes for certain differences in our way of life. Ask your students for examples. We cannot tear meat off an animal and eat it on the spot, as people did before they had means of refrigeration. We must first slaughter the animal and drain the blood. Time has to pass between the killing and the eating. Your students may recognize that such a process makes human eating different from that of an animal's.

Explain how the laws of *kashrut* are related to this prohibition. Buying meat from a *shoḥet* (ritual slaughterer) is not enough; meat has to be *kashered* (soaked and salted), liver has to be broiled, etc., to remove any trace of blood.

What are we told in reference to the spilling of human blood? Let your students find the answer in the text: God will demand a reckoning, He will demand that the murderer be punished. Who punished murderers up to this point? Your students may remember that God punished Cain. Who is to avenge murder from now on? The text tells us that *man* is responsible: "Whoever sheds the blood of man, by man shall his blood be shed" (9:6). What form will this process take? The text does not say. In later years courts were developed to take care of these cases. What reason does the text give for sanctioning retribution for spilled human blood? Man was created in God's image!

Note that also an animal that kills a human is put to death, even though we assume animals have no sense of guilt or conscience. (Later Israelite law states that if an ox gores and kills a man, it must be killed, and its flesh may not be eaten.) Why did God give laws to Noah, but not to Adam. Laws come into being when a life situation demands them. A prohibition against the shedding of blood is not likely to be given until such an event occurred. Is it easier to "be good" with laws or without them? Cain was expected to know that it is evil to kill, though there was no law. Laws make life easier. It is easier, for instance, to drive when there are traffic lights than when we have to use our judgment at every turn. Laws help to regulate human affairs.

God promises never again to cause a flood to destroy all flesh. Noah does not promise anything in return. God credits Noah for his obedience to Him. Noah may need this promise, to give him the courage to multiply and bring forth a new society. God will still punish man when he deserves it; however, never will there be another *total* destruction. The rainbow is the sign of the covenant between God and all living creatures. This is a sign for *God*, not man, although God does not need signs. You may want to discuss the value of "visual aids" in our lives (*tzitzit*, flag, etc.) What function does this "visual aid" serve for God? for Noah?

LESSON 6

A Non-Biblical Flood Story
The Epic of Gilgamesh

☐ In Preparation for Teaching

There is a Babylonian epic, part of which contains parallels to the Noah story. One way to better understand the ideas of the Noah story is to compare and contrast them with the ideas of a similar story.

Gilgamesh, the hero of the epic, is in search of immortality. He approaches Utnapishtim (the Babylonian counterpart to Noah) and is told the story of the flood:

☐ From *The Epic of Gilgamesh* (Tablet XI)

Gilgamesh said to him to Utnapishtim: . . .
Tell me, how did you joined the Assembly of the gods,
   In your quest of life?"

Utnapishtim said to him, to Gilgamesh:
"I will reveal to you, Gilgamesh, a hidden matter
And a secret of the gods will I tell you:
Shurippak—a city which you knowest,
And which on Euphrates' banks is set—
That city was ancient, as were the gods within it,
When their heart led the great gods to produce the flood. (10)
There were Anu, their father,
Valiant Enlil, their counselor,
Ninurta, their herald,
Ennuge, their irrigator.
Ninigiku-Ea was also present with them;
Their words he repeats to the reed-hut:*
'Reed-hut, reed-hut! Wall! wall!
Reed-hut, hearken! Wall, reflect!
Man of Shuruppak,** son of Ubar-Tutu,
Tear down this house, build a ship! (20)

---
*Probably the dwelling of Utnapishtim. The God Ea addresses him through the barrier of the wall, telling him about the decision of the gods to bring on a flood and advising him to build a ship.
**Utnapishtim.

Give up possessions, seek you life.
Despise property and keep the soul alive!
Aboard the ship take the seed of all living things.
The ship that you shall build,
Her dimensions shall be to measure.
Equal shall be her width and her length.
Like the Apsu* you shall ceil her.'
I understood, and I said to Ea, my lord:
Behold, my lord, what you have thus ordered,
I shall be honored to carry out. (30)
But what shall I answer the city, the people and elders?'
Ea opened his mouth to speak,
Saying to me, his servant:
'You shall then thus speak to them:
"I have learned that Enlil is hostile to me,
So that I cannot reside in your city,
Nor set my foot in Enlil's territory.
To the Deep I will therefore go down,
    To dwell with my lord Ea.
But upon you he will shower down abundance, (40)
The choicest birds, the rarest fishes.
The land shall have its fill of harvest riches.
He who at dusk orders the husk-greens,
Will shower down upon you a rain of wheat."**

With the first glow of dawn,
The land was gathered about me.
. . . .
The little ones carried bitumen,
While the grown ones brought all else that was needful.
On the fifth day I laid her framework. (50)
One whole acre was her floor space,
    Ten dozen cubits each edge of the square deck.
I laid out the shape of her sides and joined her together.
I provided her with six decks,
Dividing her thus into seven parts.
Her floor plan I divided into nine parts.
I hammered water-plugs into her.
I saw to the punting-poles and laid in supplies.
Six 'sar' measures*** of bitumen I poured into the furnace,
Three sar of asphalt I also poured inside. (60)
Three sar of oil the basket-bearers transferred,

---

*The subterranean waters.
**The purpose is to deceive the inhabitants of Shuruppak as to the real intent of the ship.
***A 'sar' is about 8,000 gallons.

Lesson 6: A Non-Biblical Flood Story

Aside from the one sar of oil which the caulking consumed,
And the two sar of oil which the boatman stowed away.
Bullocks I slaughtered for the people,
And I killed sheep every day.
Must, red wine, oil, and white wine
I gave the workmen to drink, as though river water,
That they might feast as on New Year's Day.
. . . .
On the seventh day the ship was completed. (70)
The launching was very difficult,
So that they had to shift the flood planks above and below,
Until two-thirds of the structure had gone into the water.

Whatever I had I laded upon her:
Whatever I had of silver I laded upon her;
Whatever I had of gold I laded upon her;
Whatever I had of all the living beings I laded upon her.
All my family and kin I made go aboard the ship.
The beasts of the field, the wild creatures of the field,
    All the craftsmen I made go aboard. (80)
Shamash had set for me a stated time:
'When he who orders unease at night
    Will shower down a rain of blight,
Board you the ship and batten up the gate!'
That stated time had arrived:
'He who orders unease at night showers down a rain of blight.'
I watched the appearance of the weather.
The weather was awesome to behold.
I boarded the ship and battened up the gate.
To batten up the whole ship, to Puzur-Amurri, the boatman, (90)
I handed over the structure together with its contents.

With the first glow of dawn,
A black cloud rose up from the horizon.

Inside it Adad* thunders,
While Shallat and Hanish** go in front,
Moving as heralds over hill and plain.
Erragal*** tears out the posts;****
Forth comes Ninurta and causes the dikes to follow.
The Anunnaki lift up the torches,
Setting the land ablaze with their glare. (100)
Consternation over Adad reaches to the heavens,

*God of storm and rain.
**Heralds of Adad.
***I.e., Nergal, the god of the nether world.
****Of the world dam.

Turning to blackness all that had been light.
The wide land was shattered like a pot!
For one day the south-storm blew,
Gathering speed as it blew, submerging the mountains,
Overtaking the people like a battle
No one can see his fellow,
Nor can the people be recognized from heaven.
The gods were frightened by the deluge,
And, shrinking back, they ascended to the heaven of Anu. (110)
The gods cowered like dogs
    Crouched against the outer wall.
Ishtar cried out like a woman in travail,
The sweet-voiced mistress of the gods moans aloud:
'The olden days are alas turned to clay,
Because I bespoke evil in the Assembly of the gods.
How could I bespeak evil in the Assembly of the gods,
Ordering battle for the destruction of my people,
When it is I myself who give birth to my people!
Like the spawn of the fishes they fill the sea!' (120)
The Anunnaki gods weep with her,
The gods, all humbled, sit and weep,
Their lips drawn tight, . . . one and all.
Six days and six nights
Blows the flood wind, as the south-storm sweeps the land.
When the seventh day arrived,
    The flood-carrying south-storm subsided in the battle,
Which it had fought like an army.
The sea grew quiet, the tempest was still, the flood ceased.
I looked at the weather: stillness had set in, (130)

And all of mankind had returned to clay.
The landscape was as level as a flat roof.
I opened a hatch, and light fell upon my face.
Bowing low, I sat and wept,
Tears running down my face.
I looked about for coast lines in the expanse of the sea:
In each of fourteen regions
    There emerged a region-mountain.
On Mount Nisir the ship came to a halt.
Mount Nisir held the ship fast, (140)
    Allowing no motion.
One day, a second day, Mount Nisir held the ship fast,
    Allowing no motion.
A third day, a fourth day, Mount Nisir held the ship fast,
    Allowing no motion.

When the seventh day arrived,
I sent forth and set free a dove.
The dove went forth, but came back;
There was no resting-place for it and she turned round.
Then I sent forth and set free a swallow. (150)
The swallow went forth, but came back;
There was no resting-place for it and she turned round.
Then I sent forth and set free a raven.
The raven went forth and, seeing that the waters had diminished,
He eats, circles, caws, and turns not round.
Then I let out all to the four winds
    And offered a sacrifice.
I poured out a libation on the top of the mountain.
Seven and seven cult-vessels I set up,
Upon their plate-stands I heaped cane, cedarwood, and
    myrtle. (160)
The gods smelled the savor,
The gods smelled the sweet savor,
The gods crowded like flies about the sacrificer.
As soon as the great goddess* arrived,
She lifted up the great jewels which Anu had fashioned to her
    liking:
'You gods here, as surely as this lapis
    Upon my neck I shall not forget,
I shall be mindful of these days, forgetting them never.
Let the gods come to the offering;
But let not Enlil come to the offering, (170)
For he, unreasoning, brought on the deluge
And my people consigned to destruction.'
As soon as Enlil arrived,
And saw the ship, Enlil was wroth,
He was filled with wrath against the Igigi gods:**
'Has some living soul escaped?
    No man was to survive the destruction!'
Ninurta opened his mouth to speak,
    Saying to valiant Enlil:
'Who other than Ea can devise plans? (180)
It is Ea alone who knows every matter.'
Ea opened his mouth to speak,
    Saying to valiant Enlil:
'Thou wisest of gods, thou hero,
How couldst thou, unreasoning, bring on the deluge?

---

*Ishtar.
**The heavenly gods.

On the sinner impose his sin,
    On the transgressor impose his transgression!
Yet be lenient, lest he be cut off,
Be patient, lest he be dislodged!
Instead of your bringing on the deluge, (190)
    Would that a lion had risen up to diminish mankind!
Instead of your bringing on the deluge,
    Would that a wolf had risen up to diminish mankind!
Instead of your bringing on the deluge,
    Would that a famine had risen up to lay low mankind!
Instead of your bringing on the deluge,
    Would that pestilence had risen up to smite down mankind!
It was not I who disclosed the secret of the great gods.
I let Atrahasis*
    And he perceived the secret of the gods. (200)

Now then take counsel in regard to him!'
Thereupon Enlil went aboard the ship.
Holding me by the hand, he took me aboard.
He took my wife aboard and made her kneel by my side.
Standing between us, he touched our foreheads to bless us:
'Hitherto Utnapishtim has been but human.
Henceforth Utnapishtim and his wife shall be like unto us gods.
Utnapishtim shall reside far away, at the mouth of the rivers!'
Thus they took me and made me reside far away,
    At the mouth of the rivers. (210)

---

*"Exceeding wise," an epithet of Utnapishtim.

Lesson 6: A Non-Biblical Flood Story 121

◻ Teaching Procedure

Read the above selection from the epic to your students. This is a summary of the story:

Gilgamesh is seeking everlasting life. He is told that Utnapishtim is immortal. He comes to him to find out what his secret is. Utnapishtim's answer: the gods for no reason decided to produce the flood! Ea decides, for no given reason, to save Utnapishtim. He reveals the secret of gods indirectly, by speaking to Utnapishtim's hut (so that later Ea can deny actually revealing the secret to Utnapishtim).

Gilgamesh suggests that Utnapishtim cheat the people and lull them into complacency by telling them the gods will shower upon them abundance.

Utnapishtim has all the people of Shurippak help him build a ship which he loads with gold, silver and craftsmen. (Contrast this to Noah's ark!) He hands the boat over to Puzur Amurri the captain. The flood lasts 7 days. Then the ship lands on Mount Nisir. Utnapishtim releases birds: a dove, a swallow and a raven.

When the earth has dried, he leaves the ship and brings a sacrifice "the starving gods crowd like flies about the sacrificer." (Compare to Gen. 8:21. The story has been cleaned up but pagan remnants have been left.) Ishtar promises never to bring another flood (but she cannot be trusted). The gods accuse one another for bringing the flood. Enlil then grants Utnapishtim everlasting life. (Noah remains mortal and eventually dies.)

Discuss the following issues with your students:

1. What is the motive for the destruction of mankind in each story?
2. What do Noah and Utnapishtim do about the people they lived amidst? (You may want to point out that the rabbinic Midrash finds fault with Noah who did not plead with God for the lives of the rest of the people! See above, pp. 104–105.)
3. Compare and contrast Noah's ark and Utnapishtim's ship.
4. What does each take aboard with him?
5. Who controls each vessel?
6. What is the purpose of the sacrifice in each story.
7. What is the nature of the promise at the end of each story?
8. What is the fate of the hero of each story?

LESSON 7

Noah's Sons
Gen. 9:18–29

☐ In Preparation for Teaching

Gen. 9:18–29 is not part of the flood story. Its placement at the end of the story of Noah, from whose line the whole world would be filled (see 9:7), may serve a special purpose, which we shall investigate.

Noah plants a vineyard; he drinks of the wine, becomes intoxicated and lies exposed in his tent. Ham, the father of Canaan, discovers his father Noah exposed. He tells his brothers, who cover Noah, while averting their faces. Upon awakening, Noah becomes aware of what his youngest son Ham had done. Noah curses Ham's son (his grandson) Canaan, to be the lowest of servants to Shem and Yafet.

The text does not criticize Noah for being drunk. But here, as in the story of Lot (Gen. 19:30–38), we learn that a man, when drunk, loses control over himself. Noah (and Lot) are not responsible for their actions; drunk, they are passive and vulnerable. It is clear that this story was written in a society that frowned upon seeing the nakedness of one's father. Ham, by telling about his father instead of covering him, *dishonors* him. We are not told how Noah finds out what his son Ham did while Noah was drunk.

This story comes right after the great flood and the destruction of mankind. What kind of men will populate the world now? Judging from this account, good people and bad people. Evil has not been eradicated.

Your students will no doubt raise many questions: Why is Ham referred to as the "father of Canaan" instead of the usual "son of Noah"? Why does Noah punish Canaan and not Ham? Why is Noah's curse so severe?

The answers to these questions are not to be found within the text itself; however, we can understand this chapter on another level. The Bible tells us that the people of Israel had frowned upon the customs and ways of the Canaanites since the days of

Lesson 7: Noah's Sons 123

Abraham, Isaac, and Jacob. Later Israel occupied parts of Canaan. This story may be a justification of this later act. It demonstrates that the fate of Canaan was already sealed when the nations first branched out. This kind of story is called an *etiology*, that is, a story that explains how things came to be the way they are. Etiological stories of which there are many in the Bible often are not as spiritually elevating as other stories. We find it interesting, however, that the people of Israel felt the need to explain and justify their conquering of neighboring land. Many other nations did not find it necessary to do so.

❏ Teaching Procedure

Ask your students to read verses 9:18–29. Establish the story line. What exactly did Ham do? What should he have done? How might he have described the scene inside the tent to his brothers? (You may want to talk about the later biblical command to honor one's father [Exod. 20:12].) Ham is to be one of the fathers of all people, what can be expected of the future generations of Noah? The flood, it seems, did not solve the problem of evil.

You may now want to move on to the second level of understanding. Why is Ham called the "father of Canaan"? Our attention is to be focused on Canaan rather than Ham. Note that the punishment given by Noah is not to his son Ham, but to his grandson Canaan. Ask your class what they know about the subsequent relationship between the peoples of Israel and Canaan. Mention Abraham's and Isaac's fervent wish that their sons not marry the local women. Briefly tell about Joshua's conquests. Suggest the etiological content of the story.

LESSON 8

Peoples and Language
Genesis 10

☐ In Preparation for Teaching

You may wish to "lecture" this lesson. It is not necessary for students to study this chapter with great care or know all names.

Genesis 10 records the lines of Shem, Ham and Yafet. The genealogical list begins with the ancestors of Yafet and ends with those of Shem. At the end of each list, we find this refrain (or a variation): "These are the sons of . . . according to their class and languages, by their lands and nations" (10:5, 20, 31).

Genesis 10 provides an etiology for the existence of different peoples and languages. Ancient peoples did not have a recorded memory of their beginnings. The Bible took the view that nations began with one man, who begot sons, who in turn had sons themselves. The first man of a line became the biological father of a people. Jacob (or Israel) is the father of a people called Israel, who live in a land called by the same name. The Bible attributes a similar development to all nations; thus מִצְרַיִם (Egypt) is the name of a man, a people and also a land. We find names of individuals, nations and countries jumbled together in the lists of this chapter. The genealogical lists tell us how people saw their relationship to other peoples.

According to Genesis 10, different languages developed in each nation in response to the life situations, experiences and needs of each people. Different lifestyles and life experiences forge different languages. Eskimos have many more words for "cold" and "snow" than a people living near the equator would require.

Today, most linguists do not believe that all languages stem from one single root. It is true, however, that when people who speak the same language are separated geographically and have little or no communication, they tend to develop the language in different ways. American English differs from the English spoken in Britain as well as the English dialects spoken in Australia and South Africa. During the decades of the existence of the Berline Wall, the German of East Berliners diverged from that of West Berliners. Many American idioms such as "paycheck," "coffee break," and "drugstore" crept into the language of West Berliners, just as Russian experiences had an impact on the language of the East Berliners. Israeli Arabs often complain that they feel "cut off" from the Arab cultural mainstream.

It is interesting to note that the linguistic differences between the different English-speaking countries have lessened over the past thirty years, due to advances in communication such as movies, radio and television.

Some of your students may have heard Hebrew referred to as a "Semitic" language. The term "Semitic," derived from the name "Shem," was invented by linguists in the 18th century C.E. to classify languages (*not* people!), such as Arabic, Aramaic, and Hebrew. Several nations which Genesis 10 lists as descended from Shem speak languages which are part of the Semitic language family. However, Canaan, who is listed as a son of Ham, also represents a "Semitic" language (Canaanite).

LESSON 9A

The Babel Story, I
Gen. 11:1–9

▢ In Preparation for Teaching

The Tower of Babel story in Gen. 11:1–9 is a complex story and can be understood on many levels. In essence, this is another story telling us how different languages came to be. In Genesis 10, the development of different languages is considered "normal" or evolutionary. However, in Genesis 11, the existence of many languages is attributed to an act of God. It is a device used to make people carry out God's command to multiply, scatter and fill the earth. We have dealt with such "duplications" before: two juxtaposed versions of the creation story and two versions of the Noah story combined into a single narrative.

In 11:1 we are told that all the people of the earth have one language. They migrate from the east to the Valley of Shinar, where they congregate and settle. They decide to make bricks with which they plan to build a city, and a tower as high as the sky. Their stated purposes are:

1) To make a name for themselves, and
2) To avoid being scattered.

God descends to look at the city and tower, and He disapproves. He is worried about mankind's ability, as a united force, to carry out any plans they may conceive of. God chooses to confound the language of men so that people will no longer understand one another and will scatter all over the earth. We are also told that the city's name, Babel, means confusion.

This is a perplexing story and your students are likely to raise many questions: Is it a bad thing for mankind to be united? Why shouldn't people be able to communicate? Is God afraid of man? Today we tend to see "unity" and "the ability to communicate" as desirable goals. We feel that many of our difficulties in this world are caused by the lack of unity, common goals, and a "common language." But God says: "If as one people with one language, this is how they have begun to act, then nothing that they may propose to do will be out of their reach" (11:6). This verse seems to indicate that people have banded together for evil purposes. Unity is not always used in service of a good end. God is displeased with mankind. He had ordered man and woman to multiply and scatter, to fill the earth and master it (Gen. 1:28; 9:1). Instead, people understandably want to stay together. Their decision to build a city and tower "lest we be scattered" is an act which contradicts God's plan for the world. The desire to make "a name for ourselves" by building a sky-high tower may be an act of arrogance. Who knows what they may propose to do next? (The tower never does reach heaven: God has to "go down" to see it. In 11:8 we are told that work on the tower had ceased.)

A tall tower, with its top touching the sky would have been a testimony of man's grandeur; a small, unfinished one signifies man's weaknesses and shortcomings. God does not punish mankind. The confounding of languages is rather a device, a way of forcing the people of the world to disperse.

☐ Teaching Procedure

After your class has read Gen. 11:1–9, ask your students to tell you what the subject of these nine verses is. Most students will say, "The Tower of Babel," which is, of course, correct. However, the main thrust of the story is to explain the existence of many languages. This intent is evident in the following verses:

> All the earth had the same language and the same words. (11:1)

> There the Lord confounded the speech of the whole earth; And from there the Lord scattered them over the face of the whole earth. (11:9)

Explain that this is another story which like Genesis 10 accounts for the multiplicity of languages.

What, according to the text, was the purpose of the tower? You may want to list on the board:

"to make a name for ourselves" (11:4)
"else we shall be scattered" (11:4)

Since all the people of the Earth are involved in this endeavor, whom do they want to impress?—God, or perhaps future generations of men are probable answers.

Why does God disapprove of the tower? Let's examine each of the stated motives of the tower builders:
1) *"To make a name."* Do tall buildings make a lasting name for their builders? Of course they do. We remember names of

Egyptian kings (like Raamses II) because they left temples and pyramids behind. King Herod is remembered by Jews more for his buildings (Second Temple renovations, Massada, Herodion) than for anything else he did. Making a name for oneself by building a huge monument does work. However, God does not seem to view this way of "making of a name" with favor. We shall see that in Genesis 12, God promises to make Abraham's name great, and of course He does. We all know about Abraham, the father of the Hebrew people—yet Abraham did not build any tall edifices.

2) *"Lest we shall be scattered."* There is strength and security in unity. Your students will be able to provide many examples of this fact. We find that in big cities, such as New York, people tend to live in ethnic neighborhoods: "Little Italy," "Chinatown," German "Yorktown." Orthodox Jews congregate in Williamsburg and other areas. People like being with their own group. So what's wrong with that?

Although there are benefits to unity, God had commanded both Adam and Noah *to scatter and fill the earth.* Man and woman were created (1:26) to master and rule the earth, for which purpose they have to spread out.

The settlement of the United States may serve as a good example of the importance of people spreading out, rather than remaining concentrated in a small area. When people first arrived on this continent, they settled in cities along the eastern seaboard. Later, some people forged westward. They were called pioneers. What did it take to be a pioneer? It took courage, resourcefulness and energy. A pioneer had to face many dangerous and difficult situations: attacks by Indians, wild animals, lack of shelter, food and water, exposure to the elements, disease, loneliness, etc. Why then did the American pioneers load their families and their belongings onto covered wagons and go? They were looking for a better life—for fortune, good land, maybe gold, furs or timber. It is true that people undertook this challenge for their own personal reasons; yet they were the ones who "opened up the west." This country could never have reached its potential if the pioneers had not left the security of the east coast, and forged westward.

Another example is Brazil. The Brazilians built an "artificial" capital in the middle of the country. The city of Brasilia is supposed to "open up" vast, unexplored areas of their land.

In Hebrew, pioneers are called *chalutzim* (חֲלוּצִים). Your students may know how the *chalutzim* left their homes in Europe and came to Israel. They drained swamps and eradicated malaria, irrigated waste lands and cultivated the desert. Their impact is still keenly felt everywhere you go in Israel.

Furthermore, people do not always unite for good purposes. You may want to discuss God's observation in 11:6, "If, as one people with one language for all, this is how they have begun to act, then nothing that they may propose to do will be out of their reach." It seems that people sometimes unite for evil purposes. Can you think of any groups or organizations which were formed for evil purposes—movements that unite and organize around negative goals? Street gangs, the Mafia, Ku Klux Klan, and the American Nazi Party are some that come to mind. Utilize some recent news item here.

In our story, all of mankind, unite to build a tower. They are acting against God's plan for them to scatter and fill the earth. How does God feel about the conduct of mankind? How does God enforce His will? Why are people willing in verse 11:9 to scatter to the four corners of the earth as God intended for them to do?

LESSON 9B

The Babel Story, II
Gen. 11:1–9

❐ In Preparation for Teaching

Another layer of understanding may be found in this story. You may or may not want to teach this lesson in your class. However, since the story of the "Tower of Babel" is taught in social studies classes in the public schools in some parts of the country, it is important for you as a teacher to be aware of the following information.

Clues within the text, strongly suggest that the purpose of this story is to mock and disparage the propensity for tower-building in Babylonian worship. Let us review the evidence.

Gen. 11:3 states: "Brick served them as stone and bitumen served them as mortar." That is to say, *they* used brick and bitumen in a situation where *we* use stone and mortar. From the use of the pronouns "we" and "they" we can learn something about where this story was written. It must have been written in a land where buildings were built out of stone—not in Mesopotamia, where the land is primarily silt soil. In Canaan, however, stone is plentiful. This story which deals with the city of Babel (Babylon, in English) in the Valley of Shinar, seems to have been written in Canaan.

Convincing support for this theory is found in the Babylonian creation epic *Enuma elish*. The building of the temple and the tower are described in the following manner:

> The Annunaki* opened their mouth and said to Marduk:**
> Now
> O Lord, who has caused our deliverance.***
> What shall be our homage to thee?
> Let us build a shrine!
> . . . .
> When Marduk heard this
> Brightly glowed his features, like the day.

---
*The assembly of the gods.
**The head of the assembly of the gods.
***Marduk has killed Tiamat and thereby saved the other gods from destruction.

Lesson 9B: The Babel Story, II

> "Like that of lofty Babylon whose buildings you have requested.
> Let its brickwork be fashioned,
> You shall name it the sanctuary"
> The Annunaki applied the implement. For one whole year they molded bricks.
> When the second year arrived, they raised high the head of the Esaglia* equalling Apsu.**
> They set up in it an abode for Marduk, Enlil, and Ea.
> "This is Babylon, the place that is your home.
> Make merry in its precincts, occupy its broad places."

In Babylonia, as well as other cities in Mesopotamia, archaeologists have found remnants of huge temples. They usually consist of a broad platform supporting a smaller one, which in turn supports a smaller one and so on. On the highest platform, a temple for the gods was built. One could go from one platform to the next by means of stairways. Construction followed the notion that gods would enter the temple from the top and men from the bottom. This tower was seen as a kind of meeting place for gods and men. This tower was tall; ancient man always seems to select "high places" for his sites of worship. (Moses received the Torah on Mount Sinai.) In a sense, the tower can be seen as an artificial mountain.

Enuma elish indicates that the temple in Babylon was built by the gods right after creation, in tribute to Marduk.

"Babel" was the prehistoric, pre-Semitic form of the name Babylon. The Akkadian-speaking Babylonians interpreted this name according to a popular etymology as *babilim*, "gate of the god."

The Bible, however, belittles this tower. It depicts the building of it as an act of haughtiness and disobedience to God. It tells us that the city was called a "city of confusion of languages," and that this confusion was devised by God in order to cause the people to be scattered over the earth. The Bible here is mocking the Babylonians. This story may be viewed as a satire.

❑ Teaching Procedure

Where did all this supposedly take place? Let your students find in the text the Valley of Shinar in Mesopotamia (11:2) and the name of the city, Babel (11:9).

Babel (Babylon, in English) was a real place—the mighty, rich and developed capital city of Babylonia, which was located in Mesopotamia. Its inhabitants believed it to be the "center of the

---

*The name of the temple.
**In this case, as high as the sky.

world." You may want to tell your students about the huge temples found by archaeologists in Mesopotamia. The point is that such monumental towers did exist there.

Where was this story written? Most likely *not* in Babylonia. What is our clue? Let your students do some detective work. You may have to help them find it in verse 11:3 (see above). The story was probably written in Canaan.

The people of Israel poked fun at the proud inhabitants of Babylon. They said their city was called Babel (בָּבֶל), "since there God confounded their languages (בָּלַל)—although the two words, בָּבֶל and בָּלַל have different roots. The people of Babylon, however, believed that the etymology of the name of their city was derived from *bab-ilim* , meaning "the gate of the god." This followed from their belief that in the temples, man was confronted by the gods.

Nobody knows why some ancient cities received the names they have. Even in the United States, which is a relatively young country, people often do not know the origin of their city's name. (If you live in the New York area, see if any of your students know that the Bronx was once called Bronck's, because the land belonged to a family called Bronck. Or that Brooklyn was named after Breukelen, a city in the Netherlands. In the Bible "Tel Aviv" means "the ruins of the flood (Ezekiel 3:15). Theodor Herzl, father of modern Zionism used it as the name of his imaginary Jewish city to be built in the ancient land. He and the founders of modern Tel Aviv thought it meant "Hill of Spring".)

Why is this story placed here? Genesis 12 tells us that God will choose one man to father the nation which will be instrumental in carrying out His wishes and commandments. It is therefore here that a separation of the peoples of earth into nations must take place.

LESSON 10

The Line of Shem
Gen. 11:10–32

☐ Teaching Procedure

The Torah, as we have seen in Genesis 10, assumes that all nations branched out from Noah and his three sons—Shem, Ham, and Yafet. In that chapter, all three sons are given equal attention. We are told that Ham is the youngest son (9:24), although the order in which the sons are mentioned makes Ham appear to be the middle son (9:18). Be that as it may, the important fact is that Shem, the ancestor of the people of Israel, is the oldest son! Point out to your class that the word "Semite" and the term "anti-Semite" are derived from the Hebrew name, Shem. Make sure they know the term is meant to refer to a *family of languages*, not to a *race*.

Compare the list in Genesis 10, with the present list. In this list the Torah is concerned only with Shem's descendants. Only the oldest sons are mentioned by name. Our interest is aroused in verse 11:26, with the birth of Terah, who in turn begets Abram, Nahor, and Haran. Here the list comes to a halt. The purpose of this list is to bring us up to Abram, the father of the people of Israel. We are told that Abram married Sarai, and that she is barren. Terah takes his son Abram, his daughter-in-law Sarai and also Lot, his grandson, son of Haran who had died, and begins a journey to Canaan. On the way, he wanders through the city of Haran, cuts short his journey and stays there. You may want to leave Abram with Terah in Haran until you are ready to introduce Unit V, "Stories about Abraham."

UNIT V
Stories about Abraham
Genesis 12–24

UNIT V

Stories about Abraham
Genesis 12–24

☐ Overview

The biblical account of Abraham is not a complete, continuous biography, but rather a collection of many separate stories about Abraham.

Many stories were told about Abraham. These stories were passed down orally from one generation to the next. Sometimes people told the stories differently as they passed them on, thereby creating different versions of the same story. On occasion two versions of the same story differ so much that they seem like two separate stories (i.e., the two stories about Hagar or the stories in which Abraham asks his wife to say she is his sister).

As in the earlier chapters, what really happened is not our main concern. Our purpose is to discover what the Torah is teaching through the stories it tells about Abraham's life. The stories do not always appear in a chronological sequence. Yet, there is a rationale to the Torah's ordering of the tales. Ideas develop from one episode to the next.

☐ "Historical" and "Prehistorical" Stories

The first eleven chapters of Genesis deal with all of humanity. They present a universal history of mankind. The events depicted in these chapters are set in *prehistoric* times.

The stories about Abraham, on the other hand, take place in *historical* times. You may therefore want to explain the terms "historical" and "prehistorical" to your class as you commence Unit V. Use the following material as a guide.

The historical period begins with the invention and use of writing. We can learn about the historical period directly through documents, records and other forms of written evidence left by the people who lived through the events they recorded. We can also learn about the historical period indirectly, by studying archaeological artifacts left by contemporaries of these people.

On the other hand, we can only learn about the prehistoric period—the period before people used writing—from archaeological finds, such as cave drawings, shards, arrowheads, other weapons and tools. Today we know much more about prehistoric times than did our forefathers since we have available to us significant discoveries by archaeologists who study that period.

Genesis 1–11 deals with prehistoric times. The stories about the creation of the world and the flood were not recorded at the time the events occurred. These stories were written down much later, in historical times. The Torah interjects bits of information from historic times into stories set in prehistoric times. For example, the Torah uses names of places which were known to have existed in ancient times, such as Accad and Babylon (10:10) or the Tigris and Euphrates rivers (2:14), in its prehistoric stories. Similarly, we learn of the prehistoric origins of the lyre and the pipe (4:21), musical instruments known in historical times. The fact that burned bricks were used for building temples in Babylonia (11:3), information known in historical times, is put into a story occurring at a time "when all the earth had the same words" (11:1)—in prehistoric times.

The Abraham stories, on the other hand, are set in historical times—when history was already being recorded. We have many documents other than the Bible from the period from 2000–1500 B.C.E. Archaeologists have unearthed historical sources in Mesopotamia—poems, stories, records of business transactions, certificates of marriage and adoption, etc.—which corroborate information in found the Bible about various places and the settings of various biblical stories.

However, the fact that the *settings* of biblical stories are historical does *not* mean that the Abraham *stories themselves* are historical. For instance, although the destruction of Sodom and Gemorrah may have been a historical event, the long conversation between God and Abraham prior to the destruction was not recorded by a witness to the event and cannot be viewed as historical *per se*. While a historian may make it his task to find out how much of what the Torah tells us really did happen, the Bible teacher's task is of a different nature.

How then are we to teach the Abraham stories? First, the teacher and the student should try to "enter" the story. Second, we must ask: What does the Torah teach us by means of this story?

To illustrate, first "enter" the Sodom and Gomorrah story (Genesis 18). Try to figure out why God involves Abraham in his plans to destroy the cities. Imagine how Abraham feels as he argues with God. Second, ask what the Torah teaches in this story. This story serves to guide the behavior of its readers. We are encouraged by the Torah to be as conscious of justice as Abraham is, and like him, to be an advocate for it.

LESSON 1

Abram Departs From Haran— A Beginning Myth
Gen. 12:1–9

☐ **In Preparation for Teaching**

A myth is an extended metaphor. It is a narrative or story that uses subjects and actions from known experience to express the ideas, relationships, and values which are essential to a particular culture or community. A myth is usually a story which explains how things came to be the way they are. *It must be emphasized that we are not using this term as it is commonly understood to mean "that which is not true," "a fable" or "illusion."*

Some myths deal with beginnings. Every people has a myth about their specific beginnings. Americans have documents that show how they became a nation. The birth of the United States is a relatively recent, well-documented event. The beginning myth of the United States tells the story of the pursuit of religious freedom and political self-determination.

Ancient nations, however, did not know their beginnings. They were undocumented; no reporters were there on the spot, recording how nations began and developed. How did myths about the origins of these nations evolve?

The myth usually develops after a people or a nation *already exists*. A nation's stories tell us a great deal about its people: their values, beliefs and aspirations. What a people believes about their beginnings—the circumstances of and justification for their being—determines how they will live in the present and in the future.

The Romans, for example, tell a story about their beginnings. Twin boys, Remus and Romulus, were abandoned in the forest to die. However, they were found by a she-wolf who nursed them and saved their lives. When the boys were grown, they built the city of Rome.

We may ask, why a she-wolf? Why not a sheep or a cow? People in the past believed that what one ate in some way influenced one's character. Thus, eating a lion's heart would make one brave. The children in the Roman myth were nursed by a she-wolf. Therefore, the Romans liked to believe, they and their descendants had acquired some of the wolf's characteristics (e.g., strength, courage, endurance, loyalty to the pack).

The people Israel, on the other hand, believe that they came into being as the fulfillment of God's promise to Abraham. For when God chose Abraham, He promised Abraham that he would become the father of a great nation, a nation that would be a blessing and example to all the peoples of the world. *This is the beginning myth of the people of Israel.* Thus, what Jews believe about their beginnings puts a great burden of responsibility on their shoulders.

❐ Teaching Procedures

Ask your students what we have learned about what God wants of mankind. Have them summarize the facts learned up to now.

In Genesis 1, the world is created because God wants it to be. God endows His creatures with certain powers. Man is to be God's partner. It is a well-functioning and harmonious world.

In Genesis 2, God gives people the power to make moral choices. People can choose between good and evil. From Genesis 3 on, people prove to be weak; they make the wrong choices and consequently are punished by God. After the flood, God decides to treat people with mercy, recognizing their limitations. He gives them some laws to help steer them in the right direction. He vows never again to destroy all of mankind. In Genesis 10–11, nations develop as people spread out to new locations, in accordance with God's wish that mankind fill the earth.

At the conclusion of Genesis 11 Terah leaves Ur for Canaan, taking with him Abram his son, Abram's barren wife Sarai, and Lot, the son of Terah's dead son Haran. Why did he leave Ur? Perhaps a famine had broken out, or that enemy forces had overrun the land, forcing him to leave. (We shall later learn in Genesis 24 that the rest of Terah's clan had left Ur and was living in a city called Nahor.) Why did Terah plan to go to Canaan? Maybe he had heard that it was a place of good, fertile land.

Canaan is southwest of Ur, but Terah went northwest, following the water way. He stopped in Haran and did not continue. Why? Maybe he found in Haran whatever it was he was looking for.

Ask your students to read 12:1–9. Note that Abram's leaving of Haran is different from Terah's leaving of Ur: Abram followed God's command! Abram left Haran for the purpose of fulfilling God's wish—to become the father of a great nation.

What does God command Abram to do? (Try to read 12:1 in Hebrew: לֶךְ־לְךָ מֵאַרְצְךָ וּמִמּוֹלַדְתְּךָ וּמִבֵּית אָבִיךָ) God could have said: "Leave Haran, and go to Canaan." Have your students realize how much harder God makes it for Abram to leave by emphasizing the importance of Haran for Abram. (God refers to Haran as Abram's birthplace. Possibly that is because Haran and Ur were part of the same cultural and religious milieu, or because Abram seemed to have lived in Haran for a long time, long enough to have acquired wealth and persons [12:5].)

Emigration is always a difficult undertaking. In Abram's times, when a person left his country, it was highly unlikely that he would ever see his friends or relatives again. Without telephones or postal service, regular communication between countries did not exist. Sometimes another traveler would carry news. Considering the mobility of our age, it is difficult to imagine ourselves living in the time of Abram. How did people travel in Abram's day? Most likely on foot, on donkeys, or ox carts. What dangers might Abram have faced? What character traits were needed to leave one's country?

A map of Israel and the Middle East should be available to the class, to trace the journeys of the patriarch. A biblical atlas, available in most libraries, will facilitate matching ancient names with modern locations.

LESSON 2A

The Father of a Nation
Gen. 12:1–9

☐ In Preparation for Teaching

Does any nation really ever evolve from one person, who has children, who in turn beget children? In reading the Abraham stories, we discover that Abram's "household" contains three hundred and eighteen fighting men (Gen. 14:14), and that he circumcises "all his retainers, his homebred slaves and those that had been bought" (Gen. 18:26–27). In actuality, Abram is not just an individual; he is the chieftain of a tribe. Why, then, does the Torah relate that Abram himself fathered what later became the people Israel? Here again, facts are much less important than ideas. The Torah considers all the people Israel to be descended from one man. In doing so, it teaches that *we are all brothers, and directly involved in the covenant between God and Abraham*, no matter who our ancestors may have in fact been.

☐ Teaching Procedures

Why does God make promises to Abram? God is aware of the difficulties confronting Abram and is trying to "sweeten the pill."

What does God promise Abram in 12:2–3? Your students can find answers in the text:

1) "I will make of you a great nation."
2) "I will bless you."
3) "I will make your name great."
4) "You shall be a blessing."

1) *"I will make of you a great nation."* There are two factors in the story that make this first promise difficult to fulfill: (a) Sarai is barren (Gen. 11:30). (b) Abram is already 75 years old; later we shall learn that Sarai was only ten years younger than Abram (Gen. 17:17), 65 at the time of departure from Haran.

It takes many generations to produce a nation. Even if Abram already had many children, he would not live to see them become a nation. Abram has to take God's promise on faith.

Why could not Abram become the father of a great nation in Mesopotamia? Why did he have to leave? Some possible explanations are: (a) He may have had to first prove his trust in God. (b) Mesopotamia in Abram's day was a highly civilized country. It would be difficult to forge a new nation in Mesopotamia. It might have been easier to do so in a less developed area, where temptations of assimilation were minimal.

According to the Torah, Abram is the father of our people. We are all descended from him. George Washington, the first president of the United States, is called "the father of our country." Yet, he was not the *biological* father of the American people—the term "father" is a metaphor. He was the father only in the sense that he helped to weld thirteen states into a union. Remember that the Torah often tells its stories through metaphors.

2) *"I will bless you."* The concept "blessing" was introduced in Genesis 1. A blessing flowing from God to man is a gift. What is the content of this blessing? Perhaps property, a land, a people.

3) *"I will make your name great."* What does a "great name" mean? We have touched on this subject discussing Gen. 11:1–9. It is a name that people mention with awe, respect or reverence.

4) *"You shall be a blessing."* What does the Torah mean when it says that the families of the earth shall bless themselves by Abram? People will look up to him as an example. They may say to one another, "May you be like him," meaning, "May you be as good, as fortunate or as righteous as Abram."

God has asked Abram to leave his land. To what end? What will be the purpose of the nation he is to father? Despite the record of the preceding generations, God did not give up hope for achieving a moral and harmonious world. He hoped to achieve this goal by choosing *one people* to serve as an example to others of how to live a just and upright life (Gen. 18:19).

You may want to have your class close their books and discuss Jews in general and the State of Israel in particular. How do they measure up as "examples?" Allow your students to be critical. Make sure you fully understand any example you use. Current newspaper items may be helpful. Some points to consider on the plus side are: Jews gave the Torah to the world. There have been many great Jewish humanitarians and scientists (e.g., Sigmund Freud, Albert Einstein, Jonas Salk). Israel excels in providing services for humane endeavors (e.g., absorption of refugees, land development, educational programs, prison reform, medical care for the Arab sick and wounded). On the other hand, there are examples of dishonesty and corruption, both here and in Israel. Why are we so shocked when a Jew is found guilty of fraud? It is not just because we are a minority and afraid of repercussions. We are also conscious of our responsibility and therefore dismayed at instances in which we fail to show exemplary ethical conduct.

Providing a model of social justice and personal integrity is a heavy burden. In this role, Jews have sometimes succeeded and sometimes fallen short of the mark. According to the Torah, we Jews must strive to be a good example that others can emulate.

LESSON 2B

God Chooses Abram
Gen. 12:1–9

◻ In Preparation for Teaching

Why did God choose Abram to be the father of this great nation? Why was Abram so willing to obey God's command? These are puzzling questions, which the text does not answer. The rabbis were also perplexed by these questions. To offer answers, they told stories (*midrashim, aggadot*) to provide an explanatory supplement.

◻ Teaching Procedures

Let your class discover that Abram is not told the name of the country to which he is going. Ask your students how they would feel if told by a stranger to leave their homes and follow instructions blindly. Some will probably tell you that they would refuse, or call the police. Others would ask the stranger where they would be going and for what purpose. Then ask your students how they would react to the same instruction coming from a trusted friend or relative.

Focus your students' attention on 12:4–5. In order for the story to be in logical sequence, which action takes place first, the one described in 12:4 or the one in 12:5? Obviously 12:5 must precede. Abram had *first* to take his family and *then* to leave his home and country. What does the Bible impress upon the reader by putting 12:4 before 12:5? Note the emphasis on Abram's readiness, his lack of hesitation, and the speed with which he carried out God's command. Considering our own feelings regarding a command from a stranger, what can we assume about the relationship between God and Abram? Abram seems to already have an ongoing relationship with God. It seems that God is no stranger to Abram. He reacts to God's instructions as we would react to those of a parent or an older friend.

Some students may be familiar with different *midrashim* about Abram's childhood (e.g., the breaking of his father's idols or imprisonment and rescue from a burning furnace). Make sure your students know these stories are the product of later Jewish imagination, not part of the Torah. You may want to explain how these stories came into being, or what occasioned the *midrashim*. *Midrashim* are stories related by the rabbis to explain, supplement or make plausible difficult verses in the Torah.

Like us, the rabbis were puzzled by two aspects of the story: (a) Why was Abram so ready to respond to God? (b) Considering that God's purpose was to start a new nation, why did He choose Abram, a seventy-five-year-old man with a barren wife?

The rabbis told many stories about Abram, as a way of answering these questions. According to one *midrash*, Abram refused to recognize King Nimrod as God. Nimrod punished Abram by having him thrown into a burning furnace. God then rescued Abram from the burning furnace. This story explains why Abram trusted God. He followed God's instructions immediately, without question, because he already knew that God could be depended upon.

According to another *midrash*, Abram was different from all other children. He turned against idol worship and the worship of the sun and moon, in search of the real God, Creator of heaven and earth. Abram's father Terah was a maker of idols. Abram was to sell these idols, but instead, in an effort to prove their futility, he broke them. He put a big stick in the hand of a big idol and claimed that the big idol had broken the smaller ones. His father, of course, did not believe that a stone idol could break other idols. This story serves to demonstrate that even as a child Abram knew God and took risks in order to teach others about Him. This *midrash* provides one possible explanation of why it was Abram whom God chose to be the father of the people Israel.

The biblical text itself, however, does not provide us with any ready answers.

It is interesting to note that God promises Abram land (12:7) right after Abram gives up his native land. Throughout the Abraham stories we shall see that whenever Abraham gives something up, he is compensated for it by God.

Read 12:10, the first verse of the next story. What else do we learn about Abram's new country? There was a famine—no rain, and therefore no food. Unlike Mesopotamia, which lies between the two big rivers, the Tigris and Euphrates, the land of Canaan is dependent on rainfall.

We might have wanted to pack up and return home at this point! The Torah tells us all these details to make us aware of the degree Abram's trust in God—in spite of all the hardships he encountered, he stayed on. In the rest of Genesis 12 we learn more of the hardships Abram had to face in his new land.

LESSON 3

Abram in Egypt
Gen. 12:10–20

☐ In Preparation for Teaching

Abram, confronted by famine, has to leave Canaan and seek sustenance in Egypt. As he approaches Egypt, he asks his wife Sarai to introduce herself as his sister. Since Sarai is very beautiful, Abram is afraid that an Egyptian may kill him in order to take Sarai as a wife.

Pharaoh's courtiers see Sarai's beauty and bring her to the king's harem. Abram is paid royally for her. God brings great plagues upon Pharaoh. (The nature of these plagues is unknown to us.) Pharaoh sees a connection between his afflictions and the woman Sarai. He summons Abram and accuses him of deception, for having caused him to take Sarai into his harem. (The phrase "so that I took her as my wife" [Gen. 12:19] need not mean more than having taken her into the harem because the Hebrew word אִשָּׁה can mean either "wife" or "woman.") Abram does not defend himself. Pharaoh sends him and his property back to Canaan.

Your students may react violently to this story. They may voice anger with Abram, saying he is a pimp and a coward. If he knew (as he seems to have known) what could befall him in Egypt, why did he go there? Why didn't he protect his wife? Why did he accept the gifts?

From later stories, those about Isaac and Jacob, we shall see that when famine occurred, people *had* to leave Canaan. Canaan is dependent for water on rainfall alone, while Egypt is sustained by the river Nile (although we shall see that Egypt too had famines).

Without trying to render Abram blameless, point out that it may not be fair to judge Abram by today's standards. In Abram's time, women were considered property. Until she married, a daughter would be the property of her father, who was responsible for taking care of her. A man would buy his bride from her father at a handsome price, and she would now become *his* property. Rich men could afford more than one wife.

Lesson 3: Abram in Egypt 149

The issue of "women's rights" is likely to be raised by your students. Women in America have achieved equal opportunities with men in many areas of life, so it is hard for us to understand the way in which women were regarded in biblical times. Yet it is only recently that women in Italy have obtained the right to possess property. In many countries, women still cannot vote. In Arab countries and even in Israel, you can still see an Arab husband riding a donkey, with his wife trudging behind, carrying bundles on her head. In comparison, American women have made great strides.

The respective roles of men and women vary in the societies of different times and culture. The principles of chivalry, which demanded that a gentleman must defend the honor of his lady, were only made current by the knights of the late Middle Ages. The idea that women should be equal to men in all respects would have been unthinkable until recent decades. Thus, it is unreasonable to expect Abram to lay his life down for his wife, as society may well expect of a husband in modern times.

Is it permissible to feel that Abram does not come off as well in this story as we may wish? Yes, of course! Abram is not perfect. He has strengths and weaknesses like everyone else, and the Torah presents us with both.

☐ Teaching Procedure

Have your class read Gen. 12:10–20. In the classroom discussion, you may want to share some of the information on the position of women in society in biblical times. Your students may have many questions about the story. Note them, and keep them suspended for the present.

This same story, told in a slightly different way, appears in Genesis 20, and once again in Genesis 26, where it concerns Isaac and Rebekah. It is difficult to believe that Abraham would use the same ruse again, considering the result the first time, or that the king Abimelech in Genesis 20 and 26 would take both Sarah and Rebekah into his harem. We may be dealing with three versions of the same story. The story was probably told differently by different people. Generations later, when these stories were written down, they were recorded as three different stories.

It may be useful to turn now to Genesis 20 and read the second story. How does the information in there add to our understanding of Genesis 12? We are told that God appears to Abimelech in a dream and tells him that Sarah is married (Gen. 20:3–7). The king does not approach Sarah. Abraham has to pray for Abimelech. Abraham tells Abimelech that Sarah is his half-sister. We also find out what the "plagues" in 12:17 might have been, for in the house of Abimelech no children were born (Gen. 20:17–18). In this version, Abraham attempts to defend himself before Abimelech.

In Gen. 20:11, Abraham uses the term "fear of God." What does he mean by that? Abraham assumes that people with no "fear of God" would kill a man to take possession of his wife. It is interesting to note that to "fear God" means to live according to some already well-known moral law that the Torah has not yet spelled out.

Was Sarah really Abraham's half-sister? If so, would this not have been mentioned in Gen. 11:29–30, in the genealogies of Milcah and Iscah? Could Abraham be lying? (Is it permissible to lie to save one's life? According to Jewish tradition, saving a life usually takes precedence, even when other important values are involved.)

These stories, as they stand, are not critical of Abram, but of the moral climate of the people among whom he has to live. The intent is to emphasize the hardships Abram must confront as a result of leaving his home.

LESSON 4A

Abram's Character
Genesis 12

☐ In Preparation for Teaching

In the Torah we are introduced to Abraham at the age of seventy-five. We know nothing about his youth. We can, however, observe Abraham's life from age seventy-five on, and ask what kind of man he was. We may be able to learn from his conduct in later life what kind of man he had been before God's call.

You may want to keep a running list of the characteristics of Abram as we learn more about him. Make this list as a chart that can be saved and added to for the duration of Unit V. A tentative list through Genesis 12 might be:

1) Abram trusts God.
2) He is obedient to God. (12:4–5)
3) He cares for his nephew. (12:5)
4) He is "clever" enough to outsmart the king. (20:12)

Your class may eventually want to add to this list some traits that they might consider to be negative:

5) Abram is willing to lie to save his life. (20:12)
6) He cares more about himself than about Sarai. (12:13)
7) Abram is greedy, accepts gifts in exchange for his wife. (12:16)

By all means, list these too. The Torah does not "censor" stories which are not flattering to our forefathers. Our ancestors are not depicted as gods or semi-divine beings, but as flesh-and-blood people. As such, we can surely identify with them.

LESSON 4B

Abram and Lot
Genesis 13

☐ In Preparation for Teaching

After your class has read Genesis 13, establish the following facts:

Both Abram and Lot are very wealthy cattle owners. They proceed to Bethel in stages, since herdsmen move slowly from one grazing area to the next. Friction arises between the herdsmen of Abram and those of Lot. Abram is disturbed by the quarreling and suggests to Lot that they separate. He gives Lot the right of first choice.

Lot chooses to dwell in the well-watered plain of the Jordan, and pitches his tents near Sodom. The narrator hastens to tell us that the inhabitants of Sodom were very wicked sinners before the Lord.

After Lot separates his household from Abram's, God promises Abram all the land he can see. Abram is also promised that his offspring will be as numerous as the dust of the earth. God invites him to walk the length and breadth of the land, which will be his.

☐ Teaching Procedure

Gen. 13:1–9

The herdsman of Abram and those of Lot quarrel over water and grazing rights. Tell your class something about the climate of Israel—the dryness of the Negev, the dependency on rainfall. Pictures of the Negev may help to illustrate the aridity of the area. Lack of water, and consequently of adequate grazing land, presented a real problem to Abram and Lot since both owned large herds of cattle. Abram objects to the quarreling (13:8). Is Lot aware of what is going on? If so, we do not hear of any reaction on his part.

Abram suggests that they separate. Who has first choice in choosing location? You may want to present this to your class in

Lesson 4B: Abram and Lot 153

terms of the following analogy. Suppose your mother gave you and your brother one piece of cake and suggested that one of you cut the cake and the other choose the part he wants. Which would you rather do, cut or choose?

Obviously, when you choose, you have the advantage. In the case of Abram and Lot, who should have had first choice by right? Abram, for he was the one whom God sent to Canaan to eventually inherit the land.

What does the fact that Abram gave Lot the right to choose teach us about Abram? It seems that in his estimation peace takes precedence over water and other material assets. (Students may, at this point, bring up the issue of "peace versus territory" in present Israeli politics.)

If some students felt that Abram was greedy in the previous story, this story may change their minds.

Gen. 13:10–18

Ask about Lot's value judgment. Your students will notice that he chose the well-watered plains. What else are we told about the place Lot chooses? In 13:13 we learn that the people of Sodom are very wicked sinners against the Lord. Lot seems to be oblivious to this fact. If he knows about it, he does not seem to care.

What kind of risks does a person take when he decides to live among evil people? Surely, there is the danger that one's children will be exposed to bad examples. It may be hard to find friends. One may have reason to fear one's neighbors.

Some of your students may argue that Lot did not know the people were wicked. It is true that we are not told in this chapter how much Lot knew about the people. However, as we continue reading, we shall see that this was not difficult to find out. Encourage the class not to judge Lot now, but to wait to see what happens when he finds out.

As Lot leaves Abram for the cities of the plain, God makes Abram another promise. What is he promised? Why is he *now* promised all the land as far as he can see—to the north, south, east, and west? Possibly because he gave the choice of land to Lot.

God also promises him progeny, perhaps because the departure of Lot significantly diminished the size of his tribe.

When was the first time God promised land to Abram? Look at 12:7. Under what circumstances was this promise made? Some may recall that Abram had just given up his father's house and native land. We note that whenever Abram gives something up or takes a risk, God makes him a compensatory promise.

But what are the real chances that these promises will be fulfilled? We are told that Canaanites and the Perizzites inhabit the land (13:7). And Abram still has no offspring.

In 13:17, Abram is told to walk the length and breadth of the land. What is the purpose of his walking through the land? Your students may realize that this walking is a symbolic way of taking possession. In the past, it may actually have been a ritual connected with taking possession of property. (Your students may be interested to know that Pennsylvania's boundaries were determined on the basis of how far William Penn could walk in a given amount of time.)

LESSON 5A

The Battle of the Kings
Gen. 14:1-9

☐ **Teaching Procedure**

In this lesson, it may not be worthwhile for your students to read the chapter on their own. The names of kings and places in 14:1-9 may cause students needless frustration. Do not expect students to memorize these names. It may be best for the teacher to read the first nine verses aloud and then stop to explain them.

In Genesis 14 we are suddenly catapulted into the world of general "history" of the Ancient Near East. We are told that four kings are waging war against the five kings of Sodom, Gomorrah, Admah, Zeboiim, and Zoar. We think that these cities were located near where the southern tip of the where Dead Sea is today. (A map of Israel and the Middle East should be in the classroom.)

What do we know about the four kings? Amraphel, we are informed, is king of Shinar, a city mentioned in Gen. 11:1-9 (the city of Babylon was built in the Valley of Shinar). Amraphel's allies seem to be his neighbors. According to Genesis 14, four northern kings are fighting with five kings from cities south of the Dead Sea. Why? What preceded this encounter? We learn from Gen. 14:4 that previously the five southern kings had "served" the four northern kings for twelve years; in the thirteenth year, they rebelled. (These kings should be recognized as tribal chiefs. Even a small city like Sodom had a king.)

What happened in the fourteenth year? From 14:5-7, we learn that the four kings did not directly come to subdue the five rebelling kings, but first went on a foray against a number of other kingdoms. They waged war against the Rephaim, the Zuzim, the Emim, the Horites, and the Amorites. Where were these people located? Scanning the list of places mentioned above, we recognize some names from other parts of the Bible. Mount Seir (14:6) is the country of Edom, Kadesh (14:17) is known later from wanderings of the Israelites in the desert. El-paran (14:6) is located on the Gulf of Aqaba, near today's city of Eilat. All of these peoples lived *south* of Sodom and Gomorrah. The confrontation with the five rebelling kings occurred as they were returning northbound (14:8). The four southern kings and the five northern kings met in battle in the Valley of Siddim—now the Dead Sea (or "Salt Sea"); the valley did not exist anymore at the time the story was written down (14:3).

Why do some of the cities have double names, such as Shaveh-Kiriathaim or Hazazon-Tamar? The second part of the placenames are names by which these cities were known in ancient Israelite times. When this story was written down (long *after* the eighteenth century B.C.E., when it would have taken place), the writer was aware that the cities were in his day known by different names from the ones used in the distant past. He therefore mentions their earlier names together with their contemporary names to help the reader to identify them. Try this analogy: A writer writing about the time the Dutch occupied the city of New York, might write "New Amsterdam, today's New York."

We have to contend with many questions: How did the northern kings bring their armies all the way from Babylon to the Red Sea south of Sodom? For what purpose? How did the five southern kings come into servitude in the first place? What form did this servitude take? What form did the rebellion take? The text does not tell us. However, Bible scholars have been able to learn a great deal from other sources. The route taken by the northern kings coincides with the route known in the Bible as "the King's Highway" (Numbers 20:17; 21:22). Archeologists have proved that a road once ran almost in a straight line from the north to the south all the way to the Red Sea, parallel to the river, in what today is Jordan. This road served the caravans. Between the twenty-first and nineteenth century B.C.E. (middle Bronze Age), flourishing settlements existed along this highway. These settlements were wiped out by some later catastrophe. Some scholars believe that the catastrophe was the war described in Genesis 14.

We also learn from archeological finds that the northern kings did travel far south to wage wars. Some scholars believe that the northern kings were bent on controlling the copper mines south of the Dead Sea. It is possible that the servitude of the southern kingdoms consisted of paying the northern kings tribute in either gold, silver or produce. If so, the rebellion could have been the refusal of the southern kingdoms to continue to make payments.

Most of the above information will have to be supplied by the teacher. Students can, however, participate by providing the answers to be found in the text, finding locations on the map and submitting "educated guesses" as responses to some questions. (There are hypotheses that can be defended by underlying logic, in answer to questions like "why would a city change its name?")

LESSON 5B

The Outcome of the Battle
Gen. 14:10–17

☐ **Teaching Procedure**

Have your class read 14:10–17 and establish what these verses say about the battle itself. Who won? What did the southern kings do? What did the northern kings do to the cities of Sodom and Gomorrah? What happened to Lot? Your class may note that Lot, who by now must have known the nature of the people of Sodom had moved right into the city.

This chapter deals with the political affairs of the Ancient Near East. Why does the Bible, which up until now did not involve us in world affairs, choose to do so here? The answer is that as a result of this war, Lot was captured. This, in turn, triggered Abram's involvement in "world affairs." What new information about Abram do we gain in 14:14–17? We learn that he has two allies, Eshkol and Aner. He also has 318 retainers (recruits, soldiers) who were born in his household. We suddenly realize that Abram was the chieftain of a large tribe! Abram's household must have numbered well over a thousand people to have produced 318 soldiers.

LESSON 5C

Abram in the Battle of the Kings
Gen. 14:10–24

◻ **In Preparation for Teaching**

Abram's involvement in the war is recorded in 14:10–24. Abram rescues Lot (10–17), is blessed by Melchizedek (18–20) and refuses to accept the spoils of war from the king of Sodom (21–24).

In this lesson, we will focus on Abram's rescue and refusal of reward. The Melchizedek episode somewhat interrupts the story line of Abram's involvement in the war, and you may choose to comment upon these verses last.

◻ **Teaching Procedure**

Abram is referred to here as a "Hebrew." According to some Bible scholars, the term Hebrew may be related to the people called *Apiru* (or *Habiru*) in Ancient Near Eastern sources. *Apiru* refers to any distinct social group of rootless individuals, not necessarily an ethnic group.

The people of Abraham never use the term "Hebrew" when referring to themselves, although others do (Gen. 14:13, 39:14, *et al.*). Abram's tribe may have been considered *Apiru*, but not all *Apiru* were of Abram's tribe.

Gen. 14:10–17 records Abram's rescue of Lot. You may be able to elicit some of the following from your students: As we read the Abram stories, the character of Abram seems to develop. In Genesis 12, we saw his trust in God and his courage. At the end of that chapter, we may have found some cause for criticism. In Genesis 13, he appeared a man willing to give up property and wealth for the sake of peace.

What induced Abram to wage war against the kings? After all, Abram had nothing to do with Lot's capture by the kings. You may want to ask your students to take a couple of minutes to jot down some answers to this question: What might Abram have said when told about Lot's capture? Possible answers might include: "Too bad"; "He wanted to live in Sodom—let him take the consequences"; "Am I my brother's keeper?" You may want to

Lesson 5C: Abram in the Battle of the Kings

ask your students to complete the sentence: "How would Abram have acted if confronted by _____?" Use any current situation in the news in which Jews are being imprisoned, oppressed, or persecuted. Have your students read their answers. How can we emulate Abram? You may want to discuss the "morality of war" with your class if you feel comfortable with the subject.

Can you conceivably be more ethical by fighting a war than by refraining from fighting? How do you feel about a person who would not fight Hitler? How would you have acted if you had lived in Israel during the Yom Kippur War? Would Abram have been morally superior if he had abandoned Lot to slavery or death? Many Americans today think that the United States should not have fought in Vietnam. However, it is important to open our students' minds to the fact that not all wars are alike, not all wars can or even should be avoided. On the other hand, although Abram in this particular case had to resort to warfare, force is not always the only, or best means of confrontation.

The story line of Abram's involvement in the war continues with the encounter with the king of Sodom in 14:21–24. Let us therefore deal with it first and return later to Melchizedek. What did the king of Sodom offer Abram? Why was the king of Sodom so generous? Tell your students that this was the custom: "To the victor—the spoils." Why did Abram refuse? What exact words does Abram use? (14:23–24) What reason does he give for refusing the reward? Whom does Abram consider the source of his wealth? Why did Abram take property from Pharaoh and from others, but not from the king of Sodom? Could Abram have considered Sodom's money tainted? Blood money? Did he think the king of Sodom would make claims others would not have made? Did he want to emphasize that he fought *only* to gain freedom for his kinsman? All of these are possibilities.

Returning to the Melchizedek episode (14:18–20), the priest recognizes Abram as God's chosen and blesses him (14:19), which brings to mind God's blessing to Abram (Gen. 12:3). The giving of a tithe to Melchizedek can be seen as another sign of Abram's generosity.

You may also want to tell your class that these verses shed light on when this story was actually written down. We read that Abram gave Melchizedek, king of Salem, a tenth (tithe) of his property 14:20. This is the amount that, in later Israelite society, one gave annually to the Temple in Jerusalem. Some Bible scholars suggest that Salem (שָׁלֵם) was the ancient name for Jerusalem (יְרוּשָׁלַיִם). Further, some scholars believe that the expression "God Most High" (14:19) is a reference to the God of Abram, rather than to Melchizedek's own Canaanite diety. Thus, it is possible that this part of the story was written in order to link Jerusalem to the earliest stage of the people Israel. That is, Abram worshiped God in Salem (= Jerusalem), long before it was an Israelite city.

According to 14:14, Dan is located in the north. This is another indication of the lateness of the story, since in Judges 13 and 18, the tribe of Dan still dwells in the southwest Negev near Philistia (today's Gaza Strip), having not yet moved north.

Teach as much or as little about Melchizedek as you deem proper. You may want to just read this section if you find it is too tedious for your students.

LESSON 6A

Renewing the Promise
Genesis 15

☐ In Preparation for Teaching

In Genesis 15 God reassures Abram, through a special covenant-making ritual, of the destiny awaiting his descendants. The following background information may be helpful in comprehending the text.

In 15:9–10, Abram is told to collect certain animals and perform a prescribed ritual. Among some ancient peoples a special form of oath-taking existed. According to documents found in Mari (a city near Haran) they would say they were "slayed an ass" when they entered into a covenant. It seems that they would slay certain animals and cut them in half. The parties would walk between the pieces and take an oath. The oath would express something like, "If I do not keep my part of the bargain, may I end up like these animals." Although the Bible does not explicitly describe such oath-taking elsewhere, the Hebrew language uses the expression לִכְרֹת בְּרִית, which literally means "to *cut* a covenant."

In 15:2, Abram mentions Damesek Eliezer, a servant in his household, as his adopted heir. Some knowledge of customs in Ancient Near Eastern society can shed some light on this verse.

We know from documents found in Nuzi, an ancient city in Mesopotamia, that it was considered very important for a person to have a son. First, a son would take care of one in old age. Second, he would look after one's grave after death, performing the rituals that people believed were necessary to ensure one's peace in the nether world. According to clay tablets found in Nuzi, elderly persons without heirs would often adopt a trusted slave as a son. In exchange for his freedom and an inheritance, the adopted son would take care of his aging master and later of his master's grave. Provisions in the contract were also made in the event that a child was born to the master after the adoption had taken place.

In the light of this information, it may well be that Abram, finding himself childless at an advanced age, may have considered adopting his servant Damesek Eliezer as his heir.

(The name Damesek presents a problem to Bible scholars. This may be a proper name, or perhaps Eliezer might have been from Damesek, today's Damascus.)

Some of your students may be adopted. It is suggested that you mention that the ancient practice of adopting a grown-up servant cannot be compared with today's adoptions, where an adopted child becomes unconditionally the son or daughter of the adoptive parents.

☐ Teaching Procedure

After reading Genesis 15, establish some of the following facts: God appears to Abram in a vision. God promises to be a shield to him and also promises him a great reward. Abram skeptically observes that since he has no children, any reward in the form of material possessions would at his death pass on to Damesek Eliezer, apparently a trusted slave. Thus, the reward is of no great interest to Abram. Thereupon, God promises Abram that a son of his own would be his heir and that his offspring would be as numerous as the stars. Abram is reassured by God's promise, which God considers to Abram's merit.

God renews His promise of the land. Again Abram shows anxiety. He asks, "How shall I know that I am to possess it?" (15:8). In reply, God commands Abram to go through a strange ritual. He is to take a three-year-old heifer, a three-year-old she-goat, a three-year-old ram, and two birds. He is then to cut the animals into two parts (they were, of course, killed first), except for the birds which were to be left intact. Birds of prey descend upon the carcasses but are driven away by Abram. Then a trance and a "deep, dark dread" descends upon him. These are ominous signs, foreshadowing the terrifying message that Abram is about to receive. He is told that his offspring will be oppressed and enslaved for four hundred years in a foreign land. But at the end of this time they will be released and rewarded with great wealth. By then, the "iniquity of the Amorites" will be full. A smoking oven and a flaming torch pass between the pieces of the animals.

What is this all about? Your students may need help in finding the answer to this question in the text. 15:18 states: "On that day *the Lord made a covenant between God and Abram.*" The chapter deals with the making of a covenant. The strange ceremony and God's message to Abram will be the subject of the next lesson.

What name would you give to this chapter? After listing your students' suggestions, you may want to tell them that this chapter is generally referred to as "The Covenant between the Pieces" (בְּרִית בֵּין הַבְּתָרִים).

LESSON 6B

The Making of a Covenant
Genesis 15

☐ **Teaching Procedure**

Direct your students' attention to 15:1. God comes to Abram in a vision. What does God tell him?

1) He should not be afraid.
2) God will be his shield.
3) God will reward him.

You may want to elaborate on God's promise to be a "shield" (מָגֵן) to Abram. Your students have probably seen illustrations of warriors carrying spears and shields. The shield is a symbol of protection. God promises to guard Abram from danger like a shield. Why does God use words like "fear" and "shield" at the beginning of this chapter? Abram has just been through a battle. At the head of a small army of 318 men, he defeated four kings and their armies.

If you taught Genesis 14 in Hebrew, you may want to draw a parallel between the verb מִגֵּן in 14:20 and the noun מָגֵן in 15:1. God has proven himself to be Abram's shield, or protector. Point out that this idea becomes the focus of the first blessing of the Amidah in every service—מָגֵן אַבְרָהָם. Also, the six-pointed star often referred to as a "Jewish star" is sometimes called "Star of David" or "Shield of David" (מָגֵן דָּוִד). Supposedly, King David's shield was decorated by a six-pointed star.

Why does Abram seem to be uninterested in the promise of reward? He was a wealthy man who had plenty for his own needs, and plenty for his servant to inherit, if that came to pass. How does God react to Abram's mention of possibly adopting Eliezer?

The actual making of the covenant appears in 15:7–18. Tell your class that the Hebrew word for covenant is בְּרִית. (Another kind of *berit* is referred to in the preceding chapter. We are told that Eshkol and Aner are bound to Abram by a *berit* [Gen. 14:13]. The English translation calls them his "allies"—people with whom he has an alliance, pact, or agreement. Eshkol and Aner have a pact with Abram for mutual support in battle.)

You may want to ask what the difference between a promise and a covenant is. A covenant implies something more binding than a promise, which can be made merely by word of mouth. A covenant would probably be written down, in the form of a document or contract. A covenant is characterized by a ritual act which makes the agreement more binding in the eyes of the parties. Today, too, we use a ritual act, such as a signature or a handshake, to impart a feeling of validity to an oral promise. We take an oath by placing our hand on a Bible or over our heart while reciting a verbal formula. This would be a good place to tell your class about the rituals associated with the making of covenants in Mari (see above, p. 161).

In 15:17, a smoking oven or torch passes between the pieces that Abram had arranged. You may mention that fire is often used in the Bible to symbolize God (e.g., the burning bush [Exod. 3:2], the pillar of fire [Exod. 14:24, 40:38]). It is interesting to note that this covenant, like the covenant God makes with Noah in Genesis 9, is a one-sided one. Sometimes a promise is made by a more powerful ally to a less powerful one, in order to reassure and bolster a sense of security. For instance, the United States may make binding commitments to weaker countries like the state of Israel, without asking for reciprocal commitments.

Your class will no doubt sense the elements of dread and the almost magical overtones in this chapter. The dead animals, the blood (blood often plays an important part in the sealing of pacts), the birds of prey, the trance and deep, dark dread—all of these heighten Abram's awareness of the awesomeness of this rite in which God enters into a covenant with a man and his offspring forever.

What terrible message is conveyed to Abram? Why is he not to inherit the land immediately? There are practical reasons why the land could not be given to Abram then and there. A man, or even a tribe, cannot take possession of a land; it takes many people to do so. The text, however, does not give this reason—it gives a *moral reason* for the delay. By then the Amorites would *deserve* to be dispossessed. Their measure of evil will be fulfilled.

What reason does God give for the long enslavement that Abram's offspring would endure? For this we have no good answer. Possibly they have to undergo hardship so God can exercise his saving powers. Israel will then feel obliged to Him and will accept His covenant willingly. Some see 15:13–14 as a prophecy of the future. Others say that this chapter was written *after* the enslavement in Egypt, after the Exodus. In either case, the text does not give us a good reason for the enslavement in Egypt.

LESSON 7

Hagar Bears Ishmael
Genesis 16

☐ In Preparation for Teaching

The first two verses of Genesis 16 may be baffling to your students. Sarai gives Hagar to Abram as a concubine. In the Ancient Near East during patriarchal times, a man could have more than one wife. He could also have concubines, whose status would rank below that of his wives. From the ancient laws of Nuzi (a city in the same cultural sphere as Haran, Abram's home), we learn the followin laws regarding concubines:

1) A childless wife was required to provide a concubine for her husband.
2) The concubine's child would be considered the wife's child.
3) The concubine had to respect her mistress.

In giving Hagar to Abram, Sarai may have been acting less out of her own volition than in compliance with ancient customs or laws.

☐ Teaching Procedures

In Genesis 15, Abram was told that he would father a son. He was not told that Sarai was to be the mother of his son. What takes place in Genesis 16?

Sarai gives Abram her maidservant, Hagar, as a concubine. When Hagar conceives, she becomes haughty. Sarai complains about Hagar to Abram. She considers him in some way responsible for Hagar's behavior. Abram tells Sarai to deal with Hagar in her own way. Sarai treats Hagar harshly and she runs away. Hagar then encounters an angel of God who sends her back to her mistress and encourages her to submit to the harsh treatment. The angel promises Hagar that her son will be a "wild ass of a man." Hagar returns to Abram's household where she gives birth to her son, Ishmael.

What is Sarai's reason for giving Hagar to Abram? What happened when Hagar conceived? What does the text mean when it says, "Her mistress was lowered in her esteem" (16:4)? What kind of things could Hagar have done or said to Sarai? What kind of conduct might Sarai have *anticipated* from Hagar? Obedience and humility, are possible answers. Some may feel that Sarai may have expected Hagar to be like a "baby machine," that is, providing the baby but having no personality or needs of her own. Your students may raise contemporary parallels related to surrogate motherhood. (The concubine, in contrast to the surrogate mother, remains part of the household.)

Sarai blamed Abram for Hagar's conduct (16:5). What might he have done to encourage Hagar's insolence? Your class may feel that Abram might have respected or loved Hagar, or perhaps felt grateful to her. Why then did he deliver Hagar into Sarai's hand? This was the prevailing practice at the time. Legally, Hagar was still Sarai's slave (16:8).

What can we learn from Sarai's actions about her feelings toward Hagar? Her actions indicate jealousy, bitterness and hatred. Permit your students to voice outrage at Sarai's conduct. However, let them also understand her predicament. Hagar too has her shortcomings. She seems to have been tactless and insensitive to Sarai's pain and hurt. Both women, as well as Abram, were victims of a society that permitted polygamy.

(Later, Jewish custom prohibited polygamy. Long after the prohibition had been observed, Rabbenu Gershom, around the year 1000 C.E., gave the prohibition the strength of law. This law, however, is not binding on all Jewish communities. In some places even today, such as among Jews living in Arab countries, polygamy is still practiced.)

The angel does not foresee a "rosy future" for Hagar, knowing that Hagar would be treated harshly (16:9). Yet he consoles Hagar—she would have many descendants. Some students may wonder what kind of a blessing it is to be "a wild ass of a man," one who fights all the time. Each society has its own set of ideals toward which it strives, and its own notion of who is a hero. To be a wild, untamed warrior may not be our ideal (at least not in normal peace times). However, the offspring of Ishmael did and still do idealize the reckless and fierce sharpshooting horseman.

Knowing that Abram was destined to have a son, Abram and Sarai tried to help God's plan along. However, their strategy does not seem to work. God's angel had to intervene to make Hagar return to Abram's household, and we do not foresee peace and harmony in the future of this family group.

LESSON 8

Circumcision
Genesis 17

▢ In Preparation for Teaching

Genesis 17 deals with circumcision as a sign of the covenant. Abram is commanded to circumcise all males belonging to his household.

Your students may ask what circumcision is. Explain it in a matter of fact manner, using clinical terms. The question may be a sincere one, or it may be a test to see if the teacher can be embarrassed. Throughout your teaching of Bible, you will have to deal with issues pertaining to sex. It is important to establish the fact that the teacher is not embarrassed by students' questions, and that the teacher will respond seriously.

Circumcision was known to many ancient peoples. It was practiced in Egypt, Edom, and Moab, and was usually linked to puberty or marital rites. In Mesopotamia, where Abram's family had came from, circumcision was *not* practiced. For Abram and his descendants, the adoption of the circumcision rite had a very special meaning. It was seen as the sign of the covenantal relationship between God and His people.

Circumcision gradually came to be a distinct mark of Jewishness. The Greeks did not practice it; in Hellenistic times, Antiochus IV (the infamous) forbade it. The Maccabees not only refused to comply with this decree, but forcibly circumcised Jews who had followed the ways of the Greeks. Similarly, after the Bar Kochba rebellion against Rome in 132 C.E., the emperor Hadrian prohibited circumcision. Perhaps he realized that circumcision contributed to the distinctive character of the Jewish people within his Empire.

It is interesting to note that early Christians also practiced circumcision. Christianity spread into pagan countries, away from its Jewish origin, however, and the rite of circumcision encountered resistance and was eventually dropped as a requirement of the early Christian faith.

There are various theories concerning the origin of the practice. But for Jews, circumcision has always been a sign of adherence to the Israelite covenant. Circumcision is frequently practiced amongst Jews and non-Jews in the United States today for medical or hygienic reasons. But it is most important that Jews perform circumcision *ritually*, as a *berit milah* (בְּרִית מִילָה, "the covenant of circumcision"), rather than simply undergoing a surgical operation by a doctor in a hospital. Only by participation in the *ritual* does one affirm one's attachment to the covenant.

A male convert to Judaism must undergo circumcision. If he is already circumcised, a symbolic circumcision, consisting of the drawing of a few drops of blood, must be performed.

The question arises why a man must have a ritual circumcision to become a Jew, while a woman can convert without it. It may seem somewhat unfair, but any obligation in Jewish law implies the ability to perform it. Only men can be circumcised and, normally, all men can be circumcised. Therefore, they must be circumcised to convert.

The other aspects of the conversion process are the same for men and women. For instance, they must learn about Judaism, and they must be immersed in a ritual bath (מִקְוָה).

☐ Teaching Procedure

After reading Genesis 17, have your students outline its contents: The Lord appears to Abram, changes his name to Abraham, and renews the covenant promises. God commands Abraham, his household and his offspring to circumcise the flesh of their foreskin as a sign of the covenant. God changes Sarai's name to Sarah, and promises Abraham a son by her. Abraham is incredulous. God promises Abram that his wife Sarah will give birth to a son through whom the covenant promises will be fulfilled (17:19). Ishmael is also blessed. Abraham follows God's command, circumcising himself and Ishmael, as well as all the males in his household.

The first verse tells us that Abram is now ninety-nine years old. In Gen. 16:16, we learned that Abram was eighty-six years old at the time of Ishmael's birth. Thirteen years have elapsed. How does God introduce himself in 17:1? Tell your class that agreements, contracts, and covenants often begin with a formal introduction or identification of the parties involved (e.g., the Ten Commandments [Exodus 20]). What is God's first statement to Abram? Why does God have to repeat His promise to "establish" or "maintain" a covenant with Abram (17:2)? Thirteen years have passed, apparently without further word from God. Thirteen years of waiting is a long time for a man of Abram's age.

Lesson 8: Circumcision 169

Which part of the blessing is at the forefront of Abram's mind? Your class will realize that it is the one which must be fulfilled in Abram's lifetime: the conception of a son! Is God aware of Abraham's impatience? He must be since He alludes immediately to Abraham's becoming "exceedingly numerous" (17:2). Abraham falls on his face, as a sign of respect, as one falls in front of a king (17:3).

Abram then receives a new name, Abraham. What reason does the text give for the change of name? The new name indicates his destiny, to be a father of a multitude of nations (17:5). However, "Abram" and "Abraham" *both* mean "father is exalted" in Hebrew. Probably Terah had not given his son a Hebrew name, but a name common to his time and locale, the meaning of which is not known to us. The important issue, however, is not the meaning of the name, but the fact that it was changed by God. When we studied Genesis 1 we have discussed the importance of naming. Giving a new name denotes a new turn in the life of Abram. In a sense, it means a new identity, and a new relationship between him and God. It serves as an external sign or pronouncement of this new phase (e.g., the elected President of the United States is not called "Mr. President" until his inauguration; one is not a graduate until a graduation ceremony has taken place, nor married until the proper words have been pronounced).

God details His responsibilities in the covenant. What is God's part of the bargain?

1) God will make Abraham the father of a multitude of nations. (17:5–6)
2) The covenant will be everlasting. (17:7)
3) God will give the land of Canaan as an everlasting possession to Abraham's descendants. (17:8)
4) He will be the God of Abraham's people. (17:8)

What is Abraham's responsibility in the covenant? He is to circumcise himself and all the males of his household. In the future, every newborn male is to be circumcised at the age of eight days.

Have your class find what changes take place concerning Sarai. Abraham learns that her name also is to be changed, to Sarah (17:15). Again, the emphasis is not on the meaning of the word "Sarah" as opposed to "Sarai," but on the fact that she is given a new name.

Abraham also learns for the first time that the child he is going to have would be born to his wife Sarah (17:16).

Why was Abraham incredulous? Obviously, he considered it impossible for a man of one hundred and a woman of ninety to have a child. He had given up hope for a son from Sarah, or he would not have had Ishmael. He considered the promise of an heir to have been fulfilled with Ishmael's birth. He had never been told that *Sarah* was to be his son's mother!

In 17:8, God promised to be the God of Abraham's people. What exactly does this mean? Your students will probably be able to supply some answers (e.g., He will take care of their needs, He will protect them, they will be able to depend on Him). There were also demands put on Abraham: "Walk in My ways and be blameless" (17:1).

We learn that Abraham carried out his part of the covenant (17:23–27). You may want to tell your class that the descendants of Ishmael (the Arabs) circumcise their sons at age thirteen (or before), just as Ishmael had been.

You may want to discuss the continuing importance of circumcision in Jewish life today. Ritual circumcision, or *berit milah* (בְּרִית מִילָה), is a sign of the covenant between God and the people of Abraham for all generations.

LESSON 9

The Three Visitors
Gen. 18:1–15

☐ In Preparation for Teaching

In Genesis 18, Abraham and Sarah are visited by three guests. Some of your students may refer to them as "three angels." From the continuation of the story it becomes clear that two of the visitors are "angels" or "messengers" of God and one is God Himself (18:1, 13), appearing in human form (אֲנָשִׁים, "men" in 18:1). In Gen. 19:10 we learn that these "men" have supernatural powers. In other places in Genesis we read about מַלְאָכִים. Although in later books of the Bible the מַלְאָךְ is a winged creature, there is no indication that in Genesis he is anything but a messenger of God in human form. Jacob, in his dream (Gen. 28:12), sees מַלְאָכִים going up and down a ladder. Obviously, if they had been winged, there would have been no need for a ladder.

☐ Teaching Procedure

In 18:1–6, three men announce to Abraham and Sarah that the birth of a son is imminent. The students should read the verses and summarize their contents very briefly: Three men appear to Abraham, who receives them with great hospitality. After eating of the food offered by Abraham, they tell him that a son will be born to Sarah. Sarah, who is listening at the entrance, laughs incredulously. The men, however, assure her: "Nothing is too wondrous for the Lord!"

Discuss the term הַכְנָסַת אוֹרְחִים ("welcoming guests," "hospitality"). The custom developed when there were no restaurants or hotels along the main trade routes (there were, however, inns for caravans, called "caravansaries"). Travelers could not have survived unless people offered the hospitality of their homes, providing them with water and shelter.

The custom developed mainly in inhospitable climates—the deserts of the Middle East and the frigid lands of the Eskimos. Many stories are told about Bedouin (desert Arabs) who would shelter even their enemies, but would have no qualms about killing them once they had left the shelter of their tents.

Jews today still value הַכְנָסַת אוֹרְחִים and consider sheltering others a *mitzvah*.

If הַכְנָסַת אוֹרְחִים is a custom, your students may say that Abraham does not deserve too much credit for it. The text however, indicates that Abraham is doing more than just fulfilling an obligation. Ask your students to find the verses that show effort "beyond the call of duty." For example,

- (18:2) Abraham *runs* toward his guests although it is a hot day and he is old.
- (18:3) He calls them "my Lord" and refers to himself humbly as "your servant."
- (18:4) He offers a "little water" and "a morsel of bread," belittling his own efforts.
- (18:6) He hastens into the tent and asks Sarah to prepare bread quickly (speed indicates willingness; Abraham shows no hesitation).
- (18:7) Abraham himself runs to the herd to pick a tender choice calf.
- (18:8) He himself sets the food in front of the guests and waits on them personally.

Abraham and Sarah, of course, do not know that these are God's messengers, or else Sarah would not have laughed. Why was Sarah frightened in 18:15? The strangers knew her name. They also seemed to know she was barren. They knew she had laughed, although she only laughed to herself (18:12).

(For supplementary activities related to the teaching of this lesson, see Appendix A, below, p. 319.)

LESSON 10A

Abraham's Intervention, I
Gen. 18:16–32

▢ Teaching Procedure

After your students have read 18:16–32, ask them to propose some thematic divisions. The following is one possible schema:

1) 18:16 The messengers' departure
2) 18:17–19 The Lord's soliloquy
3) 18:20–21 God's address to Abraham
4) 18:22–33 Abraham's intercession with the Lord

In 18:16, the three visitors set out for Sodom. Abraham walks with them, to see them off. Two of the men go off toward Sodom, leaving Abraham standing in the presence of God.

Why were the men heading toward Sodom? The answer can be found in 18:20–21: God tells Abraham that He has heard a great outcry coming out of Sodom and Gomorrah, a cry of anguish and despair. The outcry suggests some outrage or atrocity is taking place in these cities. God informs Abraham that He is "going down" to check if the sins of Sodom and Gomorrah are as great as the outcry seems to indicate. If so, the verses imply, the Lord will punish them accordingly.

What kind of acts would cause an outcry? Could there be an outcry without sufficient cause? And why does the Lord, who "knows everything," have to "go down" to check it out?

The sins of Sodom cause an outcry. They must be of the kind people inflict on one another: perhaps physical harm, violence, torture, prolonged oppression, humiliation, or injustice. The outcry alone, however, is not sufficient evidence to indict the people of Sodom. Consider this analogy: A little boy may be screaming his head off, although all his big brother did was touch his toy! Should the mother punish the older boy on the basis of the younger one's screams, or should she try to establish what actually took place? Our text teaches that even the Lord, who must have known what was going on in Sodom, makes sure before He punishes.

What reasons does God give for involving Abraham in His plans for Sodom and Gomorrah? Direct your students' attention to 18:17–19, and have them list the reasons on the board or in their notebooks:

1) Abraham (through his descendants) will become a great and mighty nation.
2) All the nations of the earth will be blessed through him.
3) The Lord singled him out for the purpose of instructing his children to keep the way of the Lord, to do what is just and right.

It is not clear at this point how involving Abraham in His plan for Sodom will make Abraham better able to fulfill God's plan for him.

In 18:22–33, the men (two of them, as we shall see in Genesis 19) continue on their way to Sodom. Abraham, however, remains with the third man (the Lord). He seems upset by the Lord's disclosure. What does he say? "Will you sweep away the innocent along with the guilty?" (18:23).

What was Abraham worried about? He did not want to see the innocent suffer or the Lord act unjustly. When a whole group is punished, innocent people suffer as well. This unintended consequence cannot always be avoided (e.g., wars). The Lord, however, is "the Judge of all the earth" (18:25) and should deal justly with mankind.

What else did Abraham request (18:24)? Can you describe how *this* request differs from the one in 18:23? Your students should realize that in 18:23, Abraham asked for the lives of the innocent, but in 18:24 he seems to be asking that the guilty be spared for the sake of the innocent!

The Hebrew word for justice, מִשְׁפָּט, can be divided into two components: 1) דִּין ("justice") refers to getting what one rightfully deserves; 2) רַחֲמִים ("mercy") means forgiveness, the waiving of a deserved punishment. The judicial system of the United States uses both criteria. Justice can be *demanded*. For mercy, however, one may have to *plead*.

It may be useful to have the teacher, or a student who reads well, read 18:23–32 aloud. You may want to ask, how we would feel if we had to plead with a person who had power over us. (*Never* ask a student to imagine pleading before God.) We might feel scared and nervous. Does Abraham have any of these feelings? Yes! Have your students find evidence in the text:

(18:27) "Here I venture to speak to the Lord, I, who am dust and ashes"
(18:30) "Let not my Lord be angry if I go on."
(18:31) "I venture again to speak to the Lord."
(18:32) "Let not my Lord be angry if I speak this last time."

Yet Abraham overcomes his fears. Where does he get the courage to do so? Abraham has a covenant with the Lord. In a sense Abraham is testing that covenant. How far could he go with his demands? How much pressure could he put on the Lord? What, in 18:20–22, might have encouraged Abraham to go on? Probably the fact that the Lord had involved him in His plans in the first place: God told Abraham that the fate of Sodom had not yet been decided!

LESSON 10B

Abraham's Intervention, II
Gen. 18:16–32

The Lord had approached Noah with a similar pronouncement: "I have decided to put an end to all flesh!" Noah does not try to dissuade the Lord from His intention. Your students will no doubt see that Abraham was a greater personality than Noah. It is only fair to remind them, however, that God presented Abraham with a chance to intervene, while Noah was presented with a final decision.

Why did the Lord choose to involve Abraham in the first place? Let us backtrack to the list we made on the board when we first read 18:17–19. Which of the following three statements best answers the question?

1) Abraham (through his descendants) will become a great and mighty nation.
2) All the nations of the earth will be blessed by him.
3) The Lord singled him out for the purpose of instructing his children to keep the way of the Lord, to do what is just and right.

The third statement, paraphrasing 18:19, best addresses the issue. In fact, this verse may well be the most important in the whole Abraham story. For the first time, the Lord explains why He singled out Abraham: Abraham will teach his children what is just and right, so that they will form a just and right nation—a nation that will serve as an example to all the peoples of the earth. This is the concept expressed in the prayerbook by the expressions אֲשֶׁר בָּחַר בָּנוּ ("who chose us") and אַתָּה בְחַרְתָּנוּ ("You have chosen us").

Your class may now be able to understand the connection between the Lord's plan for Abraham and His decision to involve him in the Sodom episode. Abraham was deliberately given a chance to become involved and learn about justice firsthand. What exactly did Abraham learn?

1) The Lord is willing to listen to a human. In fact he seems to *welcome* human intervention for the sake of others.

2) The Lord is willing to change His mind, if someone can convince Him to do so.
3) Righteous people have the power to save others, simply because of their being righteous.

You may want to tell your students that in Genesis 20:7, Abraham will be referred to as a prophet. One of the tasks of a prophet is to stand between God and man as an intermediary. A prophet must bring God's word to the people, admonish and warn them. On the other hand, when God's anger is kindled against the people, the prophet must intercede on their behalf and ask God for forgiveness and mercy. It seems that in 18:16–33, Abraham has earned the title of "prophet."

The "Abraham list" we commenced earlier in the unit gains several items with this chapter: Abraham intervenes for justice, he takes risks, he is willing to argue with the Lord, he cares for others, etc.

LESSON 11A

Lot Receives His Guests
Gen. 19:1–14

☐ In Preparation for Teaching

Before reading Genesis 19, it is worthwhile to summarize the knowledge we have already accumulated about Lot. Since Lot's father is dead, he joins Abram on his journey to Canaan (Gen. 12:4). Lot does not seem to be concerned about the quarrel between his herdsmen and Abram's (Gen. 13:1–13). When offered first choice of location, he seems to value material wealth over moral conduct. When he is captured in battle (Genesis 14), Abram rescues him. There is no mention of Lot giving thanks to God or Abram. In Genesis 19 we shall learn more about Lot.

Your class will, no doubt, find Lot's offer to turn over his daughters to the people of Sodom (19:8) distasteful. Encourage your students, however, to view the situation according to the norms of ancient societies. Although Lot no doubt loved his daughters, in his time daughters were considered *property*. A father took care of his daughters until they reached a marriageable age and could bring a good "bride price." Lot, in this chapter, is thus willing to give up his property, for custom seems to demand that his obligations to his guests precede those owed to his daughters. It is also possible that a homosexual assault by the people of Sodom (19:5) was considered more sinful than the act of heterosexual rape. The main point of the story, however, seems to be the fact that Lot carried little weight with the people of Sodom. They did not listen to him, nor did they respect him. Had it not been for the aid of his guests, he might have been killed.

In 19:1–12, Lot receives two visitors. When the two men (whom we know to be messengers from God) arrive in Sodom, Lot urges them to spend the night in his home. The story parallels that of Gen. 18:1–16. Lot may deserve even more credit than Abraham because, as we shall see, his act of hospitality nearly costs him his life. He must have known the risk he was taking.

Before long, "all the townspeople—young and old—all the people, to the last man" (19:4)—surrounded the house, demanding that the guests be brought out to them. Lot ventures out,

Lesson 11A: Lot Receives His Guests

closes the door behind him, and beseeches the people not to commit this wrong. He offers them his two unmarried daughters instead. The men, however, reject his offer. They call him an alien, one who has no rights in Sodom. They attempt to break the doors. The guests save Lot by pulling him back into the house and striking the people of Sodom with a temporary blindness or glare, so they cannot find the door.

What do the visitors then inquire about (19:12)? What do they tell Lot to do? How do Lot's sons-in-law regard him (19:14)?

LESSON 11B

Lot Flees Sodom
Gen. 19:15-38

☐ In Preparation for Teaching

In 19:15-26, Lot departs from Sodom prior to its destruction. At dawn, the men urge Lot to leave, but he delays and has to be physically removed from the city. Why would he hesitate? Did he doubt the men? Did he hate to leave his married daughters? Did it hurt to leave his property, his herds, and flocks behind? Surely now he would be a poor man, a refugee.

We have discussed the fact that Abraham obeyed God immediately. Lot was reluctant. Why was Lot saved? The Lord is being merciful to him (19:16). We have discussed the fact that sometimes mercy is given, although it may not be deserved. Which of Lot's acts may have earned him his rescue? Certainly his hospitality. (Your class may feel that he doesn't deserve much credit for the offer of his daughters.)

Where was Lot told to go (19:17)? The men urge him to go to the hill country, but he refused. He was afraid he would not make it. He does not seem to be aware of the fact that God is in control of the situation.

Where did Lot want to go? He suggested "a very little place" nearby. Why did Lot emphasize the "littleness" of the place? Possibly because the city would have to be saved in order to save Lot. Lot essentially told God that the favor he was asking was not a "big deal" (19:20).

Why were Lot and his wife commanded not to look back? Time is of the essence (19:17). Looking back could have wasted time. Perhaps it was just a test of obedience, for Lot was giving the men a hard time. It is also possible that the Lord did not want Lot to see the destruction. All of these are plausible answers. The story of Lot's wife may also be etiological: it offers an explanation of why there are huge deposits of salt in the Dead Sea area.

The next verses (19:27-28) describe the destruction of Sodom. The sulphurous fires (24) that rained upon Sodom and Gemorrah, and the smoke, like that of a kiln (28), seem to indicate an earthquake. The destruction of the cities of the plain was probably an actual event. Stories of the wickedness of the people of Sodom, Abraham's intercession with God, and the men's visit to Lot, are not historical. Like other biblical stories, they serve to teach us *ideas* about God and His relationship to man. The story teaches that God is just. God decided to destroy the cities because their people were wicked. (But every tragedy in life should not automatically be seen as the result of divine retribution for wickedness.) In 19:29 we find that God saved Lot not only because He had mercy on him (19:16), but also because He was mindful of Abraham. Here the Bible is making another point about God's relationship with Abraham.

The remainder of the chapter (19:30-38) deals with Lot and his daughters in the aftermath of the destruction. The daughters believed that nobody on earth was left alive for them to mate with. They plied their father with wine and conceived from him the ancestors of the people of Ammon and Moab—future enemies of Israel. (Display a map of Canaan, Moab, and Ammon.)

This story may be a "putdown" of these nations. After all, what can be expected from people born of incest? (Compare this to the last part of Genesis 9, the cursing of Canaan.) As a result, Israelites later in the Bible were admonished *not to marry* Moabites and Ammonites. Some Bible scholars give credit to Lot's daughters for wanting to fulfill their roles as mothers in spite of all difficulties.

Beginning with Genesis 13 we have become aware of the contrasts between Abraham's traits and those of Lot. By now, we may have some insight into why God chose Abraham.

LESSON 12A

Hagar Is Sent Away
Gen. 21:1–21

☐ In Preparation for Teaching

Since we have dealt with Genesis 20 in conjunction with its parallel in Genesis 12 (see Lesson 3 above, p. 148), we now proceed to Genesis 21. Here we find another story concerning Sarah and Hagar (21:1–21). Genesis 21 and Genesis 16 have a great deal in common. Once again, we seem to have two versions of the same story, with differing details. One is told about Hagar before the birth of Ishmael. The other takes place when Isaac, the son of Abraham and Sarah is weaned. (In ancient times, children were often breast-fed until the age of four or five.)

Were we to regard the Abraham stories as one continuous story, told chronologically, we would find ourselves in difficulty. Abraham was 86 at the time Ishmael was born; he was 100 at the time Isaac was born. Thus, Ishmael was fourteen when Isaac was born. By the time Isaac was weaned, Ishmael was even older. Yet Genesis 21 depicts Ishmael as a young child, young enough to be carried on his mother's shoulder.

As you study this chapter, your class may express outrage at Sarah's actions. You may want to tell your class that according to the laws of Hammurabi (an ancient Babylonian code), the sons of a slave-wife could share the inheritance of the father with the sons of the free woman, if they were recognized (or legitimized) by the father. If he did not recognize them as his sons, both the sons and their mother were to be given their freedom. Here the text leaves no doubt that Abraham had legitimized Ishmael as his son (17:24–25, 26). Sarah, however, refused to allow Ishmael to inherit along with her son Isaac. Abraham, as a father was very much distressed. He might have objected if God had not intervened, telling him to do as his wife bade him.

(Supplementary activities related to the teaching of this lesson may be found in Appendix A, below, pp. 320–321.)

Lesson 12A: Hagar Is Sent Away   183

☐ Teaching Procedure

Have your students review the events of the story: the Lord remembers Sarah and she bears a son, Isaac. Isaac is circumcised when he is eight days old. When he is weaned, Abraham celebrates with a great feast. Sarah observes Ishmael playing and insists that Abraham cast him out together with his mother Hagar. The matter distresses Abraham greatly. God, however, tells Abraham to do as Sarah instructs, since the blessing will be fulfilled *through Isaac*. As for Ishmael, he too would become a nation, since he was of Abraham's seed.

Early the next day Abraham gives Hagar bread and water, puts the child on her shoulder and sends her away. When the water is gone, Hagar puts the child under one of the bushes, since she cannot bear to see him die of thirst. An angel of God called to her, repeated God's promise to her, and showed her a well of water. Ishmael grew up in the wilderness of Paran and became a bowsman "a wild ass of a man" (Gen. 16:12). His mother found a wife for him from the land of Egypt.

In Genesis 16 we criticized both Sarah and Hagar. How do we feel about the two women in this chapter? Sarah may come out worse here. In the earlier story, Hagar gave Sarah cause for harsh treatment. Here Hagar seems to be innocent. In this story Sarah seems to be jealous of Ishmael, not Hagar. What was she jealous about? She was worried about the inheritance—money and property. She did not want Isaac to have to share it with Ishmael (21:10).

How does Sarah refer to Ishmael? "The son of *that* slave" (21:10). Referring to Hagar as "that slave," rather than calling her by name indicates disdain, contempt. In contrast, how does Abraham relate to Ishmael? He considers Ishmael to be "a son of his." Abraham had recognized Ishmael as his son and had thereby legitimized him.

Why then does God encourage Abraham to carry out Sarah's request? The alternative would have been for Hagar and Sarah to continue to live under one roof. What kind of life would Abraham have had? Would Ishmael have been happier living in Sarah's house than living in the wilderness of Paran? (Later Ishmaelites were a nomadic people who lived in the desert.) How would Isaac have fared had Ishmael stayed? These are questions the answers to which we can only guess at.

How did Isaac feel when his older brother departed? We do not know. But we do know that Ishmael joined Isaac in burying Abraham (Gen. 25:9). Therefore we learn that Ishmael did not bear a grudge against his father.

God's intervention is critical in this story. Had God not encouraged Abraham to send Hagar and Ishmael away, surely his life and that of his household would have been unbearable. Had God not intervened again in the desert, Hagar and Ishmael would have died of thirst. It seems that God usually helps those who are low and depressed.

LESSON 12B

Abimelech and the Wells
Gen. 21:22–34

☐ In Preparation for Teaching

Abraham had dug a well which was taken over by the servants of Abimelech (21:25). When confronted, Abimelech insisted that he had no knowledge of what was going on. Abraham made a pact with Abimelech. He also made Abimelech accept seven ewes from him as proof that he recognized Abraham's ownership of the well.

☐ Teaching Procedure

In your class discussion, direct your students' attention to the confrontation. The king appeared with his chief of staff, Phicol (a symbol of his power); yet, it was the foreigner Abraham who reproached *him*. This time, Abimelech was the one who had to justify himself (in contrast to Gen. 20:10–11, where Abraham had to explain his conduct before Abimelech). Does Abimelech's claim of ignorance of the situation vindicate him?

Abraham initiated the pact (21:27) and insisted that Abimelech accept the seven ewes (21:30). In accepting the ewes, Abimelech officially recognized Abraham's claim to the well. Official recognition is a public act which bestows legal status and legal rights.

This notion of "official recognition" also played a part in the first verses of this chapter. Abraham had officially recognized Ishmael as his son. This entitled him legally to an inheritance, which angered Sarah. Ishmael and his mother are given their freedom instead of the inheritance, another legal right.

To continue our "Abraham list": He had insisted on his rights and took initiative to establish them. He had obviously gained the respect of the inhabitants of the land where he was sojourning. He attributes his success to God (21:33).

LESSON 13A

The Akedah, I
Genesis 22

☐ In Preparation for Teaching

In Genesis 18, we saw Abraham test God's loyalty to the covenant: how far could he press his demands on God regarding Sodom? In this story, Genesis 22, it is God who is testing Abraham's loyalty to the covenant: how much could He ask of the man bound to Him by the covenant? The story of the *Akedah* (עֲקֵדָה, the "binding" of Isaac) embodies the most profound personal experience in the history of the patriarchs.

In this chapter we find God's last "call" (i.e., personal communication from God) to Abraham. The first call occurred in Genesis 12. Abraham's life is thus bracketed between these two chapters. (Genesis 23 and 24 deal with the future: acquiring the land and insuring descendants.) Genesis 22 in many ways echoes Genesis 12. It will be necessary to draw your students' attention to these parallels.

You will also have to help your class appreciate the differences between Genesis 12 and 22. The hardships willingly undertaken by Abraham in Genesis 12 signaled the outset of a new life for him. He was to become the father of a great nation that would inherit the land of Canaan and be a blessing to all the nations of the earth. If the promise of offspring was vague in Genesis 12, it gained momentum throughout Abraham's life. When Abraham mentioned that he expected Damesek Eliezer to be his heir (Gen. 15:2–3), God replied that he would have a son of his own (Gen. 15:4). Abraham believed that Ishmael, the son of Hagar, was the son he was promised (17:18), only to be told by God, "Sarah your wife shall bear you a son and you shall name him Isaac, and I will maintain my covenant with him" (17:19).

Not only was Isaac the son of Abraham's old age, so long hoped for, so long denied, he was also the one link to the far-off future to which Abraham's life was dedicated. To sacrifice Isaac would mean to forego all that God had ever promised him, all that he had been led to hope for by God. If we consider Genesis 12 a test of faith, how much more so is Genesis 22! Here Abraham is

Lesson 13A: The Akedah, I

asked to maintain confidence in the ultimate divine purpose, when all appears to be lost.

Up until this chapter, obedience to God (or faith) and moral conduct coincided. They were always one and the same. God judged the world in justice and righteousness and expected man to follow suit. Only in the name of what is just and right could Abraham have pleaded for the people of Sodom. In the name of justice Abraham was commanded to intercede with God for Abimelech. Abraham's act of faith in Genesis 22, however, seemed to require the suppression of his own moral judgment, the denial of all he knew to be just and good. Abraham passed this test by putting faith above all else. Abraham had to have *total faith* in God for God's promise to be fulfilled. At the end of the story, we realize that Abraham's faith in God was justified. God demanded faith of Abraham, not human sacrifice.

This test comes at the end of Abraham's life. Would he have passed it in Genesis 12? Perhaps he would not have. Abraham had to *experience* God and what He stood for throughout his life, before he could place total trust in Him.

Some of your students who have studied this story before may suggest that the main lesson of this story is the prohibition of human sacrifices. Bible scholars, however, refute this assertion. In Genesis, there is no indication that human sacrifices were offered. On the contrary, the command to Abraham is seen as an exceptional request. Also, no admonition is specifically spelled out in the story (such as "human sacrifices are an abomination!"), whereas prohibitions elsewhere are stated explicitly. Finally, it is unlikely that a story with such a concern would have taken Abraham to the brink of carrying out God's command.

The story of the *Akedah* is used for a different purpose, namely, to demonstrate Abraham's total faith in God.

▢ Teaching Procedure

Ask your students to read Genesis 22, and tell you what it deals with, saving all problems and questions for the discussion to come later. Tell your students that in Genesis 22, we find God's last call to Abraham. Ask them if they remember where the first call to Abraham occurs (Genesis 12). The class can now begin to find parallels. Read 22:2 aloud: "Your son, your favored one." Ask if they can find an echo of these words in the earlier chapter. What other parallels can they find?

You will have to supply the verses from Chapter 22. It may be helpful to pass out the chart below with only the left side filled in. Let the students fill in the right side. To save time, you could have them note only chapter and verse in class, but make sure they fill in the words later. Alternatively, you can hand out complete charts. (A list of chapters and verses has no *visual impact*, and will have no meaning to your students.) Your list should resemble the following:

Chapter 22	*Chapter 12*
[22:2] Take your son, your favored one, Isaac whom you love . . . offer him on one of the heights which I will point out to you.	Go forth from your native land and from your father's house . . . to the land that I will show you.
[22:3] So early next morning, Abraham saddled his ass. . . .	[12:4] Abraham went forth as the Lord had commanded him.
[22:9] They arrived at the place.	[12:5] When they arrived in the land of Canaan . . .
[22:9] Abraham built an altar.	[12:7] Abram built an altar.
[22:17] I will bestow my blessing and make your descendants as numerous as the stars.	[12:7] I will give this land to your offspring.

LESSON 13B

The Akedah, II
Genesis 22

◻ **In Preparation for Teaching**

In Genesis 12, God promises to make Abraham "a great nation." In the course of the subsequent chapters, this vague promise gradually focuses upon Isaac, the only son left to Abraham after the departure of Ishmael. If Genesis 12 contained the hope and promise of a new beginning, Genesis 22 brings only despair!

◻ **Teaching Procedure**

We will now turn to a close reading of the text. Read aloud 22:1-2. What do we find out in the first verse? How does our knowing that this is a *test* affect our reading? Your students may have different opinions. Some may say it releases our tension knowing that it is merely a test. Others may say that we, the readers, do not yet know what the test will entail. Perhaps it may actually involve the slaying of Isaac. Knowing this is only a test may indicate that God would not actually have Abraham slay his son, but we cannot be sure.

The fact that we know something Abraham does not know may serve to heighten our tension. Ask your students if they have ever watched a movie, a play, or a television program where they had some information the actor did not have. When this happens, one often wants to advise the actor or to alert him to some imminent danger by calling out, "Don't do it, don't do it!" or "Look behind you!"

Continue your close reading of Genesis 22. Alert your students to the fact that none of the emotional dynamics are spelled out in this highly charged episode. The terseness of the text on this score heightens its dramatic impact. We are not told what Abraham's thoughts or feelings are on that terrible night before the *Akedah*. We are only told of Abraham's actions—he rose early in the morning, saddled his ass, took his son and two servants and set out on that fateful journey. The two servants were left waiting at a distance so that they would not interfere with Abraham's task. They were assured by Abraham that the two would soon return.

Note that Abraham refers to Isaac as "boy" (נַעַר) when he talks about him to the servants. But he calls him "my son" (בְּנִי) when addressing him directly (22:7). What does this reflect?

The boy is carrying the wood for his own pyre. The father carries a knife and firestones. Isaac asks about the lamb for the offering. He mentions only the wood and the firestones, but not the knife (22:7). Is he afraid of the knife? Note Abraham's tender yet evasive answer. The boy must have sensed the truth by now, yet "they walked together," the father and his son.

At the site Abraham went about his task like a mechanical robot. Ask your students how the writer makes us sense this frantic activity. You may have to draw their attention to the verbs that rapidly follow each other: "He built an altar, he laid out the wood, he bound his son Isaac (why does the text tell us *again* that Isaac is Abraham's son?), he laid him on the altar on top of the wood (we already know this!) and picked up the knife to slay his son."

Your class may notice how many words the text uses here, focusing on each succeeding motion; the suspense becomes almost unbearable! The blade was in mid-air when God stayed Abraham's hand. The test was over; Abraham had lived up to God's highest expectations.

There was no hesitation in Abraham's action. He went about his task with meticulous concentration, indicating both his inner tension and his resolute acceptance of the inevitable. You may want to ask your students how they go about carrying out dreaded tasks. Some people carry out tasks immediately, to "get them over with." Others go in for a great deal of procrastination although they know they will eventually have to do the job. Few people could have acted like Abraham!

As on other occasions when Abraham had proved himself worthy, here too, since Abraham had not withheld from Him his son, his favored one, God rewards him with a renewal of the blessing (22:16-18).

Meanwhile, back in Mesopotamia, children are born to Nahor, Abraham's brother (22:20-24). It seems that these children are born easily, apparently without any of Abraham's struggle to ensure a line of descent. Twelve sons are born, a number which symbolizes "national completeness." Also, Rebekah was born before Sarah had died. Thus, this paragraph serves as a bridge to Unit VI, the continuation of the Abrahamic family.

LESSON 14

Total Faith
Genesis 22

☐ Teaching Procedure

Some of your students will, no doubt, be upset by the seeming immorality of God's request. You may want to take some time to discuss "total faith" (or "blind faith") with your students. Having total faith means doing exactly what is demanded of one, disregarding one's own sense of morality and conscience. Abraham has total faith in God because of his previous experiences with Him. Ask your class to illustrate this with examples from Abraham's experiences with God.

Total commitment to any man or ideal may come into conflict with one's commitment to God. (Some people will substitute conscience or moral judgment for the word "God".) Have your class list ideals which may demand one's total commitment:

1) Communism
2) Business
3) Science
4) Zionism
5) Nazism
6) Army

What is the dilemma of a medical doctor in Nazi Germany who is commanded to experiment on Jews, killing them in the process of making new scientific discoveries (e.g., comparing the brains of identical twins for genetic research)?

The doctor may have to decide if (A) his belief in God takes priority over his belief in Nazism or (B) his belief in Nazism takes priority. What would each of these decisions entail?

A	B
Life must be preserved. (God's Law)	Science must serve Nazism.
The Hippocratic oath must be followed.	It is necesary to prove that Jews are genetically inferior.
One's conscience must be followed.	The orders of one's superiors must be followed.
etc.	etc.

What might happen to the doctor if "A" won over "B"? In Nazi Germany this doctor may have been dismissed or even killed. If "B" won the upper hand, what would the doctor be declaring? That obedience to the Nazi regime was more important than obedience to God's laws. He would in effect be replacing God with Nazism.

Watch out that this lesson does not become preachy. Make your students aware of the fact that the doctor's dilemma is not an easy one. When under duress and pressure, it is very natural to try to justify acting against one's own knowledge of what is right and what is wrong.

Any item on the list of ideals that you made at the beginning of this lesson could be used in this manner. What is the dilemma of the soldier who is commanded to kill the villagers in a foreign country? Let your students discuss the different situations. You may want to let your students assume roles.

The idea you want to teach is that *one should have blind faith only in God*. Now, this does not mean that one should have no other commitments, but that whatever other commitments one has, the commitment to God and His demands must take priority.

LESSON 15

The Cave of Machpelah
Genesis 23

☐ In Preparation for Teaching

Chapter 23 tells us that Sarah died in Kiriat-Arba (later called Hebron). Sarah's death and Abraham's mourning for her is described in two verses only. The rest of the chapter deals with the purchase of the Cave of Machpelah for a burial site.

Abraham lived amongst a group of people referred to as בְּנֵי חֵת ("the people of Heth"). These are probably not the people usually described by the word "Hittites."

When Abraham "rose from beside his dead," he approached the people of Heth who dwelled in Kiriat-Arba, introduced himself as an "alien" and asked for permission to buy a burial site. The people of Heth, who respected Abraham as an "elect of God," urged him to bury his dead in whatever he considered to be the choicest burial spot, indicating that Abraham would not have to *buy* the land from its owner. Abraham refused this offer. He asked the people of Heth to intercede for him with Ephron the son of Zohar, who owned the cave that Abraham had selected, and get him to sell it to Abraham at *full price*.

We are told that Ephron was present at the scene and offered to give Abraham the land. Abraham bowed low to the people of Heth and insisted on buying the land. Ephron acquiesced: "A piece of land worth four hundred shekels, what is that between you and me?" (23:15). Abraham accepted Ephron's terms and paid him the money in front of all the people of Heth.

The field with its cave and all its trees thus passed into the possession of Abraham, in the presence of all the people of Heth who had "entered the gate of the city" (or "sat on the council of the town"). Then Abraham buried Sarah in the cave. "Thus the field passed from the people of Heth to Abraham as a burial site."

What is this story about? Abraham was not only looking for a burial site for his wife Sarah. He was also interested in purchasing the land and acquiring full title to it, so it could never revert to its original owner. We know from other sources that only property that was fully paid for could be considered a permanent purchase

(לְצָמִיתֻת, forever). With this land purchase, he also changed his status from that of an alien to a resident of the land.

❏ Teaching Procedure

After your students have read Genesis 23, ask them what the story is about. Let them tell you what took place. Do not accept any information which is not in the text.

Ask your students: What does Abraham want? He wanted to buy a burial site for Sarah. How does he introduce himself? He called himself a resident alien. (Remind your class how the people of Sodom had spoken of Lot: "The fellow [Lot] came here as an *alien* and already he acts the ruler" [Gen. 19:9]—indicating that an alien was a "second class citizen.") Why would Abraham make sure that his status was common knowledge? (Leave this open for the time being.) Write on the board: "(a) Why does Abraham introduce himself as an *alien?*"

What do the people of Heth offer Abraham? To bury his dead wherever he chooses. Abraham could take them up on their offer and bury Sarah anywhere on the land of the people of Heth. What, however, does he insist on? Write on the board: "(b) Why does Abraham insist on *buying* the land for himself?"

Whom does Abraham address in 23:3–9? He was addressing all the people of Heth. Whom did the cave belong to (23:8)? Where was Ephron at the time (23:10)? Why doesn't Abraham go to Ephron's home to discuss the purchase with him privately? Why doesn't Abraham talk directly to Ephron, who is present at the gate? Why does he want *the people* to intercede for him?

Your class may have noticed the many repetitions of the fact that the sale took place in public. If not, direct them to 23:8, 9, 10, 16, and 18. Write on the board: "(c) Why does Abraham insist on a *public sale?*"

Direct the attention of your students to 23:17–20. They may notice that it reads like a contract, a bill of sale, a legal document; if not, tell them.

Some of your students may suggest that the chapter describes how people in some parts of the world haggle in the marketplace. Your students, used to shopping in stores, may not know that in the oriental bazaars, for example, prices are not fixed. The seller will mention a high price, expecting the buyer to bargain. Both seller and buyer now enter a "haggling game" and settle eventually on a price much lower than the one first suggested.

Now, it is true that a sort of haggling does take place, but it is not the usual haggling over price. Draw your classes' attention to the fact that Ephron mentions the sum of four hundred shekels

Lesson 15: The Cave of Machpelah

(23:15), and Abraham accepts his terms immediately (23:16). Was four hundred shekels a large or small sum for a parcel of land? We do not know, since we do not know from any other source what the cost of land was at that time. Did Ephron, knowing how important the purchase was for Abraham, charge a high price? Or did he pity the poor alien and give him the land for a paltry sum?! The price may well have been high! If so, why was Efron apparently willing at first to *give* the land to Abraham? Perhaps this first offer was a formality in the haggling "ritual," which both parties knew could not be accepted.

You have listed your questions on the board.

(a) Why does Abraham introduce himself as an *alien?*
(b) Why does Abraham insist on *buying* the land?
(c) Why does he insist on a *public sale?*

(a) What does the term "alien" mean in America today? It refers to a person who is a *resident* of the United States but is not a *citizen*. How does an alien become a citizen? After a certain period of residency, one can become a citizen by taking an oath of allegiance to the United States. (If your students do not know these details, tell them.) Why would an alien want to become a citizen? Citizenship guarantees one certain rights and privileges: the right to vote, the right to run for office, the right to claim the protection of the United States when traveling in foreign countries, etc.

(b) What is the difference between buying a piece of land and borrowing or using it? Borrowing or using land does not make the transaction permanent. Abraham paid fully for the land, thus making it his.

You may want to mention that few people nowadays fully pay for the purchase of a home. Most people take out a mortgage from the bank and pay the bank a monthly payment (principal plus interest). If they find themselves unable to pay, the bank may repossess the house. Until one has fully paid for one's home, one does not own it outright.

(c) Abraham insisted on a public sale because he wanted to make sure that nobody would later say they were not aware of the fact that Abraham, the alien, had bought land.

You may want to tell your class that at one time in America only people who owned real estate had the right to vote. *Owning real estate made one a citizen.* The first Jews who came to New Amsterdam (before the American Revolution) were not allowed to buy land. The first parcel of land they were eventually allowed to buy was a cemetery.

Some Bible scholars believe that Abraham was in a similar situation among the people of Heth. Though highly revered, Abraham was an "alien." How could he become a citizen? Perhaps by buying land.

In buying this plot, Abraham had gained a foothold in the land the Lord had promised him and his descendants for a lasting possession. This was a symbolic act to show that in the future, the land of Canaan would pass into the hands of the descendants of Abraham.

LESSON 16

Finding a Wife for Isaac
Genesis 24

☐ Overview

Genesis 23 dealt with the acquisition of land, the symbolic beginning of the fulfillment of God's promise that the land would eventually belong to Abraham's descendants. Genesis 24 deals with finding a suitable wife for Isaac, the first step in insuring the continuity of the family and therefore the fulfillment of God's promise that Abraham would become a great nation.

In Genesis 18 Abraham tested the covenant; in Genesis 22 he in turn was tested by God. In Genesis 24 Abraham shows full confidence in the covenant.

Genesis 24 is a long chapter, but you should be able to teach it in two class sessions.

You may want to divide the chapter and teach it section by section. Have the students suggest a name for each section. Possible divisions and names are:

24:1–9	The Oath
24:10–14	Asking for a Sign
24:15–27	Rebekah
24:28–49	Presenting the Case to the Family
24:50–67	Mission Accomplished

LESSON 16A

The Oath
Gen. 24:1–9

☐ **In Preparation for Teaching**

Abraham commissions his trusted servant to go to Haran in order to find a wife for Isaac from among Abraham's kin. This section describes the oath that Abraham asks of the servant as a guarantee that the errand will be faithfully carried out.

It would not be correct to teach these verses as an admonition for Jews today to "marry Jewish." Rebekah was not born "Jewish," nor were Rachel, Leah, or the wives of Joseph or Moses. Abraham, and Isaac after him, were disgusted with the Canaanites, their customs and worship (see Genesis 28). They insisted on their sons marrying wives from their own background.

Today men and women who become Jewish undergo certain rituals. But in biblical times, although men who became Israelites underwent circumcision (as they do today), there was no ritual (that we know of) for women who joined the Israelite faith. Ruth the Moabite, for example, came to live in Bethlehem. Accepting Naomi's religion and customs, she became a member of the people Israel (גֵּרָה). Rebekah, Leah and Rachel joined the family of Abraham by marrying into it.

Abraham placed the greatest importance on the background of the mother who would raise the heirs to the covenant. You may want to discuss the importance of the mother and her background in bringing up children both in ancient days and in our own.

☐ **Teaching Procedure**

Abraham asked his trusted servant (who may or may not be Damesek Eliezer of Genesis 15) to put his hand under Abraham's thigh. This was a ritual manner of taking a solemn, binding oath. If he should fail to fulfill it, he would be cursed.

Ask your students what the oath consisted of. Answers should include:

Lesson 16A: The Oath

1) The servant would not take a Canaanite wife for Isaac. (24:3)
2) He would get a wife for Isaac from Haran. (24:4)
3) He would not, on any account, permit Isaac to go back to Haran. (24:6)

Why was the servant hesitant? He was concerned that the woman might not be willing to follow him to Canaan. Was his fear realistic? You may have to make your students aware of the fact that she would probably never see her family and country again. She would be going to a place she did not know, to marry a man she had never met.

Considering the importance of these matters to Abraham, why was he so willing to clear the servant of his oath should the woman refuse to go with him (24:8)? Abraham viewed the servant as a tool in the hand of God. His trust and faith in God were complete. God had promised Abraham descendants. Thus, He would undoubtedly send an angel (messenger) to assure that a wife both suitable and willing to follow the servant would be found for his son Isaac.

LESSON 16B

Asking for a Sign
Gen. 24:10–14

☐ **In Preparation for Teaching**

The servant asks God for a sign by which he may know the identity of the intended bride for Isaac.

The scene takes place at the well outside the city of Nahor. You may want to say a few words about the well and its place in society. People in biblical times did not have running water in their homes. Women and girls went to the well on the outskirts of the village to draw water. Pails or jars were lowered into the well by rope, pulled up and carried home, or emptied into a trough for the flocks to drink. In order to give water to animals, many pails had to be drawn. Women did their laundry near the well and exchanged news. The "gate" of the city was the place where business was conducted and judgments passed, but romance flourished at "the well."

☐ **Teaching Procedure**

Review the contents of 24:10–14. The servant arrived in the city of Nahor (either the city where Nahor lived, or a city in Haran called Nahor). Note that Abraham did not consider Ur his birthplace.

Was the servant aware of the fact that he was a tool in God's hands? He must have been, for in 24:14, he asks God for a sign. The sign he proposes is the following: He will ask a maiden for a drink of water. If she not only gives him water but also *offers* to draw water for his camels, he will know that she is the one designated by God for Isaac.

The servant could have asked for any kind of sign. By the one he requested, however, he would be able to learn something about the maiden. Her act would indicate hospitality, kindness, and a willingness to work hard. It would show that she was a person who did things on her own initiative, without having to be told. If the servant could learn all these things first hand, your students might wonder, why would he still insist on a sign from God? Perhaps he felt that one act was an insufficient basis for judgment.

There would be many things he still would not know about her, such as if she was of Abraham's family and if she would be willing to follow him to the land of Canaan. Only God would have the answers to these questions.

LESSON 16C

Rebekah
Gen. 24:15–27

☐ Teaching Procedure

Ask a few questions to get your students to restate or write down the events of 24:15–27. They should be able to supply the following information:

The sign came true: the first maiden to appear on the scene offered to draw water for the camels. She was indeed from Abraham's clan, but the servant does not yet know this (he doesn't find out until 24:24). In the meantime, he gives her a gift of gold jewelry as a reward. Would your students consider this the going price for watering ten camels? Although she had worked hard, the reward for her labor was excessive. The servant did not yet know for sure that his mission would be successfully concluded (24:21); yet, he gave Rebekah some of the jewelry intended for Isaac's future wife. What does this indicate about the servant's state of mind? He believed that the sign had come true, that God had led him to the maiden He had chosen for Abraham's son.

The servant now learns that Rebekah is in fact related to Abraham. She is the daughter of Abraham's brother Nahor—Isaac's cousin! The servant gives thanks to God for leading him to the house of Abraham's kinsmen (24:27).

LESSON 17D

Presenting the Case to the Family
Gen. 24:28-49

▢ Teaching Procedure

Have your students read 24:28-33. How did Rebekah's brother, Laban receive the servant? With great hospitality. It is of course possible that Laban would have been hospitable to any stranger. What, however, were some of the reasons that Laban might have been especially attentive to this guest? The man had given Rebekah costly gifts, and had come with ten camels loaded with goods. Obviously he represented a man of considerable wealth!

Read 24:34-49. The servant refused to eat until the tale was told. The matter was urgent—the servant was burdened by the oath he had taken. Therefore he presented the case at once.

Why did the servant elaborate on all the details of his errand? No doubt he wanted to impress on Rebekah's family that God had a hand in this enterprise (24:40). In great detail he told of Abraham's wealth and prosperity (24:34-36) and mentioned the fact that Isaac was his only son (that is, the inheritance would all be his). He thus stressed that Isaac was "a good catch."

The servant had done *his* part; the rest was up to the family (24:41). If they refused to let Rebekah go, the failure of the mission would not be his responsibility.

LESSON 17E

Mission Accomplished
Gen. 24:50-67.

☐ Teaching Procedure

Direct your students' attention to 24:50-60. How did the father and brother react? They agreed immediately. Ask for some possible reasons:

1) They realized it was God's will.
2) They respected and admired Abraham.
3) They wanted Rebekah to marry within the clan (see Gen. 29:19).
4) They knew the servant would have a good "bride-price" for them.

The servant gave royal gifts, objects made of silver and gold, to Rebekah and her kin. The servant was now eager to leave; however, Rebekah's brother and mother wanted her to stay ten more days. They decided to call Rebekah and ask her. What in fact do they ask her? It seems unlikely that they ask her if she is willing to marry Isaac. The servant would not have showered them with gifts before he knew that she would consent to follow him. It seems more likely that they were asking her if she would go immediately or whether she would go after a period of waiting. Rebekah agrees to go immediately.

Have your students read 24:61-67. The mission reaches fruition. Isaac is walking in the field when the servant and Rebekah approach. He has been completely passive in this search for a wife intended for him. He takes Rebekah as his wife. He loves her, and thus finds comfort after his mother's death.

LESSON 18

Abraham's Grandchildren
Gen. 25:1–18

☐ In Preparation for Teaching

These verses do not form a chronological sequel to the preceding chapter. This section also contradicts the chronology of the latter part of the chapter (25:19–34). Were we to accept the biblical ages literally, we would find that: Abraham was one hundred years old at the time of Isaac's birth; Isaac was sixty when Jacob and Esau were born. If Abraham died at the age of one hundred seventy-five, he would have died (25:8) when his grandchildren were fifteen, and not before their birth.

It seems from Genesis 24 that Abraham would be too old to take another wife and father six more children, as he does in 25:1–18. The story of Keturah and her sons probably comes to explain the presence of Semitic tribes in the area, which have not yet been accounted for.

After these sons were given their inheritance and sent away, Abraham died and was buried by his sons Isaac and Ishmael. He is buried near his wife Sarah in the cave of Machpelah which he purchased from Ephron of Heth. The concluding verses list the progeny of Ishmael.

These two stories seem to be placed at this point in order to highlight the one immediately following—that of Rebekah's difficulties in providing an heir! The six "no account" sons of Abraham, and the twelve offspring of Ishmael were born without need of God's intervention. This is not the case with the heirs to God's covenant with Abraham.

☐ Teaching Procedures

Have your students read Gen. 25:1–18 and gather the facts of Abraham's second set of children and the progeny of Ishmael. Do not dwell on the contrast between Rebekah and Keturah, or Ishmael's progeny until after they have read the story of the birth of Jacob and Esau.

UNIT VI

The Jacob Stories
Gen. 25:19–36:43

UNIT VI

The Jacob Stories
Gen. 25:19–36:43

☐ **Isaac and Jacob—An Overview**

Although Gen. 25:19 indicates that the ensuing chapters relate the story of Isaac, we immediately find ourselves in the midst of the Jacob story. There is no real "Isaac story." The stories about the early life of Isaac—his birth (Genesis 21) and the "Binding of Isaac" (Genesis 22) are integral parts of his father Abraham's story, as is the story of finding a wife for Isaac (Genesis 24). In all of these stories it is Abraham who makes the decisions.

There are two stories in which Isaac is the main character (Genesis 26). Both involve Abimelech, the king of Gerar, and both recall similar stories from the life of Abraham. Isaac is the only one of the three fathers about whom we are told that he farmed the land (the others were semi-nomadic shepherds). He is also the only one who never left the land promised to his progeny. His life stands as a symbol of the tie of the people to the land.

Bible scholars have pondered the relative passivity of Isaac. Some have said that his strong father Abraham overshadowed and intimidated him. Others have said that he never recovered from the trauma of the "Binding."

From the time Isaac's sons are conceived the emphasis moves from Isaac to his son Jacob. In Genesis 27 Isaac is already old and blind, and not in control of events happening around him. Although he will live for a long time—until Jacob returns from his sojourn in Haran—we shall not hear of him again until his death at the age of 140, when he is buried by his sons Jacob and Esau (Gen.35:29).

Jacob's life is a difficult one, full of hardships and adversities which influence him as he grows and matures. This struggle will eventually be symbolically reflected in the change of his name.

Jacob will become Israel: the one who has striven with God and men, and has prevailed.

If Abraham symbolizes the covenant with God, and Isaac symbolizes the tie to the land God has promised, it is through Jacob that the promise of becoming a great nation will be fulfilled. This destiny also is reflected in God's changing of Jacob's name: Jacob, born into the small family of Abraham and Isaac, becomes Israel, whose many children all remain within the covenant and form the beginnings of a nation.

Although the focus of the narrative will eventually move to Jacob's son Joseph (Genesis 37), Jacob remains a strong force in the story. Jacob's name will continue to be evoked throughout the remaining chapters of Genesis, and he will shape the lives of his progeny even after his death (Gen. 50:17).

LESSON 1A

Jacob and Esau
Gen. 25:19–34

❐ In Preparation for Teaching

Like Sarah before her, Rebekah was barren. Had it not been for God's intervention, she would have remained childless (in sharp contrast to the Keturah story, Gen. 25:1–4). Mothers of important men in the Bible are often described as initially barren (e.g., Rachel, Hannah, the mother of Samson). The children of these women are seen as special, almost like "miracle babies." Moses, too, was a miracle baby, since God saw to his survival.

Stories in Genesis are often etiological, that is, they offer explanations for why something is the way it is. Sometimes the stories explain some episode in the later history of Israel. The stories about Esau may be seen as stories of this kind.

By the time this story was written down, Esau's descendants were known as the people of Edom (אֱדוֹם), and they lived on Mount Seir (שֵׂעִיר). By way of explanation of these two later facts, we are told in 25:25 that from birth Esau was red (אָדֹם, like אֱדוֹם) and coverd with hair (שֵׂעָר, like שֵׂעִיר).

The Edomites were called "the people of the red city." They lived in Hasela Ha'adom, or Petra, a city carved into the red rocks of Mount Seir (in today's Jordan).

In the days of King David the Edomites were subjugated by the people of Israel, later on, they freed themselves and encroached on Israel's territory. The stories of strife and ill will between Jacob and Esau in Gen. 25:19–34 and in Genesis 27 may reflect some of this later history.

❐ Teaching Procedure

Have your students read section 25:19–34. What was special about Rebekah's pregnancy? First, the pregnancy came after 20 years of barrenness (25:26). Second, she was pregnant with twins, who were struggling prenatally in her womb.

How did she feel about her pregnancy? She was obviously upset, wondering, "Why do I exist?" She wished herself dead; she must have felt great discomfort! Furthermore, she must have felt mental anguish: if this is how her twins struggled prenatally, surely their futures would be fraught with strife and combat.

Rebekah inquired of the Lord and received an oracle from Him. We are not told by what means the message was received. (In later Israelite society, oracles would be received by means of the "*Urim* and *Thummim*" [twelve semi-precious stones symbolizing the twelve tribes set in the priest's "breastplate," which in some way would light up to answer 'yes' or 'no' questions directed to God]) or through prophets.)

Establish what Rebekah was told in the oracle:

a) Two sons would be born to her.
b) These two sons would become the fathers of two nations.
c) One nation would be mightier than the other.
d) The older would serve the younger.

The struggle that began in the womb continued during the birth process. Jacob was born holding Esau's heel. Though Esau was born first, Jacob had not given up the struggle! Did Isaac know about the oracle? Did Jacob and Esau know? Had Rebekah told them? Did her knowledge of the future influence her behavior toward her sons? The text may indicate that it did (29:28).

As in the story of Cain and Abel, here too the Bible is not interested in the childhood or youth of the boys. We are told only that Esau was red and hairy (introduce some of the background material, above), a man of the outdoors and a skilled hunter, while Jacob was a mild man who stayed in the camp. The beginning of the story is ominous. The two brothers were rivals, and the parents were split between them in their love. We are told that Rebekah loved Jacob. But we are not told why. Could it be because of the oracle? Isaac loved Esau because he provided him with game, which seems a rather shallow reason. Did he love Esau because he saw in him the aggressive man he wished he could have been? We do not always know why we love one person and not another.

Jacob is described as "mild," yet the following stories do not substantiate this fact. Do not at this point judge the brothers. Let the students develop their opinions of the characters as they read the stories.

LESSON 1B

The Birthright
Gen. 25:29–34

◻ **In Preparation for Teaching**

As in the Cain and Abel story, here too we are told of only one interaction between the brothers, one which will have a lasting effect on their lives. Jacob was cooking a stew when Esau came in, famished from the hunt. He asked Jacob to give him some of "that red stuff to gulp down" (another allusion to *Edom/adom;* see above, p. 211). Jacob demanded that Esau first sell him his birthright! Esau claimed that he was at the point of death, and therefore the birthright was of no use to him. So he sold Jacob his birthright—for bread and red lentil stew. Esau "ate, drank, rose, and went his way. Thus did Esau spurn the birthright." In these few short verses, the characters of the two brothers emerge. Neither of them earns our sympathies.

◻ **Teaching Procedure**

Discuss the brothers' actions:

Esau's request for food is worded in a rude, uncouth manner—animals gulp food down, not humans.

The birthright had obviously been on Jacob's mind, since his suggestion for a trade comes immediately upon Esau's request for food. The terms of the exchange were grossly unfair to Esau. Jacob was taking advantage of his brother.

Esau claimed to be at the point of death. If so, his claim that the birthright was of no use to him may have been true; this would put Jacob in an even worse light. On the other hand, Esau could be using an exaggerated expression, as we often do when we claim to be "dead tired" or "dying of thirst." In that case, his spurning of his birthright perhaps renders him unworthy of it.

You may want to discuss the two possibilities.

Esau "ate, drank, rose and went on his way." This is boorish behavior. He gave thanks neither to God, the source of all food, nor to his brother. His quick exit seems to indicate that he had been very hungry but not really close to death.

The remark that Esau "spurned the birthright" is provided by the narrator to emphasize the point of the story.

These are some of the character traits of Jacob and Isaac you may want to list:

Jacob	Esau
Patient	Boorish
Resourceful	Crude
Cunning	Concerned with the present
Concerned with the future	Concerned with immediate needs
Unloving	No ambition to achieve
Efficient	No sense of values
Self-assured	
Ambitious	
Goal-oriented	

LESSON 2

Isaac and the Land of Canaan
Genesis 26

◻ **In Preparation for Teaching**

In this chapter, various parallels to the stories about Abraham are evident. In 26:2–5 God repeats the promises he had made to Isaac's father Abraham. In 26:5 we are given some new information: the promise is renewed with Isaac because Abraham had kept God's commandments, laws, and teachings.

While the promises to Abraham and Isaac are essentially the same, the emphasis is new. God's promise to Abraham began with the promise of siring a great nation (Gen. 12:2). The promise to Isaac, on the other hand, begins with the land. The word *land* appears four times in God's promise to Isaac, five times in 26:1–5. Isaac's particular association with the land is emphasized by these facts: (1) Whereas Abraham had been an alien resident, Isaac's status was that of a native-born resident. (2) While Abraham was a semi-nomadic shepherd, Isaac had settled on the land as a farmer (26:12). Thus, Isaac symbolizes the part of the promise which attaches Abraham's descendants to the land of Canaan. (Later, Jacob will symbolize the part of the promise about "fathering a great nation.")

Your class will no doubt notice parallels between Gen. 26:6–11, Gen. 12:10–20, and Genesis 20. The text itself draws attention to this parallel in 26:1. We have discussed the fact that the wife-sister motif appears three times in the book of Genesis. We will not discuss it again at this point, except to mention that everything that happened to Abraham seems to have happened, in a lesser way, also to Isaac. Here the king finds out the woman is married before anything happens.

There is an interesting difference between this wife-sister story and the one in Genesis 12. In the earlier story Abraham went down to Egypt. Here, however, Isaac is commanded by God to remain in Canaan (26:2). (Your class may remember that Abraham, when seeking a wife for Isaac, had also made sure that his son Isaac would not leave the land.) Isaac's particular attachment to the land is emphasized by his dwelling there without interruption.

☐ Teaching Procedure

Have your class read Genesis 26, focusing especially on verses 12–32. These verses give us the following information: the Lord blessed Isaac (he reaped a hundred times more than he sowed). Some people were jealous of him because he had become very rich.

Your class may remember that Abraham, too, had an argument about wells with Abimelech. Ask your class to draw a comparison between Abraham and Isaac in their relationship with Abimelech. The teacher should provide one set of verses and let the class find the parallel. Since this is a difficult exercise, it should be done in class.

Abraham	**Isaac**
Gen. 20:15	*Gen. 26:16*
Abimelech says: "Here, my land is before you. Settle wherever you please."	Abimelech says: "Go away from us, for you have become far too big for us."
Gen. 21:22–26	*Gen. 19–22*
Then Abraham reproached Abimelech for the well of water which the servants of Abimelech had seized. . . . But Abimelech said: "I do not know who did this, you did not tell me, nor have I heard of it until today."	When Isaac's servants dug and found . . . a well of spring water, the herdsmen of Gerar quarreled with Isaac's herdsmen saying: "The water is ours. . . ." And when he dug another well they disputed over this one also. . . . He moved from there and dug yet another well.
Gen. 21:22	*Gen. 26:27*
"God is with you in everything . . . you do. Therefore swear to me by God . . . that you will not deal falsely with me . . . but as loyally as I have dealt with you."	"Why have you come to me, seeing that you have been hostile to me, and have driven me away from you?"
Gen. 21:30	*Gen. 26:28*
Abraham says: "You are to accept these seven ewes from	"We now see plainly that the Lord has been with you, and

Lesson 2: Isaac and the Land of Canaan 217

me as proof that I dug this well."	we thought . . . let us make a pact with you . . . that you will do us no harm, just as we have not molested you, but always dealt kindly with you, and sent you away in peace." (This is true only in Gen. 20:14, not in Genesis 26)
Gen. 21:31	*Gen. 26:31–34*
Hence the place was called . . . Beer-Sheba for there the two of them swore an oath.	They exchanged oaths. . . . Isaac's servants told him about the well. . . . He named it Shibah. The name is Beer-Sheba to this day.

The differences between the two lists should be discussed:

1) Both Abraham and Isaac are sojourners in Gerar and quarrel with the inhabitants over the rights for wells. Abraham was invited by Abimelech to stay in the land; Isaac was chased away.

2) Abraham reproached Abimelech for seizing his wells and Abimelech pleaded ignorance. Isaac, on the other hand, permitted Abimelech's herdsmen to chase him away. When Abimelech claimed that he had dealt kindly with Isaac, Isaac did not even mention the stolen wells.

3) Abraham forced seven ewes on Abimelech as proof of his ownership of the wells. In this story it is Abimelech who suggested a pact to Isaac.

4) Both Abraham and Isaac were recognized by Abimelech as the blessed of the Lord. However, the text indicates that Isaac had a special relationship with God because Isaac was the inheritor of the blessing given to Abraham (26:25), rather than because of his own merits.

5) In the Abraham story the name Beer Sheba, derived from the word שְׁבוּעָה ("oath"), is given to the city. Here, Isaac renewed the name his father had given the place.

In a way, Isaac seems a weak copy of his father. His life pattern follows that of Abraham ("like father, like son"—מַעֲשֵׂה אָבוֹת סִמָּן לְבָנִים).

LESSON 3

A Stolen Blessing
Gen. 26:34–27:45

❑ In Preparation for Teaching

Gen. 26:34–35 add another dimension to our understanding of the story which follows in Genesis 27. In the Abraham story we learned that Abraham made sure his son would not intermarry with the local women. Esau, however, married two Hittite women who, we are told, were a source of bitterness to his parents.

This note may serve to discredit Esau and disqualify him as the carrier of the Abrahamic blessing. Isaac loved Esau, and it was he whom Isaac intended to bless. Esau's marriages, however, made Isaac's choice doubtful. The Torah may provide this justification for Isaac to bless instead his son Jacob (knowingly or unknowingly). You may want to just read 26:34–35 now, and discuss these verses in depth when you read 27:46.

The story we are about to read deals with the deathbed blessing of Isaac. It is important that your students understand that in biblical times both blessings and curses were treated very seriously; both, it was believed, would come true. Deathbed blessings could not be changed or revoked (27:33).

In Genesis 25, Jacob had bought Esau's birthright. Did this entitle him to the blessing as well? Owning the right of the firstborn, Jacob was entitled to two-thirds (a double portion) of his father's estate. He would also replace his father after death as head of the household. But we do not know whether he was entitled to the blessing also. Esau accused Jacob (27:36) of cheating him out of *two things:* the birthright and the blessing. Still, what Esau said in anger need not necessarily be true! On the other hand, if the blessing was Jacob's by right, there must have been other ways for him to have acquired it.

In Genesis 25, we found Esau to be rough, boorish, and indifferent to his birthright. In this story, our hearts go out to him and his old father Isaac. Here Esau appears to be a sensitive man—one who cared deeply about the blessing, bursting out in uncontrollable and bitter sobbing at its loss (27:34). Whereas in

Lesson 3: A Stolen Blessing 219

Genesis 25 Esau sought immediate gratification, here he is able to postpone his revenge until sometime in the future, out of respect for his father (27:41).

In contrast, Jacob's only concern in Genesis 27 is the possibility of being "found out." He has no moral inhibitions or qualms about carrying out his mother's plan to deceive his father and betray his brother. This story will no doubt pose some moral problems for your students—as it did for Hosea (Hosea 12:4) and Jeremiah (Jeremiah 9:3).

Your students may notice that the two blessings, Jacob's and Esau's, do not differ greatly. Both sons are blessed with the fat of the land and the dew of heaven. The fact that Esau would at some point break his brother's yoke (27:40) may be etiological, referring to the later historical events concerning Israel and Edom.

Why did not Esau receive the Abrahamic blessing? In Gen. 28:3–4, Isaac gives the Abrahamic blessing, the covenant blessing, to Jacob. It is interesting to note that this blessing, which seemingly has nothing to do with that of the birthright, was set aside for Jacob from the start. At no point, even when Esau asked "Have you not reserved a blessing for me?" (27:36) did Isaac give him the blessing of the covenant. God had planned it that way before the birth of the boys: Jacob would be the one to carry the blessing of Abraham. Within this plan, however, Jacob was free to make his choices; and as we shall see, Jacob would have to pay for some of these. Although Jacob's destiny had been determined by God, the course of his life was not. Jacob's fate would be the result of his own making.

In our subsequent readings, we shall find that Jacob is punished for his deceptions. In the Laban story, your class will notice that Jacob is punished in kind. Jacob, who had taken advantage of his father's blindness, is given a bride under the cover of darkness; he too is unable to recognize "the wrong one." Retribution is also apparent in the Joseph story. His sons bring him Joseph's bloodstained coat and challenge him to "recognize" it. Like Isaac before him, Jacob draws the wrong conclusion!

Do not present all this information to your students now. It may be helpful to keep a list of students' questions for which answers may be found in future readings.

❒ Teaching Procedure

Have your class read Genesis 27. This story should probably be read aloud in class (by you or by a student who reads well). Establish the story line:

Isaac, fearing that death was imminent asked his son Esau to hunt for game and prepare a festive meal for him. After eating, he would bless Esau.

Rebekah, who had been listening at the doorway, overheard Isaac's command to Esau. While Esau was hunting, she told Jacob of her plan: Jacob was to fetch two young goats from the herd, and she would cook a tasty dish for Isaac. Then Jacob, pretending to be Esau, would bring the food to Isaac. Since Isaac's eyesight was failing, Isaac would not be able to recognize Jacob, and would give him the blessing intended for Esau.

Jacob was worried. What if his father touched him and noticed the smoothness of his skin? Would his father not be riled by the hoax and curse instead of bless him? Rebekah, however, told Jacob that should Isaac curse him, she would take the curse upon herself. He was not to be concerned. Jacob obeyed her without hesitation. Rebekah prepared the tasty dish; she covered Jacob's hands and neck with the hairy skins of the goats and gave Jacob Esau's clothes to wear.

Isaac, who was blind, doubted that Esau was standing before him. How could he have returned so fast from the hunt? Jacob attributed his speedy completion of the tasks to the God of Isaac. Still doubting, Isaac touched Jacob's hairy arms and declared: "The voice is the voice of Jacob, but the hands are the hands of Esau." Nevertheless Isaac decided to bless Jacob. Isaac ate and drank. As Jacob kissed his father (at Isaac's request), Isaac noted the smell of Esau's clothes. Now he was convinced. Isaac blessed Jacob. He gave him of the dew of heaven and the fat of the earth, grain and wine. He made him master over his brother, and declared that the sons of his mother would bow down to him.

It is interesting to note that all five senses failed Isaac. He is *blind* so he could not tell which son stood before him. He mistook the *feel* of goatskin for the feel of hairy hands. He mistook the *taste* of kid goats for the taste of game. He relied on the *smell* of clothes to identify their wearer. And he was unwilling to trust the accuracy of his sense of hearing.

No sooner had Jacob left the presence of his father than Esau came into his father's room with a tasty dish of game. He asked his father to sit up and eat so he could bless him. Isaac now realized his mistake! He was seized with violent trembling. Esau burst into wild sobbing. The blessing, however, had been given to Jacob; it could not be retracted.

Isaac, upon Esau's urgent request, blessed him too. To Esau he also gave the dew of heaven and the fat of the earth; but he would live by the sword and serve his brother until sometime in the

Lesson 3: A Stolen Blessing 221

future he would break his brother's yoke! Esau harbored a grudge against Jacob and declared that he would kill him when the mourning period for Isaac was over. Rebekah sent for Jacob and warned him to flee and seek refuge with her brother Laban in Haran.

You may want to divide the chapter into sections. Either ask your students to make the divisions (at home or in class), or present the class with a division schema (see below). It is also possible to use the divisions for your own teaching reference, without presenting the schema to your students. (This is recommended when time constraints require short cuts to be made.)

A suggested breakdown of Genesis 27:

1–4	Isaac's instructions to Esau
5–13	Rebekah's instructions to Jacob
14–17	Preparation of the festive meal
18–27	Isaac's doubts
28–29	The blessing of Jacob
30–38	Esau's return
39–40	The blessing of Esau
41–45	Rebekah's warning to Jacob (27:46 will be taught in connection with Genesis 28)

Isaac's instructions to Esau (27:1–4)

Have your class note the style in 27:1: Isaac called for *"his older son Esau."* We have noted before that at times the text repeats known and seemingly redundant information. These repetitions emphasize and highlight certain aspects of the story. Here Isaac's address to Esau indicates love and tenderness.

Did Isaac know that Jacob had bought the birthright? Would that have made a difference? Should Jacob have told him? We do not know. Encourage questions to be asked.

Rebekah's instruction to Jacob (27:5–13)

Ask your students to discover how Rebekah's address to Jacob is described in the text (27:6—*her* son Jacob; compared to 27:1—*his* son Esau). Point out to your class that the family relationships "your father," "your brother," "my son," are emphasized throughout the chapter. These expressions make us, as readers, more keenly aware of the tragedy within this small family. What did Jacob worry about? (27:12) What apparently *did not bother him at all*? What might he have said if asked why he did it? (His obedience to his mother was total. We do not hear anything about obedience to God or commitment to principles of moral behavior.)

The preparation of the festive meal (27:14–17)

Note how efficiently Rebekah went about her business. Nothing was left to chance! She had done all she could; the rest was up to Jacob.

Isaac's doubts (27:18–27)

What does 27:18 indicate about Isaac? Why might he have been suspicious? (Esau had returned too quickly; the voice was not that of Esau's.) Did Jacob's answer satisfy him? (27:21) What did Isaac wonder about? (27:22)

The next verses pose a problem. In 27:23 we read that Isaac felt the "hairy hands" of Jacob, "and so he blessed him." Yet in 27:24, we are told that Isaac continued to be suspicious and the blessing only took place in 27:28. There are two possible ways of dealing with the problem: Either 27:23 means "as he was *about* to bless him," or (2) that verse is an aside to the reader, telling us that Jacob would not be found out! As Isaac persists in testing Jacob's identity, the success of Jacob's deception is emphasized.

The remaining sections should be similarly treated, discussing the text line by line, using questions based on the preparatory material above (pp. 218–219) or on issues rasied by your students.

Supplementary activities related to the teaching of this lesson can be found in Appendix A, below, p. 322.

LESSON 4A

The People Involved
Gen. 26:34–27:45

☐ In Preparation for Teaching

You may want to discuss Isaac's character. What kind of a man is he? Remember all the stories about him—"The Binding" (Genesis 22); finding of a wife for him (Genesis 24), his relationship with Abimelech (Genesis 26) and the blessing of his sons (Genesis 27).

Some items your students may come up with include:

He trusts in God.
He trusts Abraham.
He is peace loving.
He is a passive man.
He is an ineffective person.
He is an inept man.

You may now want to discuss the character of Rebekah. What did we learn about her in Genesis 24, when we first met her? Your class will probably recall:

She is quick-thinking.
She takes initiative.
She is confident.
She does things on her own.
She is kind.
She is energetic.
She is resourceful.

Had Rebekah changed? She was still as confident and resourceful as before; yet she seemed unloving to her husband and older son. Could her knowledge of the oracle have made her do what she did? This is possible. In any case, your students will likely consider her shrewd and conniving.

Just a few words in Rebekah's defense: Consider the case of an energetic, enthusiastic woman like Rebekah, married to a rather passive and weak man like Isaac. It is possible that she had a better insight into the character of her two sons. Rebekah lived in a society in which men made all the decisions. It is possible that the only way a woman could exercise *any* power in such a society was through guile.

The text leaves much to the imagination. This is one possible interpretation.

You may want your students to fill in the following chart.

Characteristic	Name of Character	Evidence from Text (chapter, verse)
1. Shows self-assurance		
2. Restrained in reaction		
3. Respectful of father		
4. Taken advantage of		
5. Disrespectful of parents		
6. Disrespectful of father		
7. Bold		
8. Lies		
9. Exaggerates		
10. Takes risks		
11. Dependent		
12. Determined		
13. Disregards the feelings of others		
14. Readily expresses strong feelings		

Discuss in class.

You may want to have your students do a dramatic reading of the chapter. Let different students "try out" for each role. Or let your students role-play the different characters in various situations.

Lesson 4A: The People Involved

Divide your class into four groups: (1) Isaac, (2) Rebekah (3) Esau (4) Jacob. Have each group decide how their character would talk, think, and act. (Give them five minutes to discuss this within the groups.) Then have them choose a student from one group to have a conversation with one from another group. There are any number of possibilities. Rebekah may talk with Isaac about the children or about the future. Or she may talk with Esau, or with Jacob. Try any combination of characters! Give several students a chance.

LESSON 4B

Jacob's Departure
Gen. 27:46–28:9

☐ In Preparation for Teaching

These verses, which tell another story of the blessing of Jacob by Isaac, are apparently from another biblical source. This story seems to be unaware of the preceding story of the deception. We do not have to harmonize the two stories; we have seen that the patriarchal stories do not form a single, continuous record. If we desire, however, to understand the stories together as they stand, we must assume that Isaac had forgiven Jacob for stealing Esau's blessing, since there is no hint of anger or bitterness on Isaac's part.

The blessing Isaac now offers is the Abrahamic blessing (alluded to in Rebekah's oracle), which establishes Jacob as heir to Abraham's covenant with God.

At the end of Genesis 27 Jacob had to flee for his life. In this section Isaac appears oblivious of this fact, as well as to the existence of any family strife, other than that generated by Esau's wives. In 27:46, Rebekah presents Isaac with another reason for Jacob's departure: Jacob had to find a wife. Like Abraham before him, Isaac wanted his son to marry within the clan (28:2). Esau, we are told, was already married to two Canaanite (Hittite) women. Here the text (as in Gen. 26:34–35) may be indicating the ultimate unsuitability of Esau to carry the blessing.

We might now have expected Esau to be abusive and angry with his mother, who had cheated him out of his inheritance, and with his father, who let himself be duped. Yet Esau seems to want to please and win the approval of his parents. He takes another wife from the clan of Ishmael.

☐ Teaching Procedure

Have your class read 27:46–28:9. What is the difference between the two blessings Isaac gave his son Jacob (27:28–29 and 28:3–4)? What might have been Isaac's expectations regarding Jacob's return? (Perhaps that he would quickly return, as his father's servant had many years before.) What were the expectations of Rebekah, who had instigated both the theft of the blessing and the consequent flight? She may have been expecting Isaac's imminent death, since he had already given his deathbed blessings. She may have been counting on Esau's anger subsiding, and Jacob's early return.

Little did Rebekah, who tended to take things into her own hands, realize how little people can influence the future! When Jacob would return, more than twenty years hence, Isaac—old, blind, and senile—would still be lingering on. She herself would never see her beloved son again.

LESSON 5

Jacob's Vow
Gen. 28:10–22

☐ In Preparation for Teaching

This is the story of "Jacob's dream." Jacob, on the way to Haran, stops to rest for the night in the open. There he has a dream of angels (God's messengers) ascending and descending a stairway reaching the sky. Upon awakening, he realizes that the place where he had stopped was a holy place. He offers a prayer for protection and vows to repay the favor if his safe return is granted.

Regarding the stairway in Jacob's dream, Bible scholars have noted that the imagery calls to mind the Babylonian temple-towers that we discussed in connection with the story of the Tower of Babel (see Gen. 11:19, and above, pp. 126–127). The ladder is described as "a stairway that was set on the ground and its top reached to the sky." Moreover, Jacob exclaims: "This is none other than the abode of God, and that is the gateway to heaven" (28:17). Contrary to the Babylonians who believed that the tower served as a meeting place for God and humans (with humans ascending and God descending the stairway), here only angels went up and down the stairway. The divine and human do not meet. The angels do not represent a theophanic experience.

Bethel is regarded as a sacred place—a place imbued with the Lord's presence. "Surely the Lord is present in this place—and I did not know it!" Jacob exclaimed upon awakening (28:16). In 28:19, we are told, "he named the site Bethel."

You may want to tell your students that different religious groups often chose a site for their sanctuaries which was already considered a sacred place to an earlier religious group. Archaeologists in Israel often find a Christian church built on the ruins of a Jewish place of worship, and a Moslem mosque built on the ruins of the church. The builders of the edifice often used the stones from the previous building.

Different people give different reasons for worshipping at the same place. Some places lend themselves geographically or topographically for worship. Others are traditionally considered

Lesson 5: Jacob's Vow 229

holy. Jerusalem is sacred to Jews, Christians and Moslems, for different reasons. The mosque of Omar in the old city of Jerusalem is built on the site of the two Israelite Temples. Embedded in the floor of the mosque is a huge rock. According to Jewish tradition, this is the rock upon which Abraham bound his son Isaac (Genesis 22). According to the Moslems, the Prophet Muhammad ascended to heaven from this same rock. We call these stories etiological because they developed as explanations of why people think things are the way they are.

Genesis 28 provides an explanation, from the Israelite perspective, for using the already existing shrine in Bethel. According to this story, the place was named Luz before Jacob's arrival, and renamed Bethel as a result of Jacob's experience. Yet the name Bethel appeared in the Abraham story (12:8), designating a place of worship. Bible scholars believe that Bethel was an old Canaanite sanctuary, dedicated to the Semitic god El. This shrine was later adapted and converted into an Israelite sanctuary.

Teach as much of the above as you deem necessary. In class, focus on Jacob's vow (נֶדֶר) in 28:20–22. Ancient people often would not simply present a request in prayer; instead, they would offer a vow, presenting the request and promising something in return. Jacob vowed to show his gratitude to God in various ways if his request would be granted.

◻ Teaching Procedure

Have your class read 28:10–22. What is Jacob's frame of mind? He is worried. We have discussed earlier the lot of the stranger, who in ancient times would travel alone and unprotected, and was dependent on the mercy of strangers.

Jacob could not return home. But there were alternatives to going all the way to Haran. He could, for instance, have stayed in the vicinity and married a local girl. What would we think of Jacob's character had he made such a choice? Your students might say that he would be showing little faith in God, that he did not care about the Abrahamic blessing or about the wishes of his parents.

In spite of all his fears, Jacob continued on his way to Haran. He had self-control, he overcame his fears, and he had faith in God and in the blessing. In his dream, Jacob learned something about his destiny. Although at this point in his life he is a fugitive, he also carries the Abrahamic blessing, and therefore is part of God's grand scheme.

Your students may be critical of Jacob's vow; it sounds like he's making a deal. It would be hard to imagine Abraham pronouncing Jacob's vow: "If God remains with me, protects me, gives me bread and clothing, and if I return to my father's house, then the Lord shall be my God" (28:20–22). Yet Jacob's act was a very human one.

Have you ever taken a vow? Everyone of us has, although we may not have called it one. Tell the class of a vow you yourself may have made, e.g., "If my mother recovers, I shall never disobey or lie again," or "If the teacher does not find out that I did not do my homework, from now on I will always do my homework." Your students may be willing to tell you about an "oath" or "vow" they themselves had taken.

In Hebrew a vow is called *neder* (נֶדֶר). A vow is usually made under stress, when we need help. In times of stress, we may be willing to promise almost *anything*. Often, when the pressure is off, we tend not to keep our word. The Jewish tradition recognizes the very human tendency to make injudicious vows in times of stress. The Kol Nidre prayer, recited on the eve of Yom Kippur, asks God for release from promises made under duress. According to Ashkenazic tradition, we ask for the annulment of vows we might make in the *coming year,* under conditions we cannot now foresee.

LESSON 6A

Jacob Meets His Master
Gen. 29:1–14a

☐ **Teaching Procedure**

Read and discuss 29:1–14a. Jacob, after his stopover at Bethel resumed his journey. One afternoon he arrived at a well on the outskirts of a village and inquired about his whereabouts. He discovered not only that he had arrived in Haran, but that his cousin Rachel was approaching the well with her flocks. Surely God was with Jacob!

Jacob wondered why three flocks of sheep were lying near the well waiting to be watered instead of drinking and returning to pasture. He was told that the heavy stone covering the mouth of the well (to protect the water from dirt and evaporation and from being used by strangers) could only be moved by all the shepherds together; so everybody had to wait until all the flocks had been rounded up.

When Jacob saw Rachel, in an amazing show of strength he singlehandedly rolled the stone off the mouth of the well and watered her flock. Jacob kissed Rachel, broke into tears, and told her who he was. She ran to tell her father Laban, who in turn ran out to greet Jacob and took him into his house. Jacob told Laban all that had happened, and Laban said, "You are truly my bone and flesh."

In this love story—"boy meets girl at the well"—we learn a few more things about Jacob. The so-called mild man, who "stayed in camp," was nevertheless capable of mustering enormous physical strength when he wanted to impress a young woman. Today we know that when a person is under stress or highly motivated, a chemical called adrenalin is secreted into the bloodstream. This chemical enables a person to perform feats which he or she could not normally perform. For instance, a man might be able to lift a car off a child's body, whereas under normal conditions he would not be able to budge it at all. Perhaps Jacob's remarkable act can be explained in this way.

From this story we also learn that Jacob was capable of caring deeply and of bursting into tears. Obviously he was more sensitive and sentimental than we might have guessed! His behavior may lead us to believe that leaving home and traveling alone had taken their toll on him.

"Jacob told Laban all that had happened" (29:13). What was it that Laban would want to know? Perhaps Laban asked how Rebekah had fared since leaving home, or about Jacob's and Esau's youth, or about Isaac, his health and his wealth. What might Laban be wondering about? Possibly why Jacob had arrived empty-handed, without camels and servants, or why he had come all the way to Haran. Did Jacob really tell Laban *all* that had happened, including the deception of Isaac and the theft of the blessing? We can only guess. In any case, Laban seemed to be happy to have found his relative, and this section ends on a happy note.

LESSON 6B

Jacob's Marriages
Gen. 29:14b–30

☐ **Teaching Procedure**

Have your class read this section and tell you the events of the story.

Jacob had now lived for one month at Laban's home (14b). A good house guest, he had started work upon arrival. Laban suggested that Jacob be fairly compensated for his work. Jacob offered seven years of work in exchange for Rachel. The seven years of work would serve as a bride price for Rachel.

We have talked about the bride price in connection with Lot and his daughters. A man had to pay the father of the bride for his daughter. This money was called *mohar* (מֹהַר). A man paid according to the girl's family status, her looks and her other qualities; some brides were more costly than others. Part of the *mohar*, as we shall see later in the text, was given by the father to the bride herself to be used at her discretion.

Abraham's servant had paid handsomely for Rebekah as a wife for Isaac. Jacob, however, had no property. Instead he offered seven years of labor. Was this a high or low bride price? We do not know. However, since Jacob loved Rachel, he probably valued her highly. It is interesting to note that Laban, like Isaac, regarded it as advantageous to have his daughters marry within the family.

The seven years of working and waiting for Rachel seemed like a short time to Jacob. Some of your students may wonder why, since "waiting time" usually seems to pass very slowly. Others may realize that when one is motivated or goal-oriented, time seems to pass quickly! Maybe in retrospect, once it was over, it seemed to have been a short time.

When the seven years had passed, Jacob asked that his bride be given to him in marriage. The wedding feast took place. In the evening, when it was dark, Laban brought the bride to Jacob's tent. Only in the light of the morning did Jacob see that he had married Leah!

The text leaves much to the imagination. We may try to fill in what might have happened. Were the women kept separate from the men during the feast, as Arab women are nowadays? Had Leah participated in the deception? This is likely since she could have warned Jacob, had she wanted to. Was Rachel part of the deception? We do not know. There are a number of possibilities. Laban could have locked her up. He could have threatened her. On the other hand, Rachel may have wanted to help her sister who was unable to find a husband for herself. The rabbis preferred the second version since love between the two sisters would indicate love and peace between their progeny, the tribes of Israel. The continuation of the story, however, may point to the first version. Leave this question open, and come back to it at the end of Genesis 30.

When confronted by Jacob, Laban explained that according to the custom of the land the older daughter had to be given in marriage before her younger sister. This may have been true; nevertheless, it was a lame excuse. If indeed this was the custom, Laban could have informed Jacob of it when Jacob first asked for Rachel's hand. Laban had ample time to find a husband for his older daughter Leah.

Laban was willing to let Jacob have Rachel also, after the seven days of festivity for Leah were over. But Jacob would have to work another seven years for her. Jacob agreed. Why? There may be a number of reasons. He loved Rachel and did not want to lose her. He could not yet return home because of Esau. He had a wife but no property; therefore, he could not leave.

Also, Jacob may have accepted his fate as divine retribution: he too had taken advantage of someone who could not see. He had posed as his older brother, just as Leah pretended to be her younger sister. Jacob the conniver had met his master in Laban. You may want to draw attention to these parallels in the Hebrew text:

לָמָּה **רִמִּיתָנִי**	בָּא אָחִיךָ **בְּמִרְמָה**
What is this you have done to me? (29:25)	Your brother came with guile. (27:35)
לֹא יֵעָשֶׂה כֵן בִּמְקוֹמֵנוּ לָתֵת הַצְּעִירָה לִפְנֵי **הַבְּכִירָה**	אֶת־**בְּכֹרָתִי** לָקָח וְהִנֵּה עַתָּה לָקַח בִּרְכָתִי
It is not the practice in our place to marry off the younger before the older. (29:26)	First he took away my birthright and now he has taken away my blessing. (27:36)

Lesson 6B: Jacob's Marriages

What do we learn about Jacob's character from the way he reacted to Laban's trickery? Some suggested answers:

He has a great capacity for love.
He was able to control his temper.
He was able to bide his time and plan for the future.
He accepted reality.

Your students may notice additional parallels to earlier Jacob stories. What character traits do his mother Rebekah and her brother Laban have in common? Further, while growing up Jacob suffered from sibling rivalry, exacerbated by favoritism shown by the parents for one son or the other. Now he has married two sisters—one more beautiful and beloved than the other. No doubt there will be bitter resentment and rivalry between the sisters in the future. Why would Jacob allow himself to get into such a situation? One answer is that Jacob was in love. Logic and reason do not reign in the face of strong emotions. Also, two wives fit in well with God's plan, in that many children would be born!

LESSON 7

The Sisters
Gen. 29:31–30:24

☐ In Preparation for Teaching

Abraham symbolizes the covenant with God; Isaac represents the link with the land of Israel. Through Jacob would be fulfilled God's promise of many offspring, for Jacob's children, by his two wives and two concubines, would become the twelve tribes of Israel. The promise was divine, but it would be fulfilled by human means. Jacob's many sons were born into a tragic, strife-torn family. This strife was not the doing of God; it resulted from the actions of human beings.

Jacob loved Rachel dearly. Generally, love is an ennobling quality. It makes one put another person's needs and wants before one's own. This is true in the love of a man and a woman, or that of a parent and his or her child. Can one ever love *too much*? Yes, if a person gives *all* of his or her love to one person exclusively. In biblical times, when men had many wives, a man might love one wife to the exclusion of all others. A parent might love one child to the exclusion of all the other children. How did Jacob's love for Rachel affect Leah? The answer can be seen in the names Leah gave her children.

☐ Teaching Procedure

Have your students read and discuss 29:31–30:24. Add as much of the following information as you deem helpful.

"The Lord saw that Leah was unloved and opened her womb, but Rachel was barren" (29:31). We have already discussed that a man's reputation was enhanced by having many sons. Sons contributed to the economic wealth of the families and provided for their parents in old age. The wife who had many sons was therefore loved and respected by her husband. In this story God is the great equalizer. Since Leah was unloved, God gave her sons to compensate her. Did she win Jacob's affection? The names Leah gave her sons indicate that she did not. Four sons were born to Leah, but still she could not gain her husband's love.

How tragic! Leah had children, but was unloved by her husband. Rachel had her husband's love but no children.

Rachel declared that if Jacob did not give her a child, she would die. (Ironically, she would later die in childbirth.) Her reason for this desperate wish was clearly jealousy of her sister. Jacob attributed her barrenness to God. In the view of the Bible, men and women have children with God's help; when they do not have children, this too is considered God's doing. Rachel gave her maid Bilhah to Jacob as a concubine, just as Sarah had given Hagar to Abraham. The names Rachel chose for Bilhah's children indicate the bitter struggle between the sisters.

Was Jacob aware of the discord in his home? Could he have eased the tension? No doubt! Was he concerned about his wives' bickering? We are not told.

Then Leah gave her maid Zilpah to Jacob as a concubine, and through her Jacob had two more sons.

Gen. 30:14–21 contain the story of the mandrakes. A mandrake is a yellow small tomato-like fruit. It grows close to the ground and has an intoxicating smell. People in ancient times believed that the mandrake had medicinal powers and could make a barren woman fertile. Reuben, Leah's oldest son, found such a plant and gave it to his mother. Rachel asked Leah for it, but Leah begrudged Rachel the mandrakes and accused her of stealing her husband. Rachel traded Leah a night with Jacob for the mandrakes; ironically, it was Leah, not Rachel, who conceived. Leah bore a son, and then another son and a daughter. Rachel, in spite of the mandrakes, did not conceive. The Bible does not seem to indicate faith in the magic potion—only in the power of God!

At last, God "opened Rachel's womb" (30:22–24). She finally conceived and bore a son. The name she gave her son, "Joseph," indicates that the struggle between the sisters is not over.

LESSON 8A

Jacob Asks Leave of Laban
Gen. 30:25–31

◻ **In Preparation for Teaching**

Jacob now confronted Laban with a request: "Give me my wives and my children, for whom I have served you, that I may go" (31:26).

Jacob had served Laban for fourteen years. He had worked hard and faithfully and Laban had profited from his labor. In these fourteen years, Jacob had acquired two wives and twelve children. Why did Jacob want to leave now?

Although Jacob was Laban's son-in-law, he had lived and worked as an "indentured servant" in Laban's household. He had sold his time and labor to Laban for fourteen years; in this way, he paid off his debt to Laban for the two wives he had given him. He had wives and children, but he still had no property. It was time for him to build a household of his own.

Jacob had another reason for wanting to leave. Jacob carried the blessing of Abraham. For the blessing to be fulfilled, Jacob would have to become independent of Laban. His children would have to be under his authority, not Laban's. He would have to return to the land that God promised to him and his descendents as an everlasting possession.

Jacob asked for permission to leave (30:25) and for the right to take his wives and children with him (30:26). Why was it necessary to make this request? You may want to draw your students' attention to a later Israelite law that clarifies what the accepted practice was:

> When you acquire a Hebrew slave he shall serve six years. In the seventh he shall go free, without payment. If he came single, he shall leave single. If he had a wife, his wife shall leave with him. If his master gave him a wife and she has borne him children, the wife and her children shall belong to the master and he shall leave alone. (Exodus 21:2–4)

In a sense, Jacob was in the position of a slave. As we shall see later, Laban did indeed claim that Jacob's children were his (31:43).

Laban refused Jacob's request. He knew only too well that he had been blessed because of Jacob. What alternative did Laban propose? He offers now to pay Jacob (30:31). Why did Jacob agree to stay on? Some suggested answers: Jacob may have been aware that without any property, he could not gain real independence. Now that Laban was willing to pay him, he would have the opportunity to acquire property. Furthermore, Jacob may have still been afraid of his brother Esau. Jacob may not actually have been ready to leave at this point, but asked permission to leave in order to force the question of wages.

LESSON 8B

The Wages
Gen. 30:32–43

The deal between Jacob and Laban was quite complicated. You may want to present a concise explanation of it to your class.

It seems that most goats in the area were black and brown; most of the sheep were white. However, a small number of goats were streaked or spotted (with some white mixed in), while some of the sheep would be brown or dark. These goats and sheep would be considered "odd-colored."

Although ancient man did not have the biological or genetic knowledge we have today, they did know that solid black or solid white animals would tend to have solid-colored offspring, and only occasionally odd-colored ones. Odd-colored animals, on the other hand, would have mainly odd-colored offspring.

The text here is not quite clear, but it seems that Jacob asked for the relatively few newborn odd-colored animals as his wages. Laban agreed, whereupon he removed all the odd-colored animals from the flocks under Jacob's care. This action guaranteed that the chances of the remaining animals bearing odd-colored offspring (that would from now on go to Jacob) were minimal. Jacob, however, retaliated. His response was based on an ancient belief that one could influence the eventual characteristics of an animal by altering the environment at the time of its conception. People did not know that certain traits, such as color, are determined genetically.

In this vein, Jacob resorted to a trick. He took poplar shoots and peeled away parts of the dark bark, so that white stripes (or speckles) appeared beneath the bark. He placed these striped (speckled) shoots near the troughs from which the goats drank and where they mated. Seeing the striped (speckled) shoots, the goats would give birth to striped (odd-colored) kids. Similarly, Jacob turned the white sheep to face the black goats as they mated, and they bore black (odd-colored) lambs. Jacob did not use this ruse with the feeble or weak animals; therefore, their offspring went to Laban.

This story does not accord with our understanding of genetics and reproduction. However, our purpose in reading this story (and all biblical stories!) is not to evaluate the scientific accuracy of the story. Instead, we read this story to gain its message, namely, that in spite of Laban's cunning, Jacob outwitted him and prevailed. Our sympathies are with Jacob as he prospers.

LESSON 9

Jacob's Escape
Genesis 31

☐ In Preparation for Teaching

Genesis 31 presents a different version of Jacob's wages. We have read two versions of other stories—two creation stories, two flood stories, and two stories about Sarah and Hagar. Three stories told of a patriarch passing his wife as his sister. As we have noted earlier, each version emphasizes different ideas or aspects of the story. In Genesis 30, Jacob had decided to leave; Laban persuaded him to stay by offering him wages. Laban tried to cheat him, but Jacob refused to be cheated and rescued his wages. What transpired in that chapter is solely between Laban and Jacob; God did not intervene.

Genesis 31 tells another story of Jacob's seeking to leave Laban's household. (It is not a completely independent story; it has been edited to follow Genesis 30.) In Genesis 30, Jacob had become rich. Genesis 31 starts out on a note of envy. Both Laban and his sons (of whom we have not heard before, and who may actually have been distant heirs, kin or members of the household) resented Jacob. Forgetting that all their wealth came through Jacob, they begrudged Jacob his property. Jacob was aware of their resentment. God intervened, commanding Jacob to return to his homeland, where his destiny would be fulfilled. Jacob had his wives meet him in the field, where they could speak unobserved. He reminded them of the things that had happened to him in Laban's house, claiming that Laban had changed his wages time and again. Jacob attributed to God the fact that the flocks produced young of the type he could claim (speckled goats or black odd-colored sheep); Jacob claimed that God sent him a dream in which speckled he-goats mated with the flock. This dream made him choose the speckled kids as his wages.

If Genesis 30 emphasizes Jacob's strong will and cunning, Genesis 31 dwells on the effects of God's intervention in Jacob's life and God's protection of him. Both versions have their place: God supports and helps; yet within God's greater plan, man has to make his own decisions.

Lesson 9: Jacob's Escape

Would Rachel and Leah declare themselves willing to join their husband? What would have happened if they refused? Surely the family would have broken up. The women, however, resented their father. He had cheated them out of their share of their bride-price, using the money for himself. In spite of the tension and hatred within his household, Jacob had managed to hold his family together.

What were *teraphim* (31:30), and why would Rachel steal them? *Teraphim*, Bible scholars tell us, were small idols. Their purpose was to protect the household, and as such they were tolerated in Israelite homes. *Teraphim* also fulfilled another purpose in some parts of Mesopotamia. Their owner had a claim on a portion of the property belonging to the head of the household. Rachel might have tried to insure Jacob's claim on Laban's property by taking the *teraphim*. But we do not know whether the biblical author was familiar with this legal function of *teraphim*. (Michal daughter of Saul and wife of David also had *teraphim* in the house (1 Sam 19:13). Maybe she too had to insure her inheritance since there was tension between her father and her husband.)

☐ Teaching Procedure

This is a simple narrative. Have your class read Genesis 31 and elicit from them the information in an easy-going question-answer manner. Jacob felt it was time to separate from Laban, to see to his own future and that of his family. He took advantage of Laban's absence during a sheep-shearing that lasted several days. "Jacob put his children and wives on camels and he drove off all his livestock . . . to go to the land of Canaan."

Laban was informed. He gathered his kinsmen and pursued Jacob. Laban, with his superior numbers, could have physically forced Jacob to return with him to Haran, but God had appeared to Laban in a dream and intervened on Jacob's behalf. (Here, as in Genesis 20 with Abimelech, God communicates with people through dreams.)

When Laban overtook Jacob he bitterly complained about Jacob's sudden departure, claiming that had he known, he would have sent Jacob on his way in style, with festive music. Now it was too late for that! Why, however, had Jacob stolen his gods (*teraphim*)?

Jacob insisted on his innocence: he declared that anyone found in possession of the idols would be put to death. Why did Jacob so glibly condemn the thief to death? Jacob could not know that

Rachel had taken her father's *teraphim*. Laban went after the *teraphim* with a vengeance. In what way does the Torah belittle the *teraphim*? Rachel hid them in her camel cushion and sat on them. Laban did not find them. Was it immoral for Rachel to steal the *teraphim*? (Explain possible reasons.)

Jacob, now incensed, took up old grievances with Laban. For twenty years he had served him loyally. He had endured hardships; often scorching heat ravaged him by day and frost by night. Moreover, when an animal was killed by a wild beast he had been forced by Laban to make good the loss. That this was against the common practice is indicated by a later Israelite law:

> If [the animal] was torn by beast, [the shepherd] shall bring it as evidence. He need not replace what has been torn by beast. (Exodus 22:12)

Any Israelite who was familiar with this law would have been outraged that Laban made Jacob pay for the animal.

Not only had Jacob patiently endured all this, but Laban had repeatedly changed his wages. Had it not been for the God of Abraham and Isaac, surely Laban would have sent him away empty-handed!

Laban, ignoring Jacob's arguments and accusations, implied that all Jacob's property was rightfully Laban's. The daughters were his, Laban claimed, and so were their children. Jacob, he implied, was nothing but a runaway slave! However, Laban realized that Jacob was under God's protection, and there was nothing he could do.

Jacob and Laban made a pact, witnessed by the God of Abraham and the god of Nahor. This pact had two aspects: a personal aspect—Jacob was not to mistreat his wives or take other wives into his household (note Laban's sudden concern for his daughters), and a political aspect—neither would cross the other's boundaries with hostile intent. Then Jacob and Laban separated. The tie that bound the family of Abraham, Isaac, and Jacob to their Aramean roots was thus severed.

Gen. 32:2–3 refer to a puzzling meeting with God's angels. Whatever its significance, at the least the incident gives closure to the Laban story, in that Jacob also encountered angels when he first left Canaan.

LESSON 10

Preparing to Meet Esau
Gen. 32:4–22

☐ **In Preparation for Teaching**

Jacob left Haran. He had settled his affairs with Laban and was about to enter Canaan, where a new danger loomed—Esau, the wronged brother. In 32:4–22, Jacob agonized over what sort of reception awaited him. Was Esau still angry, intent on revenge? Or had he calmed down after all these years? Had Esau forgiven and forgotten?

Jacob sent a messenger to inform Esau of his coming. This was not the only course of action open to Jacob. He could have sneaked into Canaan and hoped for the best; perhaps Esau would not learn about his return. Why, then, did Jacob send these messengers? He may have been sending out a "feeler," to discover Esau's mood. By taking the initiative, Jacob would be better prepared for a hostile encounter. Perhaps he just wanted to get it over with, rather than live in constant fear that Esau would find out. Jacob took the bull by the horns, leaving nothing to chance.

Why did Jacob instruct his messengers to tell Esau about the wealth he acquired in Haran? Your students may recall that Jacob had acquired Esau's birthright, which meant that Jacob was entitled to a double portion of Isaac's inheritance. Could he have been reassuring his brother of the fact that he had no need of their father's wealth? Remind your class that according to the blessing (Gen. 27:27–30), Jacob was to be master over his brothers; his mother's sons were to bow down to him. How had Jacob instructed the messengers to address Esau? How were they to refer to Jacob? What, in effect, were the messengers trying to tell Esau by this choice of words? That Jacob laid no claim to Isaac's possessions. Jacob treated Esau the way a servant treats his master.

The messengers brought back the information that Esau was coming to meet Jacob, with four hundred men. Jacob was alarmed: Was Esau approaching with an army, determined to kill him? Or was he approaching with an impressive welcoming committee? Perhaps Esau wanted to show Jacob how well he had done over the years.

Jacob considered the first possibility to be more likely: "Jacob was greatly frightened" (32:8). His first response was to divide the camp into two parts, so as not to have "all his eggs in one basket." This was an act of desperation; at the same time, it was a realistic, level-headed calculation. Jacob had to act.

Jacob's next response to the threat was to pray to God (32:10–14). How did Jacob address God? Let your students discover that he addressed God as "the God of Abraham and Isaac." Why? Perhaps he wanted to establish the relationship: He was *Jacob*, the legal heir of the blessing God had given his father and his grandfather. Relate this to the fact that when Jews pray today, we often evoke the name of "the God of Abraham, Isaac and Jacob." We do so for the same reason that Jacob called upon the God of his fathers. We ask that *our* prayer be heard on account of *their* merit. This is called זְכוּת אָבוֹת ("merit of the ancestors"). When we ask for זְכוּת אָבוֹת, we acknowledging the fact that we are not perfect, and we may not be deserving of God's intervention. In all humility, we ask God to take care of us on account of the merit of our ancestors. We are asking for mercy, without which life would be unbearable.

In 32:10 Jacob claimed that he had obeyed God's command by returning to the land of his kindred; therefore God was responsible for him. The next verse is an expression of thanks and gratitude. Jacob's specific request in this prayer is for deliverance from Esau: if he were to perish how could God's promise to Abraham, Isaac and Jacob be fulfilled?

If this prayer was well-conceived, so were Jacob's subsequent actions. Jacob selected a very generous gift of livestock for Esau, and sent the animals off to Esau, drove by drove. He instructed those in charge of each drove to say that they were sent by "your servant Jacob to my lord Esau, and Jacob himself is right behind us." What would Esau expect after each drove? That Jacob would follow. What happened instead? More gifts arrived. The effect, would be overwhelming! Ten different gifts would arrive, each associated with Jacob!

What image would Esau have of Jacob, before they even met? He would understand that Jacob had become both rich and generous, and that he was someone to be respected.

(Supplementary activities related to the teaching of this lesson can be found in Appendix A, below, p. 321.)

LESSON 11

The Struggle
Gen. 32:23–33

◻ In Preparation for Teaching

In this story Jacob struggles for his life with a strange, unidentified assailant. Who was the mysterious stranger? The text refers to him as "a man" (32:25); yet the man refers to himself as a "divine being" (אֱלֹהִים; 32:29), and Jacob infers this as well (32:31). It seems that ancient Israelite folklore, like that of other ancient peoples, included tales about "divine beings"—spirits and demons, as well as angels and messengers of God.

This story explains several things etiologically: (1) the origin of the name Israel; (2) the place-name Peniel; (3) the Israelite custom of not eating the thigh tendon (גִּיד הַנָּשֶׁה) of animals.

◻ Teaching Procedure

Jacob left nothing to chance. He made several trips across the Jabbok stream, taking his wives and children across. The text does not allow us to be certain whether the struggle took place before or after the crossing of the river. In one place it says he crossed his family. In the other, that he himself crossed.

This is a strange story! Discuss some of the following aspects of the story with your students. What do we know about this divine being and its nature? (1) The assailant refused to reveal his name (32:30). We have already discussed the power of a name. Knowing the name of his adversary would have given Jacob power over him; withholding his name enabled him to stay in control. (2) He seemed to dread the dawn. This is characteristic of certain divine beings in ancient stories. It was the assailant's dread of the dawn that seems to have alerted Jacob to the fact that he was wrestling not with a human but with a divine being. (3) When the assailant realized that he could not subdue Jacob, in a last desperate effort, he wrenched Jacob's hip at the socket. We know that this was very painful to Jacob: he limped the next morning as he left Peniel (32:32). The text explicitly states here that this nocturnal encounter is the etiology of the law of *kashrut* (Jewish dietary laws) forbidding the eating of the thigh tendon (גִּיד הַנָּשֶׁה).

But wrenching Jacob's thigh did not free the man; what did he do next? He begged for his freedom. Jacob bargained for a blessing in return. What did he actually get? He got a new name, Israel. What does the name "Israel" mean, according to the stranger? "You have striven with beings divine and human, and have prevailed" (32:29). This was the essence of Jacob, to strive and to prevail. We have talked before about names. A new name indicates a new beginning, a new destiny. In what ways had Jacob changed? How was he different now?

A person is probably born with certain abilities and traits. We had described Jacob in Isaac's tent as intelligent, resourceful, patient, and able to plan for the future. We also noted some moral deficiencies: he seemed to be unloving, and lacking in sensitivity; he obeyed his mother without considering his father's and brother's feelings.

What kind of a man had Jacob become over the course of his life? Your class will have no difficulty in identifying some of the same abilities and character traits which Jacob displayed in Canaan. Jacob was intelligent and patient. He had been willing to work fourteen years for his wives, and had put up with Laban's chicanery. He had developed the ability to submerge his ego and control his temper. He was resourceful and cunning, but now in the defense of his own rights rather than in the theft from others! It was still in his nature to plan for the future; he thought of his own future and that of his family when he planned his escape from Laban and when he prepared for the encounter with Esau.

Jacob had the ability to feel, to love, to cry. He worked loyally and responsibly. Somehow he lost that former nastiness which we had found so unpleasant. He had learned to sublimate his native abilities into socially acceptable channels. Was Jacob perfect now? Of course not. He seemed, for example, totally unaware of the pain and suffering of his wife Leah. As we continue the story of Jacob, we shall find time and time again human failings and weaknesses.

You may want to discuss changes in human behavior in general: What does it take for a person to change? Your students may suggest some of the following: insight into one's own behavior; the intelligence to analyze one's actions; knowing oneself; wanting to change and working on it deliberately. People who are guided only by their emotions and have no intellectual insight into their own make-up find it very hard to change.

What do we mean when we say that someone is "good," "decent," or "generous"? We make such judgments based on a person's actions. If we see him giving, sharing or making sacrifices, we say that he is "generous." Let us imagine that this person, deep in his heart, is *not* generous, but stingy. How would he feel every time he forced himself to share? He would probably find it painful and difficult; he would have to overcome his natural instincts every time he acted generously. Would these inner feelings make him less deserving of the title "generous"? Probably not. Might his ambivalence lessen with each succeeding act of generosity? Very likely.

You may want to tell your class that according to Jewish thought, people get credit for what they do, not for what they feel or think. Of course, positive motivations usually lead to positive actions. Nevertheless, a person who gives gets full credit for his deed, despite the ambivalence of his motivations. Behavior can, in the long run, change our character.

LESSON 12

Jacob Meets Esau
Gen. 33:1–18

☐ In Preparation for Teaching

This chapter presents many possibilities, and many questions may be asked. Do not feel, however, that you have to use every question suggested below. As you know, some students are more inclined to analyze text than others, so use your own judgment. You know your students best.

In the last chapter, we saw that Jacob was fearful of Esau's approach. What do we remember about Esau?

a) He was a skilled hunter, a man of the outdoors.
b) He was careless about the birthright.
c) He was uncouth, rude, graceless.
d) He wanted revenge and had threatened Jacob.
e) He was also sensitive, careful not to hurt his father's feelings and able to control himself.

It is hard to guess how Esau would act now.

After his encounter with the divine being, Jacob might be less worried. He may have seen the change of name as prophetic. The struggle may have given Jacob confidence both in himself and in the fact that God was protecting him—he could prevail!

☐ Teaching Procedures

After reviewing what we know about Esau, read 33:1–18. Jacob obviously took no chances. He divided his family, putting the servants and their children first, Leah and her children next, and Rachel and Joseph last, furthest from possible danger. Some of your students may find this "favoritism" distasteful. If they do, you may have to remind them that in those days there were real legal differences in rank between concubines, wives and their respective children. Jacob, of course, could have left the order of his family to chance. Without prearranged groups, however, chances were greater that a disorganized group of people would panic, retreat, or otherwise display fear before Esau. That was a risk Jacob could not take. He himself ran toward Esau and bowed low to the ground seven times.

Lesson 12: Jacob Meets Esau 251

Esau's behavior must have come as a surprise (33:4). Explain that people cry not only in pain or anger, but also when they are happy. They cry with relief when a tense situation is over, (e.g., a big test or operation) or when they think of the past and feel sentimental (e.g., remembering a wedding). People who meet after a long separation often burst into tears.

Discuss with your students what Esau's original motives might have been. It is possible that Esau initially went out to meet Jacob with bad intentions, but changed his mind at the sight of the gifts. Or he might have intended to welcome his brother from the start. We do not know for sure; yet his surprise at the offer of gifts and his initial decline of taking them seems to indicate that he never meant any harm. What would this tell us about Esau? He was good natured, ready to forgive, naive and kind; Jacob did not have to fear him. Did Jacob now drop his guard and treat Esau in a free and easy manner?

It may be helpful to make a list of terms and expressions used in the brothers' dialogue. This can be done by your students at home or in class.

Jacob	**Esau**
Your servant (33:5)	I have enough, my brother. (33:9)
To gain my lord's favor (33:8)	
To see your face is like seeing the face of God.	I will proceed at your pace. (33:12)
You have received me favorably. (33:10)	Let me assign to you some of the men. (33:15)
Accept then my offer. (33:11)	
My lord knows (33:13)	
Let my lord go ahead of his servant . . . until I come to my lord. (33:14)	
Oh no, my lord is too kind to me. (33:15)	

What do Esau's statements seem to indicate?

a) Esau is eager to show his good intentions.
b) He is a generous host.
c) He holds no grudge against his brother.

What does Jacob's choice of words seem to indicate?

a) He still did not trust Esau.
b) He was "putting it on heavily."
c) He wanted to get away from Esau as quickly as possible.

Even if your class is studying Genesis in English, introduce 33:11 in Hebrew: קַח נָא אֶת בִּרְכָתִי. Your class will know that בְּרָכָה means "blessing," and they have learned that בְּרָכָה also means "gift" (Genesis 1). The use of the word בִּרְכָתִי to describe Jacob's gifts to Esau perhaps represents Jacob's symbolic returning of the בְּרָכָה that he had deceitfully taken from Esau long ago. In essence, Jacob offers to reverse his former acts, as if to make up for his regrettable past deeds.

Where did Esau invite Jacob? To his place, to Seir. Where did Jacob actually go? To Succoth! Jacob did not want Esau or any of his men with him (33:12–17). Was Jacob being unfriendly? If so, Esau was not aware of it. Jacob, of course, was very different from Esau. Esau was not one who generally prevailed, and we may wonder how he would have fared in Laban's house.

Jacob had become Israel. He was no longer a private person; he was now the potential ancestor of a people. His destiny would not be found in dwelling with his brother in Seir. He would dwell alone in the land that God had promised him—to forge his own way of life with his family and with God.

LESSON 13A

The Rape of Dinah
Gen. 33:18–34:31

◻ **In Preparation for Teaching**

Jacob, as we know, was quite wealthy (32:14–15). He owned goats, ewes, rams, camels, cows, bulls, asses, and many servants. Since all of the above are marketable commodities, he must have possessed gold and silver as well. Though rich and respected, he was still a foreigner: an alien and a semi-nomad, who camped in his tents outside the city on land purchased or rented from the city's inhabitants. He probably paid for water rights, and for permission to graze his flocks in the fields after the harvest. Eventually he would break up camp and move to the outskirts of another city, sometimes staying long enough to sow and reap a field of grain or wheat (see Joseph's dream, Gen. 37:5–8).

In 33:18–20 we find Jacob, who had returned from Paddan-Aram, encamped before the city of Shechem, where he had purchased some land. Here, in Shechem, the incident which occupies Genesis 34 takes place.

The biblical account of years, as we have noted before, is not historically-oriented and therefore need not be taken literally. If Jacob had served only twenty years in Haran; and Reuben had been born in the eighth year of his father's service, then he, the eldest, would now be twelve years old. Simeon and Levi would be ten and eleven at most. Dinah, the last of Leah's six children, would be much too young to evoke Shechem's lust, and Joseph, a babe in arms, would not be old enough to bow down to his uncle Esau (33:7).

There is no reason to bring these discrepancies to the attention of your students unless *they* bring them up. Thus, in Genesis 34 we accept the fact that Leah's four oldest sons are depicted as young adults and Dinah is at least in her early teens.

How did later Israelite society deal with rape? We find the following law:

> If a man comes upon a virgin who is not engaged and he seizes her and lies with her, and they are discovered, the man who lay with her shall pay the girl's father fifty shekels of silver, and she shall be his wife. Because he has violated her, he can never have the right to divorce her. (Deuteronomy 22:28–29)

This law deals with two aspects of rape:

1) The monetary loss of the father, who lost the "bride price" for the virgin, for which he has to be compensated.
2) The rights of the woman who had been violated, and now must be protected. The offender must marry her and is thereafter forbidden ever to divorce her.

It is important to remember that the purpose of the institution of marriage in ancient times was mainly to insure the rights of the woman. A husband was responsible for his wife's protection and sustenance. Life for a widowed or divorced woman alone was very hard. That is why the Torah admonishes us to protect the widow and her orphaned children. The law cited above (which probably pertains to *Israelites only*, not to foreigners) aims to protect the wronged woman from being abandoned. Her wishes, however, are not considered; in fact, she had little say, even under normal circumstances, in the matter of her own marriage.

The story is very rich and detailed. How much time you want to spend on these details depends on you and the interest span of your students.

The punishment Simeon and Levi meted out to the people of Shechem went far beyond what was called for. The brother, instead of killing everybody in the town, could have killed Shechem, taken Dinah, and left—the people of Shechem were in no position to stop them!

Careful reading of the text, however, will indicate that the writer of the story tries by different literary devices to arouse our sympathy for Simeon and Levi. Note, for instance, the repetition of phrases referring to the "defiling" of their sister (34:5, 13, 27). Note also that Hamor at no time acknowledges that his son had committed a crime. He does not apologize—he offers material compensation only. This may be the reason the sons mutter at the end of the story, "Should our sister be treated like a whore?" Simeon and Levi seem to be the "idealists" in the family, compared to the other brothers who

> came upon the slain and plundered the town. . . . They seized their flocks and herds and asses . . . all their wealth, all their children, and their wives, all that was in the houses they took as captives and booty. (34:27–29).

Lesson 13A: The Rape of Dinah

You may want to juxtapose the two fathers: Hamor, the loving and concerned father, and Jacob who seems to be concerned only with the practical results of his sons' act (34:30), but not with its moral implications, nor with his daughter's fate. Jacob does not answer his sons' last retort, but on his deathbed he remembered what Simeon and Levi had done:

> Simeon and Levi are a pair.
> Their weapons are tools of lawlessness.
> Let not my person enter their council;
> Or my being be joined to their company.
> For when angry they slay men,
> And when pleased they maim oxen.
> Cursed be their anger so fierce.
> And their wrath so relentless.
> I will divide them in Jacob,
> Scatter them in Israel.
> Genesis 49:5–7

(You can refer to Jacob's deathbed prophesies now, or else raise this issue when Genesis 49 is taught in class.)

All of Jacob's sons were included in the covenant blessing; but within this blessing, Simeon and Levi were cursed. This curse played itself out when the descendants of Jacob's sons grew into tribal families. The tribe of Levi never possessed its own land, and was scattered among the other tribes. The tribe of Simeon never amounted to much; it eventually merged with the tribe of Judah and lost its own identity. When Moses blessed each of the tribes before his death (Deuteronomy 33), Simeon was not even mentioned. The story of the rape of Dinah, then, may serve an etiological function. It tells us why the tribes of Simeon and Levi fared the way they did later on in the history of Israel.

◻ Teaching Procedure

Gen. 34:1–12

You might want to read this story verse by verse instead of reading the whole story first.

Dinah, daughter of Leah went out to visit the daughters of Shechem. (Being an only daughter she may have wanted female company.) Why the mention of the fact that she was *Leah's* daughter? We already know this. (Keep the answer suspended, it may later serve as an expanation of why Jacob seems to be rather indifferent to her.) Shechem, the son of Hamor, the respected chief or prince of the city, seized and raped Jacob's daughter Dinah. He subsequently fell in love with her, and asked his father Hamor to get him the girl for a wife.

Note that the rape precedes the "falling in love" and has therefore to be regarded as an act of violence and not of passion. Jacob heard of the rape—the rumor had spread to the outskirts of the town where Jacob dwelled. (In 34:26 we learn that Dinah had not returned home after the rape.) Jacob kept silent until his sons came home.

We are not told that Jacob reacted with anger or sadness; we are not told of any reaction at all. Nor did Jacob call his sons home. The brothers, on the other hand, were distressed and very angry.

Note that in 34:7 the narrator speaks of Shechem having committed an "outrage in Israel," referring to the future when Jacob's clan would be an entity called Israel. This is one way in which the narrator sways our sympathies toward Jacob's sons.

Hamor, Shechem's father came out to speak to the brothers. What proposal does Hamor offer Jacob?

1) That Dinah be given to Shechem as a wife.
2) That there be total assimilation between the people of Shechem and the people of Israel.
3) That he, Hamor, will pay any bride price, "ever so high."

Ask your class how they feel about the offer. Some may consider it a good deal. (You may want at this point to tell them about the law in Deuteronomy [above, p. 225]. Point out, however, that the law pertains to an offender who is an Israelite, not a foreigner.) Some students may say that Hamor wants to get Shechem the wife he desires and that he sounds genuine. Others may note that Hamor seems to ignore the fact that his son committed a crime. He acts as if this were a normal marriage proposal. At no time does Hamor apologize. He seems to think that he can solve the problem by paying a big sum of money.

What would Jacob's people have gained by accepting the offer?

a) They would have become citizens of Shechem.
b) They would no longer be a semi-nomadic (wandering) tribe.

What would they lose?

a) They would lose their own specific character and identity.
b) They would lose the covenant blessing.

Could the sons of Jacob agree to the deal? Discuss the pros and cons. Your class will probably say that they could not.

Lesson 13A: The Rape of Dinah

Gen. 34:13–24

What do the brothers suggest? (34:14–17)
What are we, the readers told? (34:13)
What excuse does the narrator make for the brothers?
We do not know what the "guile" consists of. What could it mean? Possible explanations might be:

a) The brothers pretend to be negotiating in good faith, but actually believe that the people of Shechem will never agree to be circumcized. (Circumcision is very painful to adults.)
b) The brothers plan that after the people are circumcized Jacob and his sons would take Dinah and escape.

Note that the brothers do not seem to be interested in the high "bride price" and the wealth offered them. They seem only interested in the need for circumcision.

How did Hamor and Shechem influence their townsmen to go along with the circumcision? They told them that a merger with the rich outsiders would be beneficial for the people of Shechem (34:23). Note the subtle change in the wording between Hamor's address to Jacob and that to his own people.

To Jacob	To the people of Shechem
Give your daughters to us and *take* our daughters for yourselves. (34:9)	We will *take* their daughters to ourselves as wives and *give* our daughters to them. (34:21)
The land will be open before you, settle and acquire holdings in it. (34:10)	Would not their cattle and substance and all their beasts be ours? (34:23)

And yet, Hamor is not really lying or misleading. Mergers are often beneficial to both sides.

Gen. 34:25–31

What do Simeon and Levi do when the young men "all who went out of the gate of the town" (i.e., the townsmen of fighting age) are hurting after the circumcision? Were they justified in doing what they did?

Note that the word *took* repeats itself within the story: Shechem *took* Dinah (34:2). Simeon and Levi *took* their sword and *took* Dinah (34:26). The other brothers *took* the booty (34:28).

Consider the actions of the various characters in the story:

a) How does Hamor regard his son?
b) How does Jacob regard his daughter?
c) The brothers are angry. Is Jacob?
d) Why does the text repeat the already known fact that Dinah is the daughter Leah had borne? (34:1) Would Jacob have reacted differently had she been Rachel's child?
e) What motivated Simeon and Levi?
f) What motivated Dinah's other brothers?
g) How did Jacob react to Simeon and Levi's act? What is he concerned with?

We do not know how Jacob felt about Dinah's rape. We know he thought Simeon and Levi were wrong. What, however, would *he* have done? We do not know. You may want to ask some or all of the above questions. Although the story is critical of Simeon and Levi, it may be even more critical of the other sons. Jacob does not come off well and, of course, neither do Hamor and Shechem. In real-life situations people in general are not good or bad, right or wrong—but somewhere in the middle, a little bit wrong and a little bit right.

When people pursue a particular objective, they usually have a range of possible *means* of reaching that objective. It is their responsibility to choose the *best* means of reaching that objective, no matter how noble the objective is. In this instance, Dinah had to be rescued, and Shechem had to be punished. But there must have been other ways of achieving both of these goals. (Similarly, years earlier, Jacob was destined to be the master of his brother. Yet he might have obtained this end by a means other than trickery.) When one uses unjust means to achieve an end, one must live with the consequences.

You may want now to read Gen. 49:5–7, Jacob's deathbed blessing of Simeon and Levi.

LESSON 14

Culminating Events
Genesis 35

☐ In Preparation for Teaching

This chapter deals with a number of matters. At first glance, they seem like "leftovers" from some of the longer stories. We may, however, be able to see a connection between some of them.

1) 35:1–7 and 9–15—Bethel
2) 38:8—The death of Rebekah's nurse
3) 35:16–21—The birth of Benjamin and death of Rachel
4) 35:22a—Reuben's misdeed
5) 35:22b–27—The sons of Jacob
6) 35:27–29—The death of Isaac

☐ In Preparation for Teaching

You may want to have your class read Genesis 35, divide it into sections, give names to the sections and discuss the contents. Present as much of the background material as you deem necessary.

Gen. 35:1–7 and 9–15 are a second version of stories we have already read. These verses merge the Bethel story (Gen. 28:10–22) with the one in which Jacob's name is changed to Israel (32:23–33). You may want to point out that the names Bethel and Israel had been given in prior stories. Here as always, we as teachers are less interested in breaking up of a story into its original components than in deriving all possible meaning from the whole text as its stands.

As the chapter begins, we find God prompting Jacob to go up to Bethel and fulfill the oath he had taken when he was fleeing from Esau. Jacob realized that he and his family had to be in a state of ritual purity before worshipping at Bethel. Jacob and his people changed their clothes. Jacob buried all the foreign gods (probably including Rachel's *teraphim*) and the golden earrings (which could be melted down to make more idols; see Exodus 32:1–4). It was customary for ancient peoples to adopt new gods upon entering a new society or culture. They would worship the new gods along with the old. Jacob's people, however, could not hold on to the old gods, since their whole faith was predicated on belief in one God exclusively—the God of Israel. Your students may find it difficult to understand how anyone could still hold onto other deities after Abraham. During the entire biblical period it is apparent that the belief in the one invisible God was not easily achieved. Throughout the generations, there was always "backsliding" among the people.

In 35:9–12, God renewed the Abrahamic blessing given to Jacob at Bethel and restated the change of name from Jacob to Israel. Since you have already taught these stories in another version, you could have your students state the facts after they read the verses, and move on.

According to the Bible, Abraham was the physical father of the people of Israel. His grandson Jacob fathered twelve sons, who in turn would become twelve tribes. The federation of these tribes would become the people of Israel.

This belief in a genealogical history is unique to the Bible. We do not know if any other people believed that they all stemmed from one father. The American people call George Washington "the father of our country," yet we do not consider him our biological father. Historically, this is not the way a people comes into being. The Bible itself tells that Abraham and Jacob were heads of great households, not of just their immediate families. Nonetheless, the image of a people descended from one father is a powerful unifying force for the Jewish people.

In 35:8 is recorded the death of Rebekah's nurse, Deborah, who had not been mentioned before. Her death may serve to blunt the news of Rachel's death, which follows.

In 35:16–22 we learn that Rachel, Jacob's beloved wife, died giving birth to Jacob's twelfth and last son Ben-oni (Benjamin), the full brother of Joseph. Typically, the Bible does not tell us anything about Jacob's feelings, but they are not hard to guess. Did he consider her death a continuation of his own punishment or possibly as a punishment for her taking the *teraphim*?

Reuben's offense (35:22a) will cost him his birthright! His immorality and its consequences are echoed in Genesis 49:3–4 and Deuteronomy 33:6. In historical terms, the tribe of Reuben never amounted to much. Together with the tribe of Gad and half the tribe of Manasseh, the tribe of Reuben dwelt on the east bank of the Jordan where they were harassed by their neighbors (Joshua 1:12; see Deut. 33:6. It is possible that the tribe of Reuben was strong in the early years and later declined. Gen. 35:22a may be the etiological explanation for this.

Gen. 22b–24 repeat the names of Jacob's sons, and 35:27–29 tell of the death of Isaac, who had receded into the background of the story a long time ago, when his son Jacob assumed center stage. These verses are discussed further in the next lesson.

(Supplementary activities related to the teaching of this lesson can be found in Appendix A, below, p. 323.)

LESSON 15

Generations of Esau and Jacob
Genesis 35–36

☐ In Preparation for Teaching

With Jacob's twelve sons, "national unity" had been achieved. Meanwhile Edom (Esau) too had become a clan, as is evident from Genesis 36. The list of names of the line of Edom may not be of great interest to us.

It is interesting to note that 36:6 claims that Esau left Canaan to live in Seir because of his brother Jacob: "For their possessions were too many for them to dwell together." We had read earlier (Gen. 33:12–16) that Esau was already living in Seir when Jacob returned from Haran. In either case, each son had amassed his own wealth. This is another case of the same story being told in different ways in order to convey different meanings or ideas. The earlier story stressed that Esau had been provided for by Isaac's blessing and had no reason to feel neglected on account of the stolen blessing. The present story stresses that the brothers got along.

Despite their differences, Jacob and Esau (Israel and Edom) acted in unison to bury their father.

It is important that your students know the names of Jacob's sons by heart. You may have them fill in a chart, such as the completed model on the next page.

SONS OF JACOB

	Leah	Bilhah	Zilpah	Rachel
1)	Reuben			
2)	Simeon			
3)	Levi			
4)	Judah			
5)		Dan		
6)		Naphtali		
7)			Gad	
8)			Asher	
9)	Issachar			
10)	Zebulun			
11)	Dinah			
12)				Joseph
13)				Benjamin

UNIT VII

The Story of Joseph
Genesis 37–50

UNIT VII

The Story of Joseph
Genesis 37–50

☐ Overview

The Joseph story is the last major section of the book of Genesis.

Up to this point we have read the stories of Abraham, Isaac, and Jacob. Abraham's story tells of God's *covenant* made with one man, a man chosen to father a people through whom all the people of the world would benefit. The story of Isaac's life symbolizes the attachment of the people to its *land*. Jacob, the father of many children, stands for the *great number of descendants* that God promised Abraham.

Jacob, however, was not the first to have many children. Abraham, too had other children—Ishamel and the sons of Keturah—but they were not included in the covenant. Similarly, in Isaac's family only one child carried the blessing of Abraham. In contrast, *all* of Jacob's sons were to carry the Abrahamic blessing.

If the stories of Abraham, Isaac, and Jacob represent the covenant, land, and peoplehood, respectively, what does the Joseph story stand for? The fact of Jacob's having many children was not enough to make a people. The sons of Jacob were thoughtless, jealous, and cruel. There were twelve of them, yet they could not be the foundation of a people. In the course of the next chapters the brothers will grow, mature, repent, and change. At first divided by hatred and jealousy, they will develop a sense of kinship and responsibility for one another. They will become a cohesive family. The Joseph story is the story of how the children of Jacob became the foundation of the people of Israel.

This story may not deal with as many abstract ideas as some other parts of Genesis. Yet the story of Joseph is one of the most dramatic tales in the whole Bible. Many storytellers and playwrights have used the Joseph theme as a basis for novels and plays. Unlike the Abraham story, this is a story with one continuous plot. There is almost unrelieved tension throughout the tale. The story deals with human nature, behavior and relationships. As with other stories in the Bible, the narration here is skeletal. Many details are omitted, left for us to "flesh out" and wonder about. We cannot be sure about the answers, but we may speculate.

Let your students read the story and enjoy it. Let them find out for themselves how Joseph, the spoiled young man, develops and changes through his ordeals and how the brothers mature and grow throughout their lives. It is likely that you will not need highly structured lesson plans for this story.

LESSON 1A

The Younger Brother
Gen. 37:1–11

☐ In Preparation for Teaching

Read the story in class in small segments. "This is the line of Jacob," we are told (37:2). Yet the story is that of Jacob's son Joseph: "and Joseph was seventeen years of age." Actually, the story began long before that, almost eighteen years earlier, before his birth. Once your students read 37:2, remind them of the first mention of Joseph (Gen. 30:22): "God remembered Rachel . . . she conceived." There we saw the tension within Jacob's family reflected in the names Leah and Rachel gave their children. Since the text does not dwell on the relationships within the family, let us imagine Jacob's household when it was first divulged that Rachel had at long last conceived.

The feelings of Rachel and Jacob are easy to guess. What about Leah? What about Leah's four oldest boys? What might Leah have said to them when she learned of Rachel's pregnancy? How did Leah's boys feel when the first son of Rachel was born and circumcised? Could they have hated and resented Joseph, even prior to his birth? Did Reuben, the oldest, even then wonder about his birthright? Was the die already cast at this early date for the course of future events? Would the course of the lives of Joseph and his brothers have been the same even if Joseph himself had not contributed to the family strife?

☐ Teaching Procedure

Have your students read 37:2–4. Help them to notice the fact that Joseph served as a helper to the sons of the concubines. At seventeen he was probably old enough to be a shepherd himself. Why then was he just a "helper," and why to the sons of Bilhah and Zilpah?

Jacob was well aware of the hardships of a shepherd's life (see Gen. 31:38–42). Was he trying to shelter Joseph from the responsibilities and dangers of being a full-fledged shepherd? Or had the sons of Leah chosen to reject and segregate him, relegating him to less important work? Raise the questions, but leave the answers open.

What do we learn in 37:2 that may strengthen our belief that Leah's sons may have rejected Joseph? He brought bad reports of his brothers to his father. From our past knowledge of the sons of Jacob, what kinds of things might he have told his father? Here are some suggestions: He could have reported acts of violence carried out by Simeon and Levi—fighting with other shepherds or amongst themselves. He may have noticed Reuben's involvement with his father's concubine, or reported that the brothers were neglecting the flocks and slaughtering animals for meat. It is also possible that Joseph made up lies about his brothers and told them to his father, causing Jacob to punish Joseph's brothers.

People who tell tales are obviously unpleasant to live with. But what else besides his being a tattletale made Joseph's brothers hate him?

Jacob loved Joseph best! He showed this by giving him a special ornamented tunic. What did shepherds generally wear? Probably rough linen garments, or in the winter garments made out of wool or fur. We do not know for sure what Joseph's garment (כְּתֹנֶת פַּסִּים, 37:3) looked like, but we do know that garments referred to by the same name were worn by royalty (2 Samuel 13:18). Surely it was an extraordinary gift for Joseph!

Like Jacob's love for Rachel, Jacob's love for Joseph seems to have been exclusive. We cannot blame Jacob for loving Joseph, but we can wonder why he chose to be so obvious about his preference for Joseph, and oblivious of the feelings of his other sons.

Read 37:5–11. Joseph had two dreams which he related to his father and his brothers. Joseph's dreams were simple. The brothers did not need a magician or sage to interpret them. Joseph never disputed their interpretation of his dreams, so it must have coincided with his own interpretation. In the Bible, dreams are accepted as signs from God. When a dream occurs twice, it has added validity (see Gen. 41:32). The hatred and jealousy of the brothers is not surprising.

Joseph could not be blamed for dreaming. But telling his dreams to his brothers may indicate that young Joseph was tactless, vain and insensitive to the feelings of others. It is also possible that he retaliated in this way for the ostracism he may have suffered.

Joseph's brothers now hated him more than ever! Yet Joseph naively continued to tell them of his dreams. Jacob chided Joseph for this, but he kept in mind the gist of Joseph's dreams, since he too believed they came from God.

The brothers' hatred of Joseph, which may have started at the time of Joseph's conception, was thus unwittingly strengthened by the actions of both Jacob and Joseph himself.

(Supplementary activities related to the teaching of this lesson can be found in Appendix A, below, pp. 322–323.)

LESSON 1B

The Plot
Gen. 37:12–24

◻ **Teaching Procedure**

Have your students read 37:12–17. Let them probe the story through your questions.

The brothers pastured their father's flocks; they were probably away from home for weeks at a time foraging for grazing pastures. Jacob and the younger children stayed in Hebron, where Jacob had settled. Jacob sent Joseph out to find out how the brothers were doing and how the flocks were faring.

In sending Joseph on this errand, what did Jacob seem to ignore? That the brothers hated Joseph so much they could not speak a civil word to him! By sending Joseph out alone, Jacob was exposing him to danger. Joseph himself seemed to have been oblivious to the danger.

Gen. 37:15–17 seem superfluous: we are told so little about the life of the brothers; why then are we told that Joseph went first to Shechem and only later to Dothan? What does the name Shechem evoke? Memories of violence, blood, deception, revenge. Its inclusion here indicates impending danger.

What did Joseph wear on his errand? What does this show us about Joseph? What kind of a person would ignore the sullen silence of his brothers and travel unafraid to the pasture in an ornamented tunic? Only someone arrogant, oblivious to the feelings of others, someone who considered himself invulnerable.

In 37:18–24, the plot is hatched. What did the brothers resent most about Joseph? The dreams, for the brothers clearly gave them credence (37:19–20). If Joseph were to die, the dreams would not come true. In a sense, the brothers were attempting to thwart God's plan.

The plot had taken shape before Joseph reached his brothers. What did Reuben suggest? He proposed that the brothers throw Joseph into pit and leave him to die instead of killing him outright.

A pit (בֹּר) is a cistern, an artificial receptacle for rain water. When full of rain, the pit served the same function as a well (which would get its water from an underground spring). We are told that the pit was empty. Joseph was in no danger of drowning, although if left there, he would die of hunger or thirst.

We, the readers, are let in on Reuben's secret plan: he intended to restore his brother to their father. Why was Reuben the one to defend Joseph? Possibly because he was the oldest. He may have felt responsible. Or perhaps because he was in disgrace in his father's eyes, he may have wanted to restore himself in the good favor of his father.

Why then didn't Reuben try to talk his brothers out of harming Joseph? Your students may come up with some of the following responses: they may not have been in the mood to listen to reason; they might have turned against him; maybe he too thought Joseph deserved a little "roughing up."

LESSON 1C

Sold Into Slavery
Gen. 37:25-36

▢ In Preparation for Teaching

Gen. 37:18-36 contains two parallel texts fused into one, with the seams still showing. In the first story, Reuben was Joseph's spokesman and defender (21-22). He suggested throwing Joseph into the pit, with the intention of saving him and restoring him to his father. In the conclusion to that story, a caravan of Midianites passed by while the brothers were absent. They pulled Joseph out of the pit (37:28a), apparently without the brothers' knowledge. Reuben was greatly dismayed when he discovered what had happened (37:29). The Midianites took Joseph down to Egypt, where they sold him as a slave to Potiphar, chief steward to Pharaoh.

In the second, parallel version, Judah is the protector of Joseph (37:26-27). He suggested selling Joseph as a slave to the Ishmaelites in preference to killing him. The Ishmaelites bought Joseph for twenty pieces of silver and brought him down to Egypt (37:28b).

In 37:28 we read: "They pulled Joseph out of the pit." Who are "they"—the brothers or the Midianites? The text is obscure on this point. Later on (Gen. 40:15) Joseph will say that he was kidnapped (by the Midianites?), but elsewhere (45:4) he will allude to the brothers having sold him. If the brothers only left Joseph in the pit, then they did not actively participate in selling Joseph into slavery. Perhaps the obsurity of the text on this point is an intentional attempt by the narrator to suggest that the brother's blame might be lessened.

▢ Teaching Procedure

Have your students read Gen. 37:25-36. The brothers sat down to eat. Usually, when people are upset, sad or excited, they forego food. The story seems to emphasize the brutality and callousness of the brothers. They had just condemned their brother to death in the pit; yet their appetites were not diminished.

Lesson 1C: Sold Into Slavery

As they looked up, they saw a caravan approaching. Judah suggested selling Joseph to the Ishmaelites. In the story as we have it, two versions are combined, much as we have seen on other occasions. In one version the brothers pull Joseph out of the pit and sell him to the Ishmaelites. In the other, the Midianites pull Joseph out (while Reuben is planning to rescue him) and sell him in Egypt. Whether it was the Ishmaelites or the Midianites is not significant. They both serve the same function, namely, as the instrument by which Joseph is brought down to Egypt.

The brothers tore up Joseph's ornamented tunic, dipped it in blood and led their father to believe that Joseph had been devoured by a wild beast. (Again Jacob was deceived; was this still part of his punishment for his own participation in a deception?) Jacob was inconsolable, but his sons seemed not to care.

Elicit the above facts from your students after they have read the verses. You may want to ask your students what they think Joseph said or did when the brothers threw him into the pit, or when they sold him into slavery. (Later we shall learn that Joseph pleaded with his brothers to spare him [42:21].)

How does Reuben compare with Judah? Your class will probably consider Reuben's secret plan more noble than Judah's proposal, but had the brothers known, they probably would have rejected Reuben's plan. For one thing, Joseph would have certainly told his father, and then Reuben would have come across as the "good guy," compared to the wicked brothers. Noble as it may appear, Reuben's plan probably would not have been practical. In any case, Judah's plan was carried out, and Joseph was sold into slavery.

Throughout the Joseph story we shall note how Reuben's powers and influence continue to diminish, while Judah's increase. This is etiological, reflecting the future fate and history of these two tribes. Eventually the tribe of Reuben would settle east of the Jordan, where it would be diminished by Moab and Ammon. The tribe of Judah, however, would become the head tribe (King David was of the tribe of Judah).

LESSON 2

Judah and Tamar
Genesis 38

◻ In Preparation for Teaching

This chapter is difficult to teach. You may choose to leave it out. Your students will probably ask why the Joseph story is interrupted by Genesis 38. Judah in Genesis 38 is contrasted to Jacob in Genesis 37 and to Joseph in Genesis 39. Judah lost a wife and two sons but we do not sense any great grief, in comparison to Jacob, who could not be consoled! Judah's lack of demonstrative grief makes Jacob's grief stand out. Also, Judah consorted with a "harlot" without much compunction. His conduct here contrasts with Joseph's self-control in in the next chapter, where he demonstrates his maturity and integrity in rebuffing the advances of Potiphar's wife. Compared to Judah's promiscuity, Joseph's behavior appears all the more commendable.

This story deals with the custom of the levirate marriage (יִבּוּם). Some Bible scholars believe this custom has roots in earlier cultures. It seems that when a married man died and left no children, his brother or close relative would have to marry the widow. The first child born of this union would be considered the child of the dead brother. This custom had some connection with the belief that a man needed a son to take care of his grave and insure the father's rest in the netherworld. Indirectly, it also insured the widow some protection. Records have been found of cases in Mesopotamia where the same woman had to go through several levirate marriages!

In Deuteronomy 25:7–10, we find the later Israelite development of this law and the custom of *halitzah* (חֲלִיצָה):

> If the man does not want to marry his brother's widow, his brother's widow shall appear before the elders in the gate and declare, "My husband's brother refuses to establish a name in Israel for his brother; he will not perform the duty of *levir*." His brother's widow shall go up to him in the presence of the elders, pull the sandal off his foot, spit in his face and make this declaration: "Thus shall be done to the man who will not build up his brother's house. And he shall go in Israel by the name of the family of the unsandaled one."

Lesson 2: Judah and Tamar 277

The purpose of this ceremony was to shame the *levir* for refusing to marry his brother's widow. After this ceremony, the woman could marry whomever she chose. In Talmudic and post-Talmudic times ḥalitzah was deemed preferable to a levirate marriage. Society had changed since biblical times, and the levirate marriage had become a burden to women. In our story, however, the custom of ḥalitzah had not yet been established. Tamar was doomed to marry one of her husband's brothers or relatives, or spend the rest of her life in her father's house. Share as much of this information as you consider appropriate. Some students will be more interested than others. You will have to use your own judgment.

◻ Teaching Procedure

Have your class read 38:1–10, and tell you the tale: Judah married the daughter of Shua, a Canaanite, and fathered three sons—Er, Onan and Shelah. Er was married to a woman named Tamar. Er's conduct was displeasing to the Lord, who took his life. We are not informed of the nature of his misconduct. We simply know that he died young, and left no heirs. Judah then gave Tamar in marriage to his second son, Onan, instructing Onan to provide an offspring for his dead brother. Onan refused to provide his brother with an offspring. In punishment for this, the Lord took his life.

Why would Onan, after having married Tamar, refuse to have a child with her? Why would he refuse to do his duty by his brother, according to custom? One possible answer concerns inheritance. Er was the oldest. According to the laws of inheritance, he would have inherited two-thirds of his father's wealth. Onan and Shelah would have had to divide the last third between them (amounting to one-sixth of the total inheritance each). Since Er had died without an heir, his inheritance would go to Onan and Shelah, each receiving one-half of the total. However, if a son were born to Tamar and Onan, he would inherit Er's portion of the inheritance; Onan's and Shelah's share would thereby revert to one-sixth each. This may have been what influenced Onan's behavior, but there is no evidence in the text one way or the other. Alternately, perhaps Onan did not want a child that would not have been considered his own but rather his older brother's. Or perhaps Onan did not like Er or did not like Tamar.

Read 38:11–30. Judah suggested that Tamar return to her father's house and remain there until Shelah the youngest, reached a marriageable age. Judah was afraid for his third and last son. He seemed to believe that Tamar had something to do with the untimely deaths of his sons, and he attempted to protect Shelah from her. Even once Shelah was grown, Judah took no steps to transact the marriage.

Tamar, not wanting to die childless, used her cunning to enforce her rights. Knowing that Judah was on his way to a sheep-shearing, she dressed herself like a harlot, veiled her face and sat on the road to Timnah, where he was bound to pass. Judah did indeed take her for a harlot and they bargained over the price. He promised her a goat's kid from the herd; she asked for his seal, cord and staff as pledges. (The seal was used to sign documents and as a sign of identification. It was a symbol of a man's standing in society.) Judah agreed.

Judah later sent his friend, Hirah the Adullamite, to redeem his pledges from the woman. The Adullamite asked for the "cult prostitute" (which may have sounded more respectable than just "the prostitute"). The woman could not be found, and Judah was afraid to inquire further, lest he become a laughing stock.

Meanwhile Judah was told that Tamar had conceived. Concluding that she had been promiscuous, he became incensed and ordered her burned, as must have been the custom of the times. But Tamar sent him the seal, cord and staff, with the message that the owner of these objects was the father of her expected child. Judah realized that he had wronged Tamar by keeping Shelah from her, and declared that she had acted more righteously than he.

The language in Gen. 38:25–26 ("Examine these: whose seal and cord are these?") reminds us of Gen. 37:33–34 ("Please examine these, is it your son's tunic or not?"). Judah is being subjected to the same type of cruel confrontation with the evidence that he had inflicted upon his father.

The Bible does not criticize Tamar for tricking Judah. Rather, she was rewarded in that she gave birth not to a single child but to twins, Perez and Zerah. We learn later in the Bible that Perez, the son of Judah, was an ancestor to David, King of Israel (Ruth 4:17–22). The fact of her ancestry to royalty seems be a further reward for Tamar, who in the face of obstacles took the initiative to insure that she fulfilled her role as a mother.

Lesson 3A

Joseph in Egypt
Gen. 39:1–6

❐ In Preparation for Teaching

Genesis 39 returns us to the stories of Joseph, who had been taken to Egypt and sold as a slave to the chief steward and courtier of Pharaoh, a man by the name of Potiphar. You may want to ask: What do we know so far about Joseph? He was spoiled by his father, he was self-centered, immature, and insensitive to the feelings of others.

What were the chances of a seventeen-year-old Hebrew slave "making it" in Egypt? His future was very unpredictable: he might have ended his life on slave-row, his master might have killed him, or he may have happened by chance to excel and better his lot and even be freed. What in Joseph's prior existence seems to indicate that his life would not end dismally? Your students may remember Joseph's dreams. We mentioned that people believed that dreams came from God. Jacob and his sons gave Joseph's dreams credence, and the brothers tried their utmost to prevent the dreams from coming true (37:20). Joseph's dreams served Joseph's life in the way that Rebekah's oracle had served Jacob's. If the dreams were to be fulfilled, Joseph would need God's special protection.

❐ Teaching Procedure

Read and discuss 39:1–6, Joseph's servitude. What role did God play in Joseph's life while in the house of Potiphar? "The Lord was with Joseph, and he was a successful man" (39:2). "His master saw that the Lord was with him and that the Lord lent success to everything he undertook" (39:3). "The Lord blessed [Potiphar's] house for Joseph's sake so that the blessing of the Lord was upon everything that he owned" (39:5).

Your class may recall another situation where one man brought blessings upon another merely by his presence: God had been with Jacob while he dwelled with Laban. Yet Jacob also had done his share to make Laban prosper by working loyally and well. What must Joseph have done to gain Potiphar's esteem? He must have learned to be humble, tactful, less irritating. He did his work, was efficient, and may have made good decisions for his master. We know that Potiphar put him in charge of all his belongings and gave his direct attention to nothing save the food he ate (possibly an allusion to Egyptian dietary taboos concerning food prepared by and eaten with strangers; see Gen. 43:32). The continuation of the story will shed more light on Joseph's character.

Gen. 39:6b sets the stage for the next events.

LESSON 3B

Imprisonment
Gen. 39:7–23

☐ Teaching Procedure

Read the next section, 39:7–23. Why did Joseph reject the advances of Potiphar's wife? Two reasons are mentioned in the text:

1) Adultery is a sin before God. Taking another man's wife is considered objectionable to God. (Abraham had implied the same in Gen. 20:11.)
2) Joseph felt he owed loyalty to his master who had been good to him and had entrusted him with all he owned.

When Potiphar's wife caught hold of Joseph, he slipped his coat off, left it in her hands and fled. To the servants who came running in answer to her screams, she complained: "Look, *he* [Potiphar] had to bring *us* a Hebrew to dally with *us*."

Your students may not be attuned to the finer nuances of this speech. Potiphar's wife used the word "us" to emphasize the distinction in her mind between the "superior" Egyptians and "inferior" foreigners, such as Joseph. First, she directed her anger against her husband: Joseph's presence in the house was *his* fault. She blurted out, "*He* had to bring *us*. . . ." (By referring to her husband as "he" instead of calling him by name, she was disrespectful of her husband in front of the servants.) Next, she directed her anger against the Hebrew slave. (Note that the word "Hebrew" was not used by Abraham's descendants; it was a derogatory term.)

Draw your students' attention to the fact that she reversed the order of events: in actuality, Joseph's escape *preceded* her screaming. What were her motivations? Your class will no doubt come up with suggestions:

1) Revenge—she was hurt by the slave's rejection of her, indignant at his *chutzpah*.
2) She might have been afraid that Joseph would report *her*, and decided that attack would be the best defense.
3) She had to explain why Joseph's coat was in her room.

Potiphar put Joseph in prison for attempted rape. (It is interesting that he permitted him to live. One might expect a slave to be killed for such an act.)

What happens in our society when a person is accused of an offense? Without going into our judicial system (and its problems) in detail, you may want to establish the point that in our society the accused has the right to an attorney to defend him and a jury to hear his case, before judgment and sentencing. Joseph, on the other hand, had no way of defending himself. Who would take the word of a slave against that of his mistress?

From the pit, Joseph had gone down to Egypt into the depth of slavery. Now he was imprisoned even more deeply, in a dungeon. Joseph must have known despair. The next step down would be into the grave. But still, there were Joseph's dreams—his promised destiny! And God was with Joseph (39:21). The chief jailer took notice of Joseph and put him in charge of all the other prisoners. Joseph became the one in authority. Joseph had begun his climb out of the depths.

In order to find favor first with Potiphar and then with the jailer, Joseph must have grown, must have achieved a measure of wisdom and maturity. Surely resisting Potiphar's wife indicates discipline, self-control, and awareness of what one owes to God and to one's fellow man. God protected Joseph and gave him his opportunities; the rest was up to him.

LESSON 4

Dreams Once More
Genesis 40

☐ **Teaching Procedure**

Read and discuss this chapter. If God's intervention had been needed to help Joseph in Potiphar's home, how much more so was it needed in prison! Potiphar had been the master of Joseph's fate. The chief jailer, however, was not. He could extend kindnesses to Joseph but did not have the power to release him. Only a power *outside* the prison could free him. But who cared about or even knew of the young Hebrew slave, who reputedly had had a "falling out" with his master? In the normal course of events, Joseph would have ended his natural life in prison. But this was not to happen.

One day both the king's cupbearer and his baker were confined to prison for some transgression we can only guess at. These were respected officers at Pharaoh's court. You may want to let your students venture some reasons for the cupbearer's importance. For example:

1) Poison was often used to kill rulers. The king had to trust his cupbearer with his life.
2) After a number of drinks, the king might have divulged information that was not meant to be public knowledge. He would therefore need a trustworthy cupbearer, who could keep a secret.

We learn from Egyptian sources that the Egyptians (and certainly Pharaoh and his court) were gourmands (fond of good food). Fifty-seven kinds of bread were known in Egypt, as well as thirty-eight different kinds of cakes. Thus, the king relied heavily on his baker.

Joseph's dreams had been simple. Jacob, Joseph and his brothers all understood their meaning immediately. Not so the Egyptians' dreams. For dreams such as these, one would need a magician or a wise man. Joseph was no magician; yet he had the ability to interpret dreams. He declared God to be the source of this special ability.

In the cupbearer's dream, the cupbearer was serving the king. Joseph predicted that the cupbearer would be restored to his former office. He was so sure of his interpretation that he put in a plug for himself! Joseph implored the cupbearer to mention him to Pharaoh, telling him that he had been kidnapped from his country (apparently a reference to the version of the story in which the Midianites pulled Joseph out of the pit) and was innocent of any wrongdoing.

When the baker heard the favorable prediction, he eagerly told Joseph his dream, in which his baked goods had been stolen by birds. But Joseph predicted that the baker would be put to death.

Three days later both of Joseph's predictions came true!

Once restored to his position, however, the cupbearer, forgot about Joseph (40:23). How could he forget? Ask for possible explanations. Some suggestions: He might have wanted to forget an unpleasant event. He did not want to remind Pharaoh that he had ever been in disfavor. He might have been an ungrateful person. Or the chance may not have presented itself.

LESSON 5

Ascent to Power
Genesis 41

☐ **Teaching Procedure**

This is a simple narrative. Have your class tell you orally what took place. Let them enjoy the story.

Two years had passed since the events of the last chapter. Pharaoh dreamed two dreams. In the first dream seven ugly, lean cows devour seven fat, healthy ones. In the second dream seven healthy ears of corn are swallowed up by seven thin and scorched ones. There was no one who could interpret Pharaoh's dreams.

Reluctantly the cupbearer reminded Pharaoh of his brief stay in prison. He told him about Joseph, who had correctly interpreted his dream and that of the baker. Joseph was summoned from the dungeon, cleaned up and brought before Pharaoh. Joseph told Pharaoh that both dreams carried the same message: God was informing Pharaoh that seven years of great abundance would come to Egypt, followed by seven years of severe famine. Joseph offered a suggestion: Pharaoh should appoint a prudent man as overseer of Egypt. This man would gather the surplus food and grain during the seven years of plenty, and store them for the seven lean years. In this way, the country would not perish in the famine.

Pharaoh recognized "the spirit of God" in Joseph, since God had chosen him to reveal His plans. He put Joseph in charge of all the land of Egypt. Joseph was dressed in fine linen and given Pharaoh's signet ring, with which he could sign documents in the king's name. He rode in a chariot with heralds running before him. Pharaoh called Joseph by an Egyptian name—Zaphenath-paneah and gave him Asenath, daughter of Poti-phera, priest of On for a wife. Joseph was now thirty years old. The seven years of plenty came, and Joseph, according to plan, bought produce in large quantities. During these years, he had two sons, Manasseh and Ephraim. With the onset of the seven lean years, famine set in—not just in Egypt but in the surrounding countries as well. Joseph opened his enormous granaries and rationed out food to the Egyptians who came to him. Other people heard that there was grain to be had in Egypt, and they too came to Joseph.

To capture the flavor of ancient Egypt, you may be able to provide your class with pictures of clothes, chariots, etc. If you live in a large town, a trip to a museum that contains Egyptian art may be a meaningful experience (e.g., the Metropolitan Museum in New York).

The names of Joseph's sons may cause some question. He named his first son Manasseh: "God has made me *forget* completely my hardship and my parental home" (41:51) (that is, ". . . the hardship *in* my parental home"). Had Joseph really forgotten all the hardships he had endured on account of his brothers? The meaning here is that he was finally able to put these events behind him, out of his mind. Joseph's sudden ascent from the dungeon to the second highest office in the land had compensated him for his years of hardship in Canaan and in Egypt—for the strife he had known in his father's house, for the hatred, the loneliness, the rejection which even his father's love could not make up for, for his being sold into slavery, and for the years of suffering which followed. The emotional pain he endured as a result of these experiences possibly exceeded his physical pain and discomfort.

Joseph named his second son Ephraim: "God has made me fruitful in the land of my affliction" (41:52). Egypt, which had been the land of Joseph's affliction, was now the land of his fruitfulness and prosperity. Slavery and prison were now over and done with. God had elevated Joseph to the rank of vizier to the king.

All this had been God's miracle. Yet Joseph himself had to take advantage of the opportunities God provided. God had helped him to interpret the dreams, but the suggestion to hoard the food during the years of plenty was Joseph's. Furthermore, it was Joseph himself who saw to it that the plan was successfully implemented. Joseph had grown to be a man of discernment and wisdom, as Pharaoh had immediately recognized.

LESSON 6

The First Trip to Egypt
Gen. 42:1–38

◻ **Teaching Procedure**

This is an action-packed chapter your class should enjoy. We will read the story in sections:.

1–5	Down to Egypt
6–17	The Encounter
18–26	Benjamin Is Summoned
27–28	Discovery on the Road Home
29–38	Return to Canaan.

1) Down to Egypt (42:1–5)

Jacob was old, yet still very much in command. Noticing his sons' lack of action in the face of starvation, he took the initiative and sent them down to Egypt. He kept Benjamin, the youngest (but by no means a child) at home. Your students may recognize the parallel to Joseph, who had been kept at home when the brothers went out to pasture the sheep. (As we watch Joseph and his brothers grow and change throughout these stories, Jacob seems to remain a "constant.")

2) The Encounter (42:6–17)

Upon reaching Egypt the brothers came face to face with Joseph. Joseph recognized his brothers, but they did not recognize him. Why not? It is often hard to recognize somebody in unexpected surroundings. (We may fail to recognize the butcher in a regular suit at the movies.) Joseph now wore royal Egyptian clothes. Moreover, he was seventeen when they last saw him; now he was a man of thirty-eight or thirty-nine. (He became vizier at thirty. By this time, seven years of plenty, and one or two years of famine had passed).

Joseph, on the other hand, had some clues to go by. The brothers probably still wore the same kind of clothes. There were ten of them; he had only to recognize one in order to draw his conclusions. Also, the brothers were already grown when he last knew them; adults change less in appearance over time that do younger people.

What was the first thing Joseph thought of when he saw his brothers? The dreams! As his brothers bowed down to him, he remembered that this had been predicted. What else did Joseph possibly think of as he remembered the dreams? That the dreams caused his downfall; what the brothers had done to him; all the hardships he had endured.

Joseph could have identified himself to his brothers. Instead he pretended to believe that they were spies who had come to find out how the land could be conquered. Why? Your class no doubt will identify Joseph's act as one of revenge. Revenge may have had a place in Joseph's treatment of his brothers. But as the story develops, we may find other, stronger motives for his behavior.

The brothers' description of their family circumstances may be seen as a typical reaction on the part of unjustly accused persons. Feeling they had nothing to hide, they blurted out all sorts of random information—including embarrassing details about the brother who "is no more." An unjustly accused person typically feels that the more his accuser knows about him, the more obvious his innocence will become. Their protestations of innocence were to no avail; Joseph had his brothers confined to prison.

3) Benjamin Is Summoned (42:18–26)

The brothers are sent back to Canaan with a request to bring Benjamin to Egypt. Joseph released his brothers after three days in prison because, he claimed, he was a "God-fearing" man. We have already read in the Joseph story that a "God-fearing" man does not commit adultery. Now we learn that to be "God-fearing" also means to be just, i.e., refraining from condemnation until guilt has been established. Joseph singles out Simeon to stay in prison. Joseph might want to separate him from Levi, his partner in the Shechem affair.

Originally, Joseph had said that only one brother would go back to Canaan; the other nine would be imprisoned. Now he changes his plan. He would retain one and let the rest go. The reasons for this change of plan may be:

1) One person cannot carry enough food to Canaan—Joseph does not want to deprive the family.
2) He wants them to relive their coming home without one of the brothers.

Why did Joseph want Benjamin to be brought down to Egypt?

Lesson 6: The First Trip to Egypt 289

Your class may venture some guesses, such as: Joseph missed his full brother and wanted to see him. Or, Joseph might have wanted to force Jacob to come to Egypt by means of detaining Benjamin. For the time being, such conjectures seem to be plausible answers. Keep this question open, however, until later in the story. If the twelve sons of Jacob were to be united in the Abrahamic blessing, Jacob's family would have to be reunited. Past grievances would have to be forgiven, if not forgotten. Your class, however, cannot be expected to anticipate the end of the story.

To what did the brothers attribute their present situation? In 42:21-22 we see that they regarded it as a well-deserved punishment for the brutality they had accorded their brother Joseph. Little did they know that the Egyptian vizier understood Hebrew, and hence, their private exchange! Ask your class what prompted Joseph's secret crying in 42:24. He might have felt sorry for himself, thinking of that day in the pit. He realized that his brothers had not forgotten that day either! How often had they thought of him? Did they regret their cruel act? The text does not tell us. What made them think of Joseph *now*? Possibly the fact that they were now about to lose another brother.

(Supplementary activities related to the teaching of this lesson can be found in Appendix A, below, p. 313.)

4) Discovery on the Road Home (42:27-28)

On their way back to Canaan, one brother discovered that his money had been returned to him, along with the grain he had purchased. Why did Joseph return the money? It is possible that he did not want to take money from his own kin. But he also knew that his brothers would be greatly alarmed and intimidated by this surprise. This was obviously part of Joseph's plan. Because of the unexplained money, they would be uneasy about returning to Egypt. We may wonder about Joseph's apparent lack of concern for his old father's feelings of anguish.

How do the brothers react to the discovery? They consider it yet another punishment from God.

5) Return to Canaan (42:29-38)

Upon returning home, each brother found his money in his grain sack. The brothers were dismayed (42:35). Why did they consider this such a serious problem? If the Egyptian authorities were to discover that the brothers had not paid for their grain, it would strengthen the accusation of spying. It would thereby threaten their access to a food supply during the famine and would also make it impossible for them to free Simeon.

How did Jacob react to the detention of Simeon and the summoning of Benjamin? Jacob considered the loss of Simeon an accomplished fact—he says, "It is always *me* you bereave . . . these things always happen *to me*" (42:36). He clearly felt that life had treated him harshly. He had lost Rachel, Dinah, Joseph, and now Simeon. Was he to lose Benjamin also? Losing the last surviving son of Rachel would surely be more than he could bear. There is also some hint of accusation in Jacob's tone: *You*—my sons—bereaved me! Did he suspect that his sons were involved in Joseph's disappearance? We can only guess.

What did Reuben suggest, and what in his suggestion strikes you as ridiculous? (42:37) How did Jacob react to this suggestion? Jacob's retort sheds a new light on his relationship to Benjamin (42:38). Evidently, Benjamin had taken Joseph's place in the affections of his father. Jacob said: "He alone is left," which could be taken to mean that his other ten sons were of little consequence. Knowing Jacob's sons, how would you expect the brothers to regard Benjamin? Some of your students will assume the brothers hate him. Others may suggest that a change had occurred in the brothers as they matured and mellowed. They seem to accept and tolerate their old father now, despite his flaws and obvious "favoritism" to Benjamin.

LESSON 7

Return to Egypt
Genesis 43

☐ **Teaching Procedure**

Read the exciting climax of this story in sections:.

1–14	Taking the Risk
15–25	The Second Encounter
26–34	The Banquet

1) Taking the Risk (43:1–14)

"But the famine in the land was severe" (43:1). The word "but" links this chapter to the previous one in which Jacob refuses to let Benjamin be taken to Egypt. Reuben, the oldest son, had failed to sway his father, with his extravagant vow. Judah was now more successful in fending the accusations and objections of his father, in part, no doubt, because the family had once again run out of food and was facing starvation. Taking Benjamin to Egypt was a risk they would have to take—or they would all perish. Judah vowed to take full responsibility for Benjamin's safe return.

Even in anguish Jacob planned each act in his characteristic way. He instructed his sons to bring gifts and delicacies to the Egyptian vizier (echoes of his meeting with Esau). We must note the depth of Jacob's love for Benjamin, contrasted with the seeming disregard for his other sons. Every effort was made to insure Benjamin's safety; on the other hand, there is no thought given to retrieving the imprisoned Simeon.

2) The Second Encounter (43:15–25)

The brothers, including Benjamin this time, returned to Egypt. When Joseph saw Benjamin in the company of his brothers, he gave orders for a reception and banquet in their honor. The brothers were frightened and alarmed by the unexpected gesture of being asked to Joseph's home. They feared it had some connection with the money they had found in their sacks. The steward of Joseph's house, however, denied any knowledge of the money. He brought Simeon out to them, gave them water to bathe their feet and food for their pack animals. They spread out their gifts for the vizier and awaited his arrival at noon.

The Banquet (43:26–34)

Joseph arrived at his home, where the brothers awaited him. Upon seeing Benjamin, Joseph was so overcome with emotion he hurriedly sought privacy to weep. After regaining composure and washing his face to remove evidence of his tears, he returned to the banquet and ordered that the meal be served.

It is necessary to explain why three separate tables were set. Egyptians would not eat with foreigners—not even with Joseph, who was second to the king. Thus, Joseph could not sit at the table with the Egyptians. Joseph could not eat with his brothers without divulging to them his non-Egyptian origins. So Joseph ate alone, and the Egyptians and the sons of Jacob ate at separate tables (43:32). The brothers would assume that Joseph ate alone because of his elevated status, and the ruse could continue. To the brothers' amazement, they were seated according to their ages; the brothers must have assumed that the vizier possessed magic powers of divination. Benjamin was offered portions several times larger than those of the others. Why? Because Joseph loved Benjamin, his only full brother and the only brother who had not been present when Joseph was thrown into the pit. Also, Joseph may have been looking to rouse feelings of jealousy toward Benjamin.

LESSON 8

The Test
Gen. 44:1–17

❐ Teaching Procedure

You may have discussed Joseph's possible motivations for demanding Benjamin's presence in Egypt. Some of your students may have suggested that Joseph simply wanted to see him again. If that was the case, surely the time had come for Joseph to reveal himself. The "game," however, continued.

Other students probably said that Joseph's motivation for all of this was revenge. While the motive of revenge may have been present, it seems that Joseph's elaborate plan included something else besides simple revenge. In 44:1–10, Joseph instructed his servants to return the money to the bags of grain; he also told them to discreetly slip his silver goblet into Benjamin's bag.

As soon as the brothers departed, Joseph dispatched men to overtake them and charge them with the theft of the goblet, which the vizier used for divination (e.g., to "learn" how the brothers ranked in age). The brothers, in their innocence, declared that if the goblet was found in the possession of any one of them, that one would die and the rest would become slaves to the vizier! (This echoes Jacob's declaration to Laban regarding the *teraphim* in Gen. 31:32.) The stewart graciously declined the offer; only the one in whose bag the goblet was found would be held as a slave.

To heighten the tension, the search began with the bag of Reuben, the oldest, and proceeded one by one to Benjamin, the youngest (44:12). The suspense mounts! At long last, the goblet was found in Benjamin's bag. All the brothers returned to Joseph's house. There was nothing Judah could say in their defense. He offered that they all remain in Egypt as slaves to the vizier. Joseph declined the offer. Only Benjamin would have to stay; the rest were free to leave.

The brothers knew, of course, that Benjamin was innocent. Twice had their money been returned to them! Obviously the Egyptians had tampered with their bags. Judah had promised Jacob to protect Benjamin with his life. What would he do now?

Now at last Joseph's strategy becomes clear. Joseph had succeeded in separating the interests of Benjamin from the interests of the rest of the brothers! Benjamin had taken Joseph's place within the family and in Jacob's affections. Like Joseph, he was loved, cherished and over-protected. Although he may not have provoked the brothers as Joseph had, they had reason enough to resent him. Here was an opportunity to rid themselves of Benjamin as they had rid themselves of Joseph many years before. Would they now abandon Benjamin? Would they deal this fatal blow to their aging father? Joseph obviously had set up a *test*. He had duplicated as closely as possible the conditions of his own story. The brothers had been imprisoned without cause (as had Joseph), leading them to search their conscience for a reason why God may have wanted to torment them. Would the brothers repeat their earlier conduct? Or did they regret their former deeds? Had they acquired a sense of conscience, compassion, and responsibility? Had they become what brothers should be—each other's keeper?

Make explicit to your students the two alternatives available to the brothers: (1) to abandon Benjamin to his fate and return home with the grain, or (2) to attempt to save him and perhaps end up sharing his fate. What would the choice of each alternative reveal to Joseph (and to us) about the present characters of the brothers?

LESSON 9A

A Second Chance
Gen. 44:18–34

◻ Teaching Procedure

Judah's presentation is masterful in its utter sincerity. He gave a detailed account of their relations with the vizier. At no time did he declare Benjamin's innocence; this could not be done without implicating the vizier and his servants. His pleading was for the old father, who would go down to the grave (Sheol) grief-stricken at the loss of his youngest, best-loved son. Poignantly, Judah described how Jacob's life was bound up with that of Benjamin's. He then proposed the extreme sacrifice: he volunteered to take Benjamin's sentence upon himself. He would serve as a slave in place of his youngest brother. Remind your students of Judah's promise to Jacob—on no account would he return without Benjamin.

The test had been passed with flying colors. Where once had been a household torn by hatred and strife, there now stood a cohesive, united family. The brothers proved to be mutually responsible and concerned for their old father whose shortcomings they knew and forgave.

You may want to deal with the concept of repentance (תְּשׁוּבָה), which averts punishment for misdeeds. *Complete* repentance (תְּשׁוּבָה גְמוּרָה) takes place only when a person has the chance to repeat an evil deed—but refrains from doing so. The brothers had performed תְּשׁוּבָה גְמוּרָה!

LESSON 9B

The Reunion
Genesis 45

☐ **Teaching Procedure**

The test was over. If revenge had been on Joseph's mind, surely the brothers had suffered enough. The time had come for Joseph to reveal himself. Understandably, the brothers were stunned by the revelation. Joseph attempted to alleviate their fears by telling them: "God has sent me ahead to insure your survival. . . . So it was not you who sent me here, but God" (45:7–8).

The fact that God planned to bring Joseph to Egypt, however, does *not* render the brothers' act morally acceptable. Within God's plan, man still operates as a free agent. He is free to choose between good and evil, and is ultimately responsible for the morality of his acts. Joseph, in a forgiving mood, nevertheless, tried to ease his brothers' minds.

Joseph's first question pertained to his father: "Is he still alive?" Joseph must have been aware of the additional trauma he had caused his father with the detention of Simeon and the summons for Benjamin. Yet, Joseph could not have tested the brothers without causing his father anxiety. He commanded his brothers to hasten back to their father and prepare their families to sojourn in Egypt for the remainder of the famine. Then Joseph embraced his brother Benjamin and all his half-brothers. Only then (and possibly for the first time in their lives!) were the brothers able to talk to Joseph (45:15).

Pharaoh heard of the emotion-filled reunion and authorized Joseph to supply wagons for Jacob and the brothers' kin. Pharaoh promised Jacob's family some of the best land in Egypt. Joseph also gave his brothers gifts and warned them "not to be quarrelsome" on the way (45:24). Why was Joseph concerned? What kind of things might the brothers have quarreled about? (Open discussion.) Suggestions: Reuben might have reproached the others for selling Joseph in the first place. They might have argued about how to tell Jacob that Joseph was alive. Would they have to tell him the truth? If they made up a story, would Joseph back them up?

The text gives us no information about this. Do you think they ever told Jacob the truth? Is it always kind to be honest? (Open discussion.) The text only tells us that "when Jacob heard that Joseph was alive and a ruler over the whole land of Egypt, his heart went numb for he did not believe them" (45:26). However, when he saw the wagons that Joseph had sent on Pharaoh's order, "his spirit revived" (45:27). Evidently he remembered Joseph's dreams. He decided to go and see Joseph before he died.

LESSON 10A

Jacob's Departure
Gen. 46:1–27

☐ **In Preparation for Teaching**

Once again Jacob had to leave the land he was to inherit. In Beer Sheba, as had happened many years before in Bethel (Gen. 31:13–16), God appeared to Jacob in a vision to renew His covenant with him. Again God promised Jacob His protection: God Himself would go down to Egypt with Jacob and there make his family into a great nation. Although Jacob would die in the land of Egypt, God would return Jacob's children to the land He had promised Abraham as an everlasting possession.

Jacob's descent into Egypt was more than a family visit to a long lost son. In Egypt the sons of Jacob (Israel) would become a people. Often in the Bible, as momentous decisions are made the text stops to give us a history of the hero or heroes involved, a sort of census, as we find here (46:8–27), to tie up loose ends. It is not important for your students to know the names of these descendants, although they may enjoy seeing the names of Judah's sons if they studied Genesis 38. They may be surprised to find that Benjamin was already a father of ten sons.

LESSON 10B

Settling in Goshen
Gen. 46:28–47:12

☐ In Preparation for Teaching

In 46:28–34, we discover the beginnings of a problem and its solution—namely, that of survival in exile. Joseph realized that if Pharaoh knew the sons of Jacob were shepherds (owners of sheep and goats), he would permit them to live in Goshen, separate from the Egyptians, who were herdsmen (owners of cows, bulls and oxen).

This is a reflection of the deep enmity that has traditionally existed between herdsmen and shepherds in many ages and places (including the United States). It seems to stem from the fact that sheep and cows cannot use the same land for grazing. Sheep pull out grass by it roots. Cows graze high and permit the grass to grow back.

As we shall see, Joseph was correct. The sons of Jacob (Israel) were allowed to dwell separately. (There are conflicting reports in the book of Exodus concerning the proximity of Israelite and Egyptian dwellings. On the one hand we learn that the Israelites were spared the plagues since they were segregated in Goshen. On the other hand, blood on the doorposts was needed to differentiate Israelite homes from those of Egyptians. Moreover, the Israelites "borrowed" gold and silver from their Egyptian "neighbors.")

In the book of Exodus, hundreds of years later, the sons of Israel still maintained their unique identity. Although this distinction caused the sons of Israel enslavement and suffering in Egypt, it also enabled them to eventually return to their homeland and become a great and unique nation, as God had prophesied to Abraham (Genesis 15:13–15).

☐ Teaching Procedures

Have your students read 46:28–34 and 47:1–12. Jacob sent Judah ahead to point out the land of Goshen. It seems that Judah had become the official spokesman for the family, long ago replacing Reuben in this role.

When the caravan reached Goshen, Joseph ordered his chariot and went to meet his father. A tearful reunion ensued. Joseph asked his brothers to tell Pharaoh they were shepherds. Why? We have already learned a number of facts about the Egyptians: (1) Potiphar would not permit Joseph to prepare his food; (2) Egyptians would not eat with foreigners; (3) Egyptians abhorred shepherds.

Joseph knew that Pharoah would segregate the sons of Jacob on account of their profession. Why might Joseph have wanted to segregate his brothers from the Egyptians? Joseph might have wanted to protect his family from abuse and disdain. On the other hand, he might have been thinking of the future. Their unique destiny made it imperative for them to keep their own traditions and way of life intact. To integrate or assimilate into the Egyptian population would be to forego their national fate.

Joseph presented five of his brothers to Pharaoh (which ones? Judah? Benjamin?) As Joseph had foreseen, Pharaoh asked the brothers about their occupation. They told him that they were shepherds, as their fathers and forefathers had been, and that they had to sojourn (dwell temporarily) in the land of Egypt because of the famine. They asked to be permitted to dwell in the land of Goshen. Pharaoh consented to their request and suggested that they take care of his livestock too.

Joseph then presented Jacob to Pharaoh. When Pharaoh asked his age, Jacob declared the days of the years of his life had been short and hard, as indeed they had been. Help the class recall the events of his life: As a child, he struggled with Esau. He had to flee his father's house. He was repeatedly cheated by Laban. Dinah had been injured. His life had been endangered by the rash act of Simeon and Levi. He had lost his beloved Rachel and he had lost Joseph. Simeon had been held in captivity. He had weathered a famine. He had to part with Benjamin. If his early life had been less than noble, surely in the course of his life Jacob had suffered for the misdeeds committed in his father's house.

Joseph supported his father's household with food throughout the years of famine.

LESSON 11

Egyptian Economics
Gen. 47:13–27

☐ **Teaching Procedure**

Up to this point in the story we have been so involved in Joseph's family affairs that we have not discussed his "economic miracle." Now we are told what Joseph had been doing all these years in the employ of the Pharaoh. For seven years Joseph had been buying up all the surplus grain from the farmers (Gen. 41:47–49) and paying them in gold from the king's treasury. In each city he built granaries to store the grain locally.

With the years of famine, the time had come to reverse this practice. The doors of the storehouses were opened to sell grain to the farmers of Egypt and neighboring countries. Joseph obviously made a profit for the king by demanding more for the grain than he had originally paid (Gen. 41:53–57). In this way, Joseph acquired most of the money that was to be found in Egypt and Canaan for Pharaoh's treasury (Gen. 47:14).

When the farmers ran out of money, they brought their livestock in exchange for food. (Some of your students may note that sheep are mentioned among the livestock. Although Egyptians abhorred shepherds, some must have kept sheep.) When they had sold all their animals they started selling their land, fields and orchards. Joseph moved the farmers from their former fields to others areas, thus depriving them of the hope of ever regaining their land. They became serfs to the king—working his land and producing crops for him. They retained only a certain percentage of the crops for themselves. Thus Joseph inaugurated a feudal system in ancient Egypt. Joseph's loyalty obviously was to the king of Egypt, not to the populace. On the other hand, his forethought averted starvation in the land. Obviously Pharaoh was deeply indebted to Joseph. This explains Pharaoh's willingness to provide for Joseph's clan.

You will be able to elicit some of this information from your students.

LESSON 12

Jacob's Blessing
Gen. 47:28–48:21

❏ In Preparation for Teaching

Jacob's life and the spectacular career of Joseph were both drawing to a close. The last chapters of Genesis reflect on the past and look toward the future. These chapters should be read and briefly discussed.

Later in the history of Israel, when the name of each of Jacob's sons would represent a tribe, there would not be a tribe of Joseph. In its place would be two tribes: the tribe of Ephraim and the tribe of Manasseh. Sometimes they are referred to as one, "the House of Joseph" (בֵּית יוֹסֵף; 2 Samuel 19:21). Ephraim would eventually become the leading tribe of the Northern Kingdom, while Manasseh would become a weaker tribe, geographically divided by the Jordan River (half on one side of the Jordan, half on the other).

Try to obtain a reproduction of Rembrandt's famous picture of Jacob blessing Ephraim and Manasseh to use in class.

❏ Teaching Procedure

Jacob realized he was about to die. He summoned his son Joseph and made him take a vow to bury him at Machpelah, not in the land of Egypt. Joseph took the oath. Why was it Joseph that he asked this of? Joseph was the only one who had the power to carry out this faraway burial. Why was this so important to Jacob? What was on his mind? He was probably thinking about his covenant with God and his tie to the land of Canaan. He wanted his remains to be part of the land that his seed would eventually possess.

Have your students read Genesis 48. Joseph, accompanied by his two sons, came to see his old and ailing father. Summoning his strength, Jacob sat up in bed. Perhaps he was remembering the Abrahamic blessing given to him by God in Bethel (Gen. 28:19). The time had come to pass this blessing on to his own family.

Lesson 12: Jacob's Blessing

Jacob recognized that God had always been with him, protecting him and preserving him from disaster. The God of Abraham and Isaac had become also the God of Jacob. Now he asked God to extend this protection to his grandchildren. He also asked that his name and the names of his fathers be recalled in them.

What reason does Jacob give for wanting to adopt his two grandchildren, the sons of Joseph? Perhaps he adopted the sons of Rachel's son simply because he had loved her and felt a special fondness for *her* grandchildren.

This chapter, as others before it, suggests the presence of different versions. The story, as it appears, contains echoes of other tales: Jacob whose eyes were dim with age (like Isaac) had not been aware of the fact that the boys had come with Joseph. He then became aware of their presence and asked for their identity. Joseph brought them closer to Jacob. Manasseh, the older of the two, faced Jacob's right hand and Ephraim faced his left, waiting for Jacob to bless them. Jacob, however, crossed his arms and placed his right hand on Ephraim's head and his left on Manasseh's.

Thinking his father had made a mistake, Joseph tried to move Jacob's right hand to Manasseh's head; but Jacob insisted that though both boys be blessed, Ephraim, the younger son, would be greater than the older one—as indeed his tribe turned out to be. This story recalls the story of Jacob's receiving the blessing meant for the older son, Esau.

Read 48:20. You may want to teach your students the words with which parent begins the blessing of the children on the eve of the Sabbath:

(for boys): יְשִׂימְךָ אֱלֹהִים כְּאֶפְרַיִם וְכִמְנַשֶּׁה

(for girls): יְשִׂימֵךְ אֱלֹהִים כְּשָׂרָה רִבְקָה רָחֵל וְלֵאָה

LESSON 13A

The Heritage of the Twelve Tribes
Genesis 49

☐ **In Preparation for Teaching**

Chapter 49 is a difficult chapter. Some of the blessings allude to subsequent events in the life of the tribes about which we know nothing. It may therefore be easier to concentrate on Joseph and the four oldest sons of Leah: Reuben, Simeon, Levi and Judah.

The symbolic representation or "emblem" for each tribe is derived from this chapter. Show your class pictures of the Chagall windows and study them. Although all the sons were included in the Abrahamic blessing, the fate of all the sons was not to be identical. Reuben lost his birthright. Taking his father's concubine indicated rebellion against his father; this deed was not forgiven. Simeon and Levi were punished for the happenings in Shechem. The Levites were to be divided amongst the other tribes. Simeon later merged with Judah. In the blessings Moses gives shortly before his death (Deuteronomy 33), Simeon is not even mentioned. The blessing of the first born is given to Judah, Leah's fourth son, and to Joseph, son of Rachel (through Ephraim). From Judah, the young lion, descended the Davidic dynasty of kings. Joseph, the wild ass, was promised success in battle, and the fruits of the land and the womb.

LESSON 13B

After Jacob's Death
Genesis 50

☐ In Preparation for Teaching

Jacob (Israel) was now dead. In this chapter we learn that he was mourned and was prepared for burial in the Egyptian manner. You may want to tell your class about Egyptian embalming. If you cannot take your class to a museum to see mummies, bring pictures to class. Look up embalming in the encyclopedia (or let some of your students do so) and give the class a short oral description of the process. Preserving the body after death was of vital importance in ancient Egypt. The Egyptians believed that the body continued a physical life in the world of the dead. The treasures buried with the dead were intended for use in the netherworld. Jews do not embalm their dead. In Jacob's case, however, this might have been necessary, since Jacob was to be buried far away, at Machpelah.

☐ Teaching Procedures

Joseph asked Pharaoh for permission to bury his father in the land of Canaan, as he promised he would do. A large troop accompanied Joseph. Although Jacob had already been mourned in Egypt, he was now mourned again in Canaan, in the Israelite manner, for seven days. Jacob was buried in the cave of Machpelah, which Abraham had bought. In this way, the bond between the people of Israel and the land of Canaan was maintained. Joseph, his brothers and the entire retinue, however, returned to Egypt. The Egyptian phase of the history of the sons of Israel had barely begun.

What were the brothers worried about after Jacob's death? They had never been able to rid themselves of their guilt concerning their brother Joseph. They were afraid that Joseph would take revenge upon them. As long as Jacob was alive they felt safe, for Joseph would not act against them, out of respect for their father. (Similarly, Esau was willing to postpone his revenge against Jacob, out of respect for his father [Gen. 27:41].) Now that Jacob was dead, would Joseph seek revenge?

The brothers sent a message to Joseph saying that Jacob had left instructions asking for Joseph's forgiveness. Did Jacob actually leave such instructions? If so, what would this indicate? It would show that Jacob knew the whole truth, and that he was worried about Joseph's conduct after his death.

What are some other possibilities to explain 50:15–21? The brothers could have invented these instructions themselves. What would that indicate? That the brothers never really believed that Joseph had forgiven them. Did Joseph need such instructions? Your class will probably agree that for Joseph, the matter had been settled when the brothers stood up for Benjamin.

Joseph remained in Egypt and died there at the age of 110 years. Before he closed his eyes, Joseph made his brothers swear to carry his bones back with them to Canaan when God brought them back to the land He had promised to Abraham, Isaac, and Jacob (Exodus 13:19).

That time, however, was a long way off. Many hardships would befall the children of Israel in Egypt before God would bring them back to the land He had promised them.

(For supplementary activities to use in reviewing Joseph's life, see Appendix A, below, pp. 327–329.)

APPENDIX A

Supplemental Classroom Activities

Miriam Brunn Ruberg and Susan Wall

APPENDIX A

Supplemental Classroom Activities

Miriam Brunn Ruberg and Susan Wall

☐ Introduction

The primary learning activity in the Melton Bible materials is inquiry, focusing on discussion, analysis and close reading of the biblical text. However, many teachers also want to use other kinds of classroom activities to enrich discussion and vary the pace of the lesson. To assist in this process of enrichment we have prepared a set of sample activities that the teacher can use at his or her discretion. Some of these activities may, on occasion, replace the discussions suggested in the main body of the *Guide;* more often, activities can be used as a supplement to the inquiry. When choosing whether to use an activity in addition to an inquiry or as a substitute for an inquiry, the teacher must decide how much time he or she has available and to what extent the learning from the activity duplicates the learning from the inquiry.

These activities, when used judiciously, can be appropriate in many different contexts. Below is a list of basic techniques that teachers can use in teaching virtually any text. Following this list is a set of sample supplemental activities keyed to specific lessons in the *Guide*. In addition to enriching their particular lessons, these activities can serve as models for further activities that the teacher may wish to develop.

☐ A Guide to Classroom Techniques

1. Role Playing

Role playing allows students to put themselves in the role of characters so that they can better understand the characters' motivations, actions, and feelings.

Set up chairs (one for each character) facing each other. You might want to put labels or signs on the chairs indicating which character is being represented. Select one student to portray each character, and clarify which part of the text the students are to act out. The role-players should closely reflect the text in their actions, while also speculating about the motives and feelings behind these actions. Guidance can be offered to a student to aid him or her in portraying the character. (See p. 320, below, for a sample of the application of this technique to a specific lesson.)

2. *Diorama*

A diorama is a three-dimensional portrayal of a poem, verse, event, scene, etc., permanently placed in a box or on a piece of wood or cardboard. Students use various supplies and scrap materials for this project. (See p. 317, below, for a sample of the application of this technique to a specific lesson.)

3. *Fishbowl*

In this group activity, students sit in two concentric circles, with both sets of chairs facing inward. The teacher introduces the topic to be discussed. Those in the inner circle speak, while those in the outer circle listen—in order to react later. The roles are then reversed, with those on the outside moving to the inner circle in order to speak, and those in the inner circle moving to the outside to listen. (The teacher may ask the students in the outer circle to take notes on what they observe.) The instructions are identical for each group. The same time period is set aside for each. The teacher should only give the instructions and should try not to become involved in the discussion.

At the very end, an open discussion is held, at which time people share their reactions to what was happening. Note: A fishbowl is most effective when it involves discussing feelings or memories that are personal, as opposed to facts. (See p. 321, below, for a sample of the application of this technique to a specific lesson.)

(Special thanks to Bernard Reisman's useful work, *The Jewish Experiential Book* (Ktav) for his discussion of some of these activities.)

4. *Whip*

A whip is a technique used to elicit short answers from as many students as possible in a short period of time. The teacher starts a sentence and goes around the room asking students to complete the same sentence. Remember: The whip is a type of nonjudgmental brainstorming—*any answer is acceptable*. Do not stop to comment on a child's response. Move quickly around the room. You might want to record the children's answers or have someone jot down some of the ideas. Or you might want to list some on the board after you have gone around the room. You can refer back to them after the text study. (See p. 319, below, for a sample of the application of this technique to a specific lesson.)

5. Four Corners

This group activity forces each participant to express his or her opinion by choosing one of four options. It works best with mature students. An open-ended statement is made. In each of the four corners of the room there is a sign with one possible ending to the open-ended statement. For example:

Statement:	"My favorite day of the year is . . ."
Four signs:	My birthday
	Thanksgiving
	Hanukkah
	The last day of school

Each child goes to the corner with the answer that most closely reflects his or her own response to the statement. Note that the student's specific opinion may not be on one of the signs, but he or she must pick the sign which most closely reflects his or her own feelings.

Once all the students have chosen a corner (this should only take two minutes), they discuss with others in that corner why they selected that corner. One person in each corner volunteers to make a brief presentation to everyone in the class, explaining why the people who chose that corner did so. The teacher may choose to encourage cross-corner discussions and challenges. Students may be allowed to rethink their decision and move to a different corner. A culminating discussion should follow. (See p. 322, below, for a sample of the application of this technique to a specific lesson.)

6. Adapted TV Game Shows

In the sample exercise below on p. 323, we use the "Jeopardy" format but other popular TV games, such as Concentration, Tic Tac Toe and College Bowl can be adapted to review factual material. Sports games, such as baseball, football, and basketball can also be used. Make up a list of questions based on the facts you want to review. Then draw a diagram of the game board or playing field for the game or sport you have chosen. Adapt the rules of that game or sport to give points for correct answers. For example, in baseball, an easy question might be worth a single, while a more difficult one might be worth a home run. Instead of playing the game on the chalkboard, locations in the classroom might be designated as bases so that students would walk from base to base as they answer correctly.

If you would like to make a permanent game board for Concentration or Tic Tac Toe, try to obtain library card pockets, which could be glued onto a large piece of oak tag. They hold 3 x 5 cards on which questions can be written.

Many other games can be found in a useful book entitled *A Jewish Tapestry*, published by the Dolores Kohl Educational Foundation, 161 Green Bay Road, Wilmette, Illinois 60091.

7. Puppet Show

Puppets can be put to many uses. They can be used to review the text itself. They can be used creatively in an original presentation (for example, with an original midrash) or to express a character's feelings (such as those of Abraham in the Binding of Isaac). This activity lends itself well to small groups and does not require a lot of teacher supervision. Let the students use their imaginations.

Professionally made puppets and a theater are not necessary, but could be used. Finger and hand puppets can be made out of old socks and stockings, paper bags, etc. See *Jewish Holiday Crafts* by Joyce Becker (New York: Bonim Books, 1977). See also the activity described immediately following, which as a variation could be done in conjunction with puppets.

8. Radio Show Interview

Audio tapes offer various opportunities for creative projects. One such project is a radio show interview. Students can interview famous biblical personalities or others who supposedly knew them. The students can write their own script and present a show in class reviewing a certain story. Examples are "On the Scene With Noah," and "An On the Scene Report of the Destruction of Sodom and Gemorrah."

Audio tapes can also be used in conjunction with other activities. Students themselves will often suggest their own creative ideas. Some suggestions include taping music or sound effects for a play or puppet show.

9. Collage

A collage is a visual representation of a story or scene using a variety of pictures or other materials mounted on a piece of burlap, oak tag, or other board. In addition to drawing, students can use magazine pictures, as well as three-dimensional objects or materials (macaroni, cotton, bark, etc.). The elements of the collage need not be placed in any order and can even be placed overlapping each other in various directions.

The finished collage makes an attractive bulletin board. Some suggested themes are "The Flood," "Creation," "The World before Creation Garden of Eden," "Joseph's Dreams," and "Pharaoh's Dreams."

10. Creative Dramatics

In this technique of dramatic presentation, no script is used because the story is known. This activity can be used as a review of factual material or as a creative medium to allow students to interpret a story.

Creative dramatics can be applied to the Genesis material in at least two ways. One way is to dramatize the story *before* the students study the material together in class. They would read the passages on their own and then act them out, sticking closely to the text. The teacher could then "freeze the action" wherever an inquiry is needed. For example, on pp. 288–289 above, an inquiry is suggested regarding Joseph's motive for wanting Benjamin brought to Egypt. When the students reach that part of the story in their dramatic presentation, the teacher stops the action and asks the questions suggested in the *Teacher's Guide* lesson material.

A second way to use creative dramatics is as a review of material that has already been completed. To give some structure to the activity, the teacher may want to serve as the narrator. The students should make up the parts, based on their knowledge of the text and what they have learned from their studies. The teacher should word the narration so that it is very clear who is to speak next and what they are to say. For example, the teacher (narrator) might say: "Jacob called his sons to him to send them to Egypt for food a second time. Judah, remembering what Joseph said about bringing Benjamin, said to his father: . . ." The student playing the role of Judah then would continue the drama.

You might want to have the students dress up or use props. These could be available on a table to be used as the children see fit. The presentation might be done within the class, or it could be done for another class. It is not meant to be a polished performance—the "script" is composed as is it being performed. Encourage the students to imagine themselves as the character they are portraying, using facial and vocal expressions, body movement, etc.

❒ Sample Lessons Using Supplemental Activities

A. Creation of a Moving Picture Show

This project provides students with the opportunity to review the day-by-day sequence of creation. Students can work in small groups, in pairs, or as individuals. If a class is working in small groups, each group could be assigned to work on a separate day of creation.

Fairly durable paper (e.g., construction paper, large brown mural rolls of paper) should be used. Students work on the paper, holding it horizontally. Using paints, magic markers, or crayons, students depict their assigned day of creation. To depict a day on which several things were created, such as the third and sixth days, students might draw several different panels.

Individual sheets should later be attached to each other with tape on the back, or colored bookbinding tape on the front, which gives a frame-like affect. After the sheets have been attached in one roll, the roll is fastened at both ends to dowel sticks, empty paper towel rolls, or poster canisters (depending on the size of the paper) with a good glue, reinforced with tape. The result is a moving picture creation story.

Introductory and concluding panels should be attached telling what the show is about and who made it. An audio cassette utilizing the biblical text could be made to accompany the pictures.

A further enhancement would make use of a box slightly taller than the paper. Make holes in the box so that the sticks fit through them. As the sticks are turned, the story is revealed, one panel at a time (see illustration).

Supplemental Classroom Activities 315

B. Nature Walk

This activity should be done *before* students begin their study of the texts describing the creation of the world and all aspects of nature. Before they begin, they have an opportunity to focus on the world and its beauty. People rarely take the time to enjoy and look at nature and see each aspect as part of an orderly and continuous system.

Students should take paper and a pencil (and crayons, if you would like them to draw as well) and go as a class to a pretty wooded area. Before going, have students choose (or assign each student) one specific thing in nature. Here is a list of suggestions (be sure to assign only those things that will actually be found by the students in your locale):

grass	berries or fruit
flowers	brook or stream
roots of a tree	soil
leaves	the wind
bark of a tree	rock or stone
a tree	weeds
petals of a flower	shrubs, vines, little plants
an animal	worms
a bird	ants or other crawling creatures
the sky	bees
the sun	clouds

Explain to the class what you will be doing: "Class, today we will be going to a wooded area as part of our introduction to the study of creation. I want you to carefully observe and concentrate on your assigned item. I am handing out a sheet with some guidelines for what to look for. Use it as a guide, but please spend most of your time looking at your object and making your own observations."

On the following page is a sample guide sheet that could be distributed to the students. The teacher should review the guide sheet with the students, making sure they understand what it asks them to do.

Nature Walk—Students' Guide Sheet

Item to Observe: _____

Not *all* of these questions will apply to your assignment. Choose those that do and add your own ideas as well. Examine (look at, smell, feel, listen to, etc.) your assigned item carefully. Then respond to many of the following as apply. BE SPECIFIC!

1. What color is it? What effect does that color have? _____
   _____

2. Describe its smell. _____
   _____

3. Describe the way it feels. _____
   _____

4. What system is it part of (plant world, animal world, solar system)? _____

5. What *specific* other things (e.g., food, sun, rain, shelter) does it need to survive? _____
   _____

6. How is your item beneficial or important (e.g., it is useful, it is beautiful)? _____
   _____
   _____

7. Does it always look like this, or does it change (e.g., a caterpillar changes into a butterfly)? If so, how and when? _____
   _____
   _____

8. Other observations: _____
   _____
   _____

9. If you would like to, draw a picture of your object on a separate sheet.

C. Noah Builds the Ark

This activity should help students visualize the ark that Noah built by having them build or draw a model of it. The students will see that what Noah was told to build was a box with no means of steering or propelling itself.

This activity may be done at home or in class. *Keep in mind the amount of time you wish to spend on this!* If you opt for building a model in class, be aware that it will take several class periods. Drawing or making a model as a home assignment is less time-consuming.

If working in class, the teacher might want students to work individually or in small groups. Decide whether you want the students to simply draw a model of the ark, or actually build it (using wood, cardboard, clay, etc.). If building in class, make sure you have all the necessary tools and materials, as well as adequate adult supervision for any carpentry.

Give students the following instructions: "Read Gen. 6:14–16. Draw (or build) a scale model of the ark, sticking as closely to the biblical instructions as is possible."

Follow up with questions (possibly written on a worksheet) such as:

1. What does the ark look like to you? What does it remind you of?
2. What is missing that is usually found on a boat?
3. Would you be willing to sail off in this type of vessel?

After completing the activity, refer utilize the *Teacher's Guide* material, emphasizing how much Noah put his trust and faith in God.

D. Diorama: Garden of Eden (see above, p. 310)

This project can be used successfully by all teachers—those who enjoy art projects and also those who tend to shy away from them. This project allows students to use their imaginations in visualizing various Bible stories. It also encourages them to read the text carefully for detail. Other stories for which this activity might work well are:

The Binding of Isaac
Joseph and his dreams
Joseph with his brothers in Egypt
Joseph in prison

Have students bring in a shoebox (or another box with a similar shape). During the class period immediately preceding the project explain what will be done. "Today each of you will choose a verse or part of the story that we have been studying. I will ask you to write the verse down. Between today and our next session think of how you will depict your scene. We will have all kinds of materials available, such as clay, pipe cleaners, fabric, cotton, etc."

On the day of the project, set up the room *before* the students arrive. Place all supplies on a centrally located table or front desk. Cover the students' work areas with newspaper. Students should each have a pencil, scissors and glue. Make sure you have extra shoeboxes.

Students should be encouraged to be as independent and creative as possible. The project should take two one-hour class periods *at the most*. Students can work alone, in pairs or in small groups. (The activity is also well suited as an extended homework assignment or an extra credit project.)

Once the project is completed, students can try to guess what verses their fellow students chose, by looking at the dioramas. This could be done in the form of a game. For example, you could divide the class into teams and have them write down the verses they think the other dioramas portray. The finished dioramas should also be displayed in the classroom or in a hallway showcase. Displaying them at a P.T.A. meeting would also provide an opportunity for parents to see their children's' work.

Suggested Supplies

    clay for people and buildings
    wood and twigs for trees and plants
    construction paper for people, scenery
    cotton for clouds
    yarn or hair to connect things
    buttons, beans, and macaroni as small props
    shells and stones as small props and ground
    pipe cleaners for people, animals
    cardboard for buildings
    swatches of material, rug scraps, and gift wrap paper
        for clothes and scenery
    felt-tipped markers
    paint
    crayons
    scissors
    paste or glue

E. *Whip on Hakhnasat Orḥim* (see above, p. 310)

This activity is to be used as a short (five- to ten-minute) introduction to Gen. 18:1–8 (pp. 172–173). Its purpose is to help students to better understand the mitzvah of *hakhnasat orḥim* (extending hospitality to guests). This exercise, like the *Teacher's Guide* material, is designed to help the students to better understand the lengths to which Abraham went to welcome his guests.

The lesson might go as follows:

"To start our lesson today, we are going to use a technique called a "whip." I am going to start a sentence which I would like each of you to complete. Please be sure that your answer is no longer than five or six words. If your answer are too long, it can ruin the effectiveness of the whip. Let's try one as an example."

"My favorite day of the year is _____ because _____." (Go around the room and have some students fill in the sentence.)

"That should give you some idea of how it works. As we do the next ones, please give the best answer you can think of as quickly as possible. We will go around in order. If your answer is the same as someone else's you may repeat it, but try to think of your own. Or, if you really cannot think of any answer, you may pass. Let's begin."

"If I wanted to make a stranger feel comfortable in my home, I would _____." (Go around the room, getting the students to respond. Repeat the first part of the statement periodically, as you feel it necessary.)

"Now that we've dealt with this idea a bit, let's take it a little further. If I wanted to *really* extend myself for a favorite guest, I would _____." Now, teach the textual lesson on hospitality, above, pp. 172–173. After studying the text, compare the students' comments to Abraham's actions, enumerated above, p. 173.

Other Applications for the Whip

Whips may be used whenever a teacher wants to get quick responses from many students. They are also good for helping students try to put themselves into the role of a particular character, for example:

Character	"Whip Statement" to Complete
Abraham:	When God told me to leave I felt _____.
	I went because _____.
Isaac:	When my father placed me on the altar I _____.
Rebecca:	When I realized that in order to marry Isaac I would have to leave my family, I _____.

Jacob:	I tricked my father Isaac to get his blessing because _____. I felt _____.
Simeon:	When Joseph was "lording it" over us, I _____.

Note: Whips need not always be oral. In some cases you might want to hand out a ditto with several whip questions. Ask students to quickly complete them and then use them as a basis for a discussion.

F. Role Playing: *Abraham, Sarah and Hagar* (see above, p. 309)

This activity ties into the *Teacher's Guide* material found on pp. 182–184 and also refers back to pp. 165–166. Review with your students the content of Genesis 16 and 21, to make sure they understand the text. Select three students who are willing to play the roles of Abraham, Sarah and Hagar. Explain that they will have to speak to each other while the rest of the class listens. Have them sit in the designated seat, and hand each one a card or a slip of paper with information that will help them to act out their character. Here are some examples:

Abraham
Text. Sarah has finally given you a son. She has asked that you expel Hagar and Ishmael. You are distressed. God has reassured you that it will be okay.
Role-Playing. You have to face Hagar and explain your difficult decision to send her and Ishmael away.

Hagar
Text. Abraham has given you some bread and water and has told you that you must leave.
Role-Playing. You're hurt, angry and upset. You start the action by confronting Sarah and Abraham with the events of Genesis 16 and with how you are feeling and why.

Sarah
Text. You have demanded quite firmly that Abraham send Hagar and Ishmael away. You still remember the way she acted after she bore a son for Abraham when you could not.
Role-Playing. You must face Hagar as she challenges the justice of the decision to send her and Ishmael away.

Remind students that they are to speak in the first person. For example, Abraham might say: "I feel badly that I have to send you away, Hagar, but. . . ."

After role-playing, the teacher might want to ask some questions to wrap up the activity, such as:

Do you see any of the characters differently now? If so, how?

Do you have a better understanding now of what might have happened? If so, in what way?

Other Options

1. Allow students in the "audience" to ask the characters questions after they have done some role-playing. For example, "Abraham, weren't you still upset even after God reassured you?"
2. Allow one student to represent all three characters by moving from chair to chair. This makes the differences very dramatic.
3. Stop the action in the middle and have your three actors trade roles with each other.
4. The teacher might want to involve more students. Stop the action and have other students take the roles.

A similar activity, with Isaac, Rebekah, Esau and Jacob, is recommended above, pp. 224–225, in a lesson dealing with the stealing of the blessing.

G. *Fishbowl: The Reunion of Jacob and Esau* (see above, p. 310)

This activity is to be done before the students read the story of the reunion of Jacob and Esau (above, pp. 245–246 and 250–252). The objective is to help students identify with Jacob's feelings in confronting his brother Esau, by getting the children to recall a conflict situation which they have faced in their lifetime. By sharing these situations with their classmates, the students may begin to understand the build-up of emotions involved in the brothers' meeting.

Before the students arrive, set up chairs in two concentric circles, with both sets of chairs facing inward. As students enter the classroom, instruct them to sit wherever they wish (unless you have a reason for designating seats). The teacher then goes on to explain: "Today I am going to ask you to think back to certain situations in your life which may help us to better understand Jacob's actions in the next section we will study. Those of you who are sitting in the inside circle will have ten minutes to tell each other (one at a time) about an event in your life which you dreaded or did not look forward to and how you dealt with it. We are very interested in hearing about the kinds of feelings you had in anticipation of the event. It could be the visit of an unfavorite relative, being invited somewhere and not wanting to go, having lost something, or having done something wrong and knowing you will have to face the consequences, etc."

Give them a minute or two to think, and then ask, "Would anyone like to start?"

During this time, those in the outside circle will listen carefully, possibly taking notes. (The teacher should only intervene to help keep the discussion from wandering needlessly.) The teacher should warn the group in the inner circle when their time is almost up.

The students in the two circles exchange, and the activity is repeated.

When the time is up for the second group, discussion should follow. Have those who were in the first outer circle give their reactions and comments about what was said. (You might also decide to allow the inner circle to respond.) Repeat the same procedure with the second outer circle.

The teacher should then make the bridge to the Jacob–Esau reunion as follows: "We are about to begin to study the reunion of Jacob and Esau. Remembering how their relationship was when they parted, we could expect a difficult meeting. As we read the text, I want you to keep in mind the activity we just did and *your* feelings about facing a difficult situation. When we have completed studying the text, we will discuss and compare what the brothers experienced with your own experiences."

H. Four Corners: Favoritism in the Joseph Story (see above, p. 311)

This activity can be done after teaching the lesson on pp. 269–270, above. It can also be done with the Jacob and Esau story, pp. 218–227.

One of the motifs of the Joseph story is favoritism of a parent toward a particular child. The object of this activity is to help students better understand the interactions of Joseph, his father, and his brothers, by gaining greater insight into the effects of favoritism in a family.

The teacher introduces the activity to the class: "Students, today we are going to do a special activity. It is called "four corners." It may seem to be only a game, but it is meant to be taken seriously, as we will be using the results in our text study. I am going to start a sentence, but I will not end it. In each of the four corners I will place a possible ending to my sentence. You will go to the corner which completes the sentence in the way you most agree with. It is possible that no corner will reflect exactly what you're thinking, but choose the one that comes the closest. Please be honest in choosing a corner. Do not be influenced by what your friends decide."

Supplemental Classroom Activities

At this point, the teacher may want to give an example of "four corners," such as the one mentioned above, p. 311, so that the students will have a better understanding of how the activity works.

Once the class is ready the teacher recites the following phrase, and uncovers the choices in the four corners.

"In my family, when only I (and not my brothers and sisters get a special privilege from my parents, I feel...." (Children who do not have siblings should replace "brothers and sisters" in this sentence with "friends" or "cousins.")

Follow the steps outlined above, p. 311, in proceeding with the activity. Limit the time to 10–15 minutes. Do not have the culminating discussion; rather, continue with a second "four corners," using the following statement:

"When my brother or sister gets special privileges, I feel...."

Follow the same procedure as for the first exercise, limiting their time to 10–15 minutes. At the end of this time period, have students return to their seats. Draw out any insights the students have gained, summarizing the main points that were made.

I. *Jeopardy Game: The Life of Jacob* (see above, p. 311)

The purpose of this activity is to review the events in the life of Jacob. (By changing the questions, it can be used to review any unit or body of material.) This particular game can be used after completing Genesis 35 and the material up to p. 261, above.

This activity is a modified version of a TV game called "Jeopardy," with which children might already be familiar. However, rather than giving answers in the form of questions, our game simply involves giving answers to questions. We made this change based on our experience that students find it difficult to give answers in the form of questions.

Basically, the children will be answering questions that have been placed in one of several categories. The teacher may have as many categories as he or she wishes, but it is preferable to have at least four. Catchy titles for the categories should be chosen if possible. Each category contains several questions, all dealing with the same theme, arranged in order of difficulty, with corresponding point values (from 10 to 40, or whatever the teacher wishes). Each category should have the same number of questions.

To play the game, divide the class into three or four teams. Allow one child to choose the first category. The teacher reads the question, and the first child to raise his/her hand gets a chance to answer. If the answer is correct, that child chooses the next question. If incorrect, the last person who gave a correct answer chooses the next question. Children may go from category to category, but must go in numerical order. That is, a 40-point question cannot be asked before 10-, 20-, and 30-point questions have been asked.

The game ends at the end of a designated amount of time, or when all the questions have been asked. The team with the highest score wins.

A sample Jeopardy game featuring the life of Jacob is found on the facing page.

The Board

There are several ways to set up the board. The easiest way is for the teacher to list the names of the categories on the board with numbers under them, like this:

Run for Your Life	Sister Troubles
10	10
20	20
30	30
40	40

When a category and a point value selected, the teacher reads the corresponding question from his or her own sheet and erases that number from the board.

A fancier technique would be to write each question on a piece of construction paper, using the same color for all questions in one category. On the back of each piece of paper write the point value for that question. Tape the papers to the board so that only the point value side shows. When a student selects a question, turn it around and tape it to the board so the question shows.

Supplemental Classroom Activities 325

Sample Game of Jeopardy:
The Life of Jacob

	Which Twin Will Win?	The Great Deception	Run for Your Life	A Match Made in Heaven	Fathers-In-Law	Sister Troubles
10	What was Jacob holding onto when he was born?	Who persuaded Jacob to deceive Isaac?	Why did Jacob run away from home?	What did Jacob see in his dream?	What was Jacob's original deal with Laban?	Who was older, Rachel or Leah?
20	Who was "the man of the field"?	Where was Esau when Isaac was blessing Jacob?	Where was the home that Jacob ran away from?	What did Jacob do with the stone he laid his head on?	What excuse did Laban give for tricking Jacob by giving him Leah?	What did God do for Leah because she was "hated"?
30	Explain this quote: "The older will serve the younger."	What did Rebekah put on Jacob's arms and on the back of his neck?	Where did Jacob go?	What did God promise Jacob?	What did Rachel do upon leaving Haran that brought about a confrontation between Jacob and Laban?	Who was Rachel's firstborn?
40	What explanations are given for Jacob's Hebrew name?	What did Isaac say that indicated he wasn't sure it was Esau?	What was Isaac told was the reason that Jacob left home?	What did Jacob call the place where he had the dream?	What division of property did Laban and Jacob finally make?	How many children did Leah have, and who was her firstborn?

A more permanent Jeopardy board could be made in the following way. Take a large piece of poster board. Leave about 4 inches at the top. Take library card pockets and paste them onto the board, one under another in 4 or 5 columns. Label the pockets in each column from 10 to 40. Your questions can then go on 3 x 5 cards which fit into the pockets. Category names can be fastened to the top of the poster board with paper clips. To use the board for different games, simply change the questions and the category names.

Another Option

Use the same questions for a "college bowl." Divide the class into teams. Ask the easier questions for "toss-ups" (the first person to raise a hand gets to answer). If the student answers correctly, the team gets to work together to answer a "bonus question" (a more difficult question from the same category). Point values are assigned to toss-up questions and to bonus questions.

J. Crossword Puzzle: The Life of Joseph

Across

1. Because Joseph refused the advances of his master's wife, she had him "framed" and put in _____.
3. When Joseph brought Jacob and the rest of his family to Egypt, they settled in _____.
5. Jacob showed his special love for Joseph by giving him a multi-colored _____.
8. Joseph's only "full" brother (born of his same mother and father) was _____.
10. Joseph's second-born son was named _____.
11. Joseph's brothers sold him to a caravan of Ishmaelites headed for _____.
13. Joseph's firstborn son was named _____.
15. Pharaoh asked Joseph to explain his dream in which he saw _____ healthy cows and _____ ugly, sickly cows.
16. As a youth, Joseph dreamed a dream in which he and his brothers were binding sheaves. His brothers' sheaves _____ down to his.
18. Benjamin was Joseph's _____ brother.
19. Joseph's brothers dipped his coat in the _____ of a goat and then brought it to their father Jacob.

Down

1. Joseph explained to Pharaoh that the healthy cows in his dream represented years of _____.
2. The Ishmaelites sold Joseph to an Egyptian official named _____.
4. In Joseph's second dream as a youth, the moon, the sun and eleven _____ bowed down to him.
5. When Jacob saw Joseph's coat, he assumed that Joseph was dead. He mourned for him and refused to be _____.
6. _____ convinced his brothers not to kill Joseph, but rather to put him in a pit (planning to later come back and rescue him).
7. In jail, Joseph acquired a special reputation for his skill in _____ dreams.
9. The ugly, sickly cows represented years of _____.
12. Joseph's "cellmates" were the king's butler and _____.
14. Judah suggested to his brothers that they take Joseph out of the pit and _____ him to a caravan of Ishmaelites.
16. Jacob made Joseph promise not to _____ him in Egypt.
17. Jacob loved Joseph more because he was the son of his _____ age.

Crossword Puzzle:
The Life of Joseph

Solution to Crossword Puzzle

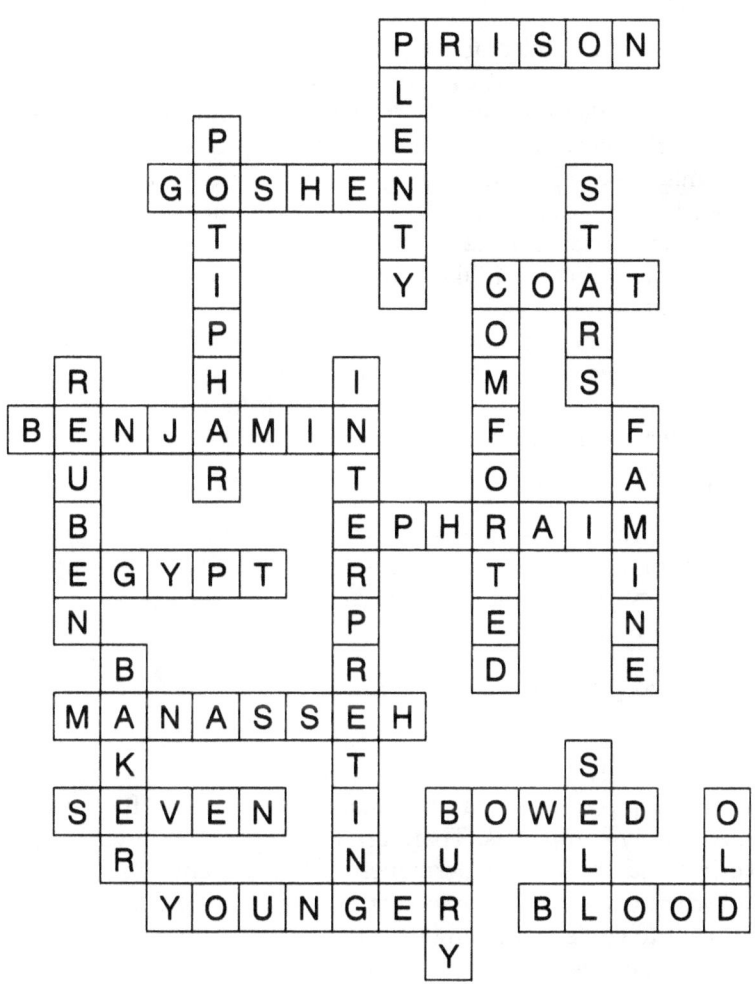

☐ Using the Overhead Projector

We use the creation story here as one example of how the teacher might use an overhead projector.

Ways to Use the Overhead Projector

The overhead projector can provide a visual means of teaching or reviewing material. It can be used in many different ways for Bible studies. Pictures can be drawn on the transparencies (the clear plastic sheets that are used with the projector). This technique might be especially appropriate for the creation story (see below), Joseph's dreams, portrayal of life in ancient Canaan, etc. (Some commercial transparencies covering this period in history are available from the Millikin Company.)

In addition, any material that you might put on a worksheet or on the board, can be put on a transparency. One advantage of the overhead projector is that, unlike material written on the board, the transparencies can be stored and reused. Another advantage is that the teacher is able to face the students while pointing to the appropriate material on the transparency, something very awkward to do when using the board. A third advantage of the overhead projector is that it allows you to build upon or take away from any visual image by using overlays—placing one transparency on top of another (see the project below for an example of this).

How to Make a Transparency

The most common way to prepare a transparency is to draw or write directly on the clear plastic sheet. There are special pens for this purpose, which can be obtained from most office supply or art supply companies. There are two types, those with washable ink and those with permanent ink. Washable ink pens are used when you do not care to keep what you have done, or when you want to circle something on a permanent copy to point it out to the students but you need to erase it afterwards. For the project mentioned below, you should use permanent markers.

Try ordering just a few pens until you get the type you really want (there are fine tips, regular tips, etc.). There are also cardboard frames that can be placed around the transparency for storage and protection. These can be purchased where you buy the pens and transparencies.

Transparencies can also be made on most photocopy machines. Any material that can be photocopied on paper can also be photocopied directly onto a transparency. Note: Special transparencies that can be used in a photocopier must be obtained. Using the regular transparencies used for writing and drawing in a photocopier will severely damage the photocopier.

The Project

The purpose of this project is to enable students to learn what was created on each of the days. The finished project can be kept and reused by the teacher as a teaching tool in a follow-up lesson or with another class to provide a visual backdrop for teaching the days of creation. This project could be done by the whole class or by a small group for extra credit (or even by the teacher alone). If it is to be done in the classroom, set aside about two one-hour class sessions.

Explain to the children that they will be making six different transparencies, each portraying what was created on one of the days of creation. You might want to have them work in small groups, deciding what will go into their picture. The class as a whole should go over these plans to check the accuracy of what is in each (e.g., that the sun is included in Day 4, not Day 3). After this, each group may begin its work.

The children can draw their own pictures freehand. Or they can look through magazines for pictures of what they want to include, cut out the picture, place it under the transparency and trace it.

You might want to have the children use a single color for all the things created on a particular day. For example, the sun, moon and stars would all be yellow, while the fish and birds would be brown.

The final goal is to use all the transparencies laid one on top of the other in order to show the total picture of creation. Ideally, the students should collaborate so that when the transparencies are placed on top of each other, each drawing occupies a different spot. This can be accomplished in two different ways:

1. Simply assign one-sixth of the paper to each group so that no two groups can draw on the same area.

2. Use a piece of paper the size of your finished transparency to make a composite sheet. Have one representative from each group fill in their group's design, being careful not to draw over anyone else's. When the picture is complete, it should look like the world at the end of creation. Make a photocopy of the composite for each group. Each group then clips a transparency on top of the

composite sheet and draws their artwork on the transparency, using the composite as a guide for size and spacing.

The following examples may be helpful:

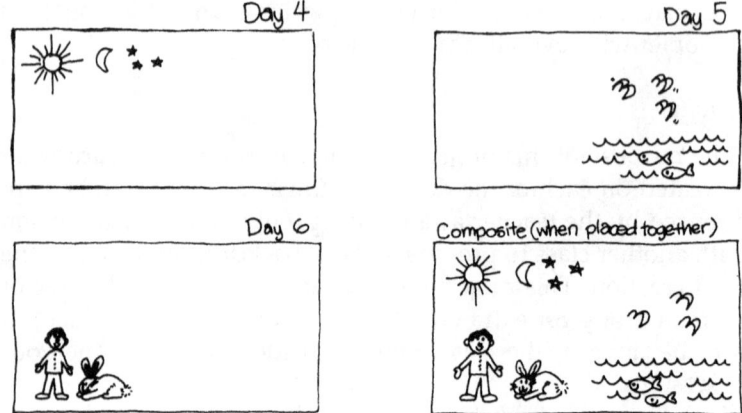

Note: Without careful planning, Day 1 and Day 2 are difficult to work into a composite. Also, in assigning work to various groups, be aware that Day 1 and Day 2 may take a much less time to illustrate than other days. Perhaps one group should be assigned both of those days.

APPENDIX B

Truth and Metaphor in the Bible: An Essay on Interpretation

Fritz A. Rothschild

APPENDIX B

Truth and Metaphor in the Bible: An Essay on Interpretation

Fritz A. Rothschild

> What good is a program of religious instruction in which the teacher does not believe in what he teaches and in which the student is not supposed to believe in what he is taught—a program which only passes in silence over that which should be articulately fought? I must admit that at times I totally despair of this situation. . . .

These words, although written in 1840 by Abraham Geiger in a letter to his friend Joseph Dernburg, sound contemporary and relevant to every Jewish educator who has tackled the task of teaching the Bible. The modern teacher is confronted with the double task of conveying to his students the literal, plain meaning of the *Ḥumash* and at the same time transmitting a religious faith and outlook which is not only grounded in the ancient Torah text, but is also intellectually respectable and in agreement with the results of our scientific and moral outlook. All too often the tension between these seemingly conflicting requirements causes the teacher to abandon either the faithful rendition of the "traditional" sacred message or the use of the Bible as an instrument for the building of a viable and coherent world-view.

It is understandable, if not excusable, that some teachers solve this problem by selecting only those stories which agree with modern views. The result is a bowdlerized version of Genesis in which the chapters on Creation, the Garden of Eden, the Flood, etc., have been omitted because they clash with modern knowledge. Other teachers cling to what they believe to be the sense authorized by tradition, without introducing the "subversive" material of modern biblical scholarship.

Ironically, however, both the "modernists" and the "traditionalists" share three assumptions: (1) There is only one meaning of the text that has been authorized by tradition; that meaning was taught in our religious schools until the onset of modern scholarship and secular culture. (2) Attempts to study the Bible in the light of contemporary science and philosophy must lead to a break with the traditional understanding of the text. (3) The present-day confrontation of the tradition and modern scholarship constitutes a new and radical crisis for the contemporary Jew, and presents us with an unprecedented problem in our educational enterprise.

Accepting these common assumptions, modernists and traditionalists draw opposite and often unhappy conclusions. The modernists often feel guilty of having betrayed the age-old legacy of ancestral faith; and the traditionalists realize that the challenges of biblical criticism, science, and philosophy cannot really be met by passing them over in silence. Many a loyal traditionalist must have felt like the two old Victorian ladies who, when first learning of Darwin's theory of evolution, said: "Let's hope it's not true, and if it is, let's hush it up!"

Now it cannot be denied that the modern scientific revolution has created tremendous problems for Jewish religion in general and for the teaching of the Bible in particular. Historical scholarship, the study of comparative religion, the documentary theory of the Pentateuch—whether in Wellhausen's or Yehezkel Kaufmann's version—all these and the implications of modern science present formidable challenges to traditional formulations of Judaism. But it would be wrong to accept without *questioning* the assumptions which we mentioned earlier. We shall try to show in this paper that the idea of a single timelessly valid and authoritative sense of Scripture is a figment of the imagination.

The reasons why such a single meaning cannot exist are both sociological and theological. Sociologically, the meaning of any document depends to some extent on the cultural resources, the linguistic skills, and the particular interests of the reader.[1] The theological assumption that faith in the divine nature of the Torah necessitates a monolithic and unchangeable interpretation of it is a mistaken notion, as is reflected in the history of Jewish Bible interpretation. On the contrary, the view that the Bible contains God's message to man has led to ever new interpretations, since it constantly forced believing readers to reconcile the words of the sacred text with whatever they held to be true on the basis of their own experience, the canons of logic, contemporary science, and their moral insights.

Certainly, the non-believer is under no compulsion to reject older interpretations of the text which contradict the truth of his time and thus denigrate the value of the Bible; while the traditionalist will always feel called upon to interpret the text so that it reflects not ancient error but the highest standards of trustworthy knowledge and insight of his own time. If one believes that the Torah contains eternal truth and valid guidance, it follows that its teachings should be explained and applied to changing situations. Indeed, this is a pre-condition for the sort of appreciation of the Bible that alone can command the loyalty and trust of intelligent people. To freeze a particular understanding of the text and canonize it as the only legitimate one makes its message irrelevant and defeats its very purpose.

Since the traditional study of the Bible adapts itself to changes and advances in knowledge (contrary to the first assumption above), it follows that the study of the Bible in the light of contemporary knowledge, far from leading to a "break with tradition" (the second assumption) is in fact a continuation of traditional practice. Thus the third assumption, that the present-day confrontation of traditional piety and modern scholarship has no parallel in our history, also breaks down. Without denying that the present crisis is more radical and in some ways unique, we ought to realize that basically we face the type of challenge which has confronted our sages and thinkers in every epoch of Judaism.

◻ A Historical Survey

Far from being guilty of having betrayed our heritage, the teacher who expounds the Bible in the light of the best available knowledge stands within the authentic tradition of our faith.

Philo of Alexandria (20 B.C.E.–45 C.E.) was committed to the belief that the highest philosophical knowledge, theology and ethics, or, as he calls them, "the worship of God" and "the regulation of human life," are to be found in the Torah of Moses. Although he emphasized the superiority of Scripture revealed by God over philosophy which represents the imperfect gropings of the human mind, he demanded that we never interpret the Bible in a manner contrary to reason or expectation (common-sense), or unworthy of the dignity of God's inspired words. His opinion on what is worthy of God's dignity reflects the intellectual ideals he had imbibed from the great philosophical schools of Greece. He distinguished the *literal* or *obvious* meaning of a text from the *underlying* or *allegorical* meaning which explains a text in terms of something else. In the case of Philo this something else is his understanding of an inner, deeper, more spiritual meaning and his denial of anthropomorphism. The words "God is not a man" (Num. 23:19) is understood by Philo as enunciating the principle of denying physical attributes to the Deity. While believing that the laws of the Torah are to be observed literally, Philo seems to vary in his opinion on the historical narratives of the Pentateuch, sometimes accepting both the literal and the allegorical meaning, and sometimes denying the literal sense of a passage in favor of an intellectually or morally instructive interpretation.

Although Philo did not have any traceable, direct influence on Jewish exegesis, his indirect effect was immense. The Christian Church Fathers took over his allegorical method, and from them Islamic thinkers borrowed it and thus transmitted it to the great medieval Jewish philosophers. His distinction between the literal and the underlying sense of the Torah, and his conviction that Holy Scripture yields the most profound spiritual and moral truths to the enlightened interpreter, have been influential even where the particular results of allegorical exegesis were rejected by later generations.

Rabbinic literature dealt with the problems not only of scriptural passages which taken at face value were unworthy of the dignity of God, but of statements which seemingly contradicted the moral standards the Rabbis had learned from the Bible, and of others which denigrated the honor and worth of the Jewish people and its heroes.

The statement in the fifth commandment that God "rested on the seventh day" clearly did not seem to agree with the idea of Divine omnipotence and led to the rhetorical question of the *Mekhilta:* "And is He subject to such thing as weariness?" The solution which is offered proves, by the use of other biblical quotations, that the *peshat* (plain or literal meaning) must be abandoned. We quote it in full to show how the Sages justified their changed interpretation of the text:

> Has it not been said: "The Creator of the ends of the earth fainteth not, neither is weary" (Is. 40:28)? And it says: "He gives power to the faint" (ibid. vs. 29). And it also says: "By the word of the Lord were the heavens made," etc. (Ps. 33:6). How then can Scripture say: "And rested on the seventh day?" It is simply this: God let it be written about Him that He created His world in six days and rested, as it were, on the seventh. Now by the method of *qal va-ḥomer* you must reason: If He, for whom there is no weariness, let it be written that He created His world in six days and rested on the seventh, how much more should man, of whom it is written: "but man is born to toil" (Job 5:7), rest on the seventh day.[2]

Changed ideas about the religious factor in social and family behavior also led to significant re-interpretations by the aggadists. Ruth, the Moabites says to her mother-in-law: "Entreat me not to leave you and to return from following you; for where you go I will go, and where you lodge, I will lodge; your people shall be my people, and your God my God . . ." (Ruth 1:16). The text says nothing about Ruth having made her decision on religious grounds; on the contrary, her resolve not to abandon Naomi and to stick with her through thick and thin is the guiding motive which (since ethnic loyalty could not be separated from religious loyalty) makes her accept even Naomi's God. Now, to the rabbis who saw in Ruth the exemplar of the true proselyte, it was inconceivable that her conversation was merely the by-product of her loyalty to her mother-in-law. Hence they had to re-interpret the passasge in the light of their convictions:

> "Entreat me not to leave you" . . . In any case, I had made up my mind to convert to Judaism, and it is best to do so through you and not someone else! When Naomi heard this she began to expound (to Ruth) the laws concerning converts . . .[3]

The popularity and near-canonizaiton of Rashi's commentary on the Torah by generations of Jews can largely be attributed to the fact that he combined a genius for explaining the text according to the *peshat*, with a sensitivity for those passages where the plain meaning led to the kinds of difficulties which we have mentioned. Whenever that happened, he fell back on the fund of "revisionist" aggadic interpretations, of which we have offered some instances, and incorporated them in his work. Thus Rashi supplied what seemed to many readers "the" correct and authoritative interpretation of the Torah. It also explains why his particular reading of the text—reflecting as it does the needs of a particular phase in history—cannot possibly be accepted as the only authentic interpretation in perpetuity.

Saadya Gaon (892–942), in his *Book of Beliefs and Opinions* (*Emunot ve-Deot*), is the first medieval philosopher of religion who supplies a methodological guide for biblical interpretation.

He justifies deviation from the *peshat*, where it is demanded by one of four factors: sense perception, reason, other scriptural statements, and tradition. This approach had a liberating influence on all subsequent exegesis. Since it leaves to the interpreter the task of reconciling the claims of the literal sense with rational and empirical considerations and the oral tradition, it makes reason—namely the interpreter's—the dominant factor in the understanding of Scripture.

Maimonides (1135–1204) developed biblical hermeneutics based on rational considerations to a point where an "inner" speculative meaning beyond the "outer" and common meaning of key terms and narratives was presented as the true and primary meaning of Scripture. The *Moreh Nevukhim* (*Guide of the Perplexed*), although not written as a commentary on the Bible, is nevertheless devoted to

> biblical exegesis of a particular kind. That kind of exegesis is required because many biblical terms and all biblical similes have an apparent or outer and a hidden or inner meaning; the gravest errors as well as the most tormenting perplexities arise from men's understanding the Bible always according to its apparent or literal meaning.[4]

Maimonides was convinced that fasting and praying were not sufficient to enable men to come close to God; intellectual knowledge is required in addition to the observance of the *mitzvot*. Thus, for example, affirmation of the necessary existence, unity and incorporeality of God is essential for Jewish faith. Physics (*ma'aseh bereshit*) and metaphysics or theology (*ma'aseh merkavah*) are the noblest topics of true religious knowledge.

The need for a novel branch of hermeneutics, philosophical exegesis, follows inevitably if we consider Maimonides' basic presuppositions: 1) The Bible contains God's word and hence theoretical as well as practical guidance. 2) Since it is intended for the instruction of all the people and not only the intellectual elite, it operates on two levels, the exoteric (outer) and the esoteric (inner). 3) It must be possible to extract from the Bible the highest theoretical knowledge, that of nature (*ma'aseh bereshit*) and of the Deity (*ma'aseh merkavah*), as far as these are within the grasp of man. 4) But the Bible does not in its surface meaning contain such speculative information couched in philosophical language. 5) Therefore it must be possible to understand biblical terms and figures of speech in such a way that they can be translated into doctrines of philosophy and theology by the enlightened, while conveying to the uninitiated useful exoteric instruction.

In the *Guide*, where the philosophically competent reader is addressed, thirty-two chapters are "lexicographic," i.e., devoted to a discussion of biblical terms, and the initiated reader is shown how the esoteric truths of Judaism ("the true knowledge of the Torah") can be extracted. In the first book of the *Mishneh Torah*, the indispensable minimum of theology necessary for meaningful and saving faith is rendered in more popular fashion for the benefit of the general reader.

Apart from the intrinsic philosophical merit of Maimonides' work (which is, of course, the most important aspect to the theologian), his emphasis on figurative language, simile, and metaphor focuses on problems of biblical interpretation which will occupy us even though we may not be concerned as he was with the Bible as a textbook of philosophical theology.

The *Kabbalah* as crystallized in the Zoharic corpus[5] uses the form of biblical commentary to expound mystical doctrines which to the critical reader seem to be less interested in what can be found *in* the Torah than to read *into* it the theosophical teachings of its author(s). But we ought to be careful when making such a distinction. David Neumark, historian of Jewish philosophy, once said that "even the critical reader is occasionally plagued by doubts whether the true interpretation of certain passages of the Torah may not after all be found here (i.e., in the *Zohar*) and nowhere else.[6]

The Zohar, like the exegesis of Maimonides and other medieval philosophers, is also driven to doctrine of inner (*setima*) and outer (*galya*) meaning. If God's word contains the highest knowledge attainable to man, then it simply cannot be limited to stories of mundane happenings as recounted in so many biblical passages.

> Come and behold: there are garments that everyone sees, and when fools see a man in a garment that seems beautiful to them, they do not look more closely. But more important than the garment is the body, and more important than the body is the soul. So likewise the Torah has a body, which consists of the commandments and ordinances of the Torah, which are called *gufey torah*, "bodies of the Torah." Fools see only the garment, which is the narrative part of the Torah; they know no more and fail to see what is under the garment. Those that know more see not only the garment but also the body that is under the garment. But the truly wise, the servants of the Supreme King, those who stood at the foot of Mount Sinai, look only upon the soul, which is the true foundation of the entire Torah, and one day indeed it will be given them to behold the innermost soul of the Torah.[7]

It is in identifying the nature of the inner meaning that the Zohar diverges from the philosophical exegetes. The aim of mystical enlightenment is not intellectual knowledge of physics and metaphysics, but intuitive understanding of the hidden Divine life which pulsates from its source, the *En Sof*, through the realms of the ten *sefirot*. The Torah is at once an organism, a cosmic pattern and a symbolic description of the Divine life process. Functioning on many levels in the ontological realm the Torah is also seen as functioning in the realm of communication (or revelation), as the source of multiple, perhaps even infinite meanings. Thus a distinction is made between the Primordial Torah, the Written Torah and the Oral Torah, corresponding to the *sefirot* of Ḥokhmah (Wisdom), *Tiferet* (Compassion) and *Malkhut* (the last *sefirah* of Divine Judgment). Another distinction among levels of exegesis found in the Zoharic corpus is the fourfold division symbolized by the term *Pardes: peshat*, the literal meaning; *remez*, the allegorical or philosophical meaning; *derash*, the talmudic or aggadic interpretation; and *sod*, the deepest mystical or theosophical meaning.

Strange as the threefold distinction of primordial, written and oral Torah and their assignments to three levels of the "sefiratic" hierarchy may appear to modern readers, it embodies a principle which, when reformulated in less esoteric terms, is a valuable tool in dealing with certain aspects of Torah interpretation. The belief in Divine revelation implies the absolute and infinite nature of the Giver of the Torah and the limited, time-and-language-bound nature of its recipients. The tension implicit in this polarity cannot be avoided by anyone who takes the claim of the Torah as Holy Scripture seriously. It forces him to face the problem that the giving of the Torah is complemented by the ongoing activity of appropriation and acceptance of the message in every generation. Since the medium of Torah is *language*, and since language is never self-explanatory, acceptance of Torah necessitates the activity of interpretation. The supernal or primordial Torah may be of infinite potential meaning, but in order to become available to finite man it has to be expressed in a fixed text. This text, combining the allusiveness and depth of its ineffable inspiration with the ordered structure of literary formulation, in turn becomes the source for the oral tradition which allots meanings and allows for their application to specific situations.

The reader who has followed us so far is doubtless aware that our bird's-eye view of a few selected types of exegesis cannot have been intended as a handy guide to the history of Jewish Bible interpretation. Its aim is rather to introduce some of the problems which face the contemporary teacher of the Torah, and which, to some extent, face anyone engaged in the understanding of an important text.

Words by their very nature are not self-centered, immanent and isolated entities; they function as intermediaries ("media"), and their function is the joint result of a variety of factors. A word is spoken (or written) *by* someone and refers *to* something *for* someone else. It stands for something other than itself. If we realize that most words function in multi-stage pointings beyond themselves, it will become even clearer how formidable the basic problem of interpretation is. Apart from (though not independent of) matters of historical, syntactical, and other contexts, the chief problem of interpretation is the relation between primary (first order) meaning and metaphor.

☐ Peshat and Metaphor

The critical reader may feel that, despite our parade of authorities, no convincing case has been made for rejecting the literal sense of Scripture. He might be tempted to quote the talmudic dictum: "A biblical passage never loses its literal meaning" (*Shabbat 63a*). He might point out that the authorities we have cited had recourse to metaphor, allegory or esoteric meanings only when the plain meaning led to difficulties or inconsistencies. Philo and Maimonides were aware that the allegorical method, if applied by radicals to *mitzvot* of the Torah, could lead to an explaining away rather than explaining of the obligatory nature of religious law.

Let us deal with this issue by taking a verse which challenges the teacher of Genesis at the very beginning: "God said: 'Let there be light'; and there was light . . ." (Gen. 1:3). Many teachers have pondered the question of its interpretation. Do we really mean to teach the plain sense of this verse, namely, that God did in fact at the outset of His creative work say these words and then light appeared? Or are the fanciful interpretations that reject the *peshat* so many attempts to hide the fact that we have no real faith in the truth of the literal sense of our verse?

We think that the way of meeting this question head-on is by asking a counterquestion: What *could* the 'literal' meaning of the verse possibly be? Does the advocate of the *peshat* maintain that God at a certain moment of time (but there was no time in our sense before Creation) uttered two Hebrew words? (But to utter words presupposes a vibration of air by a being equipped with physical organs such as vocal cords, in order to reach the ears of other sentient beings—and there was no air, and no possible listener, and the idea of God as "speaking" in the literal sense of that word is anthropomorphism of the crudest kind!) We do not have to belabor the point. Suffice it to add that if the verse could be accepted as a plain statement, questions such as "Did God speak with a loud voice?" or "Did He use the Ashkenazic or Sephardic pronunciation of Hebrew?" would be legitimate. But to frame such questions is to indicate their absurdity. It is clear that in this passage (and many others) the real issue is not our acceptance or rejection of the *peshat*, but our inability to ascertain what the *peshat* is in the first place. Metaphor, simile, analogical language and myth, far from undermining our ability to take the text seriously, are frequently the only way in which we can hop to penetrate to its true meaning.

Saadya was trying to convey what he took to be the real

meaning of our verse when he translated it "And God *willed* that there be light." Maimonides was trying to find the true intention of the passage when he wrote:

> "By the word of the Lord were the heavens made, and all the host of them by the breath of His mouth" (Ps. 33:6). In this verse God's acts are likened to those that proceed from kings, whose instrument in giving effect to their will is speech. However, God, may He be exalted, does not require an instrument by means of which He could act, for His acts are accomplished exclusively by means of His will alone; neither is there any speech at all. . . .[8]

No wonder that the compiler of an anthology on the "plain meaning of Scripture" from traditional sources comes to the conclusion that perhaps the best definition of *peshat* is "all those Scriptural interpretations which our sages—early and late—*thought* to be the *peshat*. . . .[9]

If the reader has learned from the foregoing that a simplistic approach to the problems of exegesis leads to *reductio ad absurdum*, he will be in a position to see the efforts of commentators from Philo to the *Zohar* not as attempts to evade the true understanding of the Torah, but as attempts to take the text seriously and to read it in the light of the best methods at their disposal.

When we find it difficult to accept these interpretations of the text, we should realize that the difficulty results from their having been deduced by a method which we find unacceptable. This is due to the fact that methodologies change in the light of available knowledge. If we wish to understand the Bible in the twentieth century we have an obligation to bring to bear upon its interpretation the best conceptual tools of our time and the fullest historical and philological scholarship at our disposal. In other words: we shall need all the knowledge that the philosophy of language and symbolism can contribute to the analysis of the text as well as the results of scholarship dealing with ancient Near Eastern cultures and comparative religion.

To show how that can be done, we shall devote the rest of this essay to the application of this principle to the Creation story. We shall do this in two steps: firstly by using linguistic analysis to clarify some aspects of metaphorical language, and secondly by applying this analysis to selected materials from comparative religion and the Genesis narrative.

Now it is sometimes thought that metaphor or simile is mainly used by poets to relieve the monotony of everyday locutions, to make language more "colorful" and ornate. But where we have to depend on the accuracy of our statements we eschew such poetic trappings and say directly and unambiguously what we want to communicate. According to this view metaphorical language is inaccurate at best and misleading at worst.

But this is a misconception. Metaphor is not a mannerism of poets or rhetoricians; it is inherent in all language. Only the words for the most primitive and obvious physical objects and qualities are non-metaphorical in most languages. As soon as ideas more abstract or subtle are to be expressed, the process of metaphorization sets in. Our language is well equipped to handle spatial reality with "first-order" terms that stand directly for their designata. As soon as "higher-order" experiences are to be described we have a tendency to use spatial terms metaphorically, i.e., as "second-order" simile or pointers.

For example, what has been called the transitive character of words involves the same principle that generates metaphor. The word "Lord" functions as a word precisely because it refers not to itself but to the entity it denotes, a human being who is a master or a commander. But if we push this operation one step further, if we carry the meaning from the area of inter-human relations to the area of human-divine relations, we apply the term "metaphorically" to God (*Adonay*). It is possible to carry this process even further and say that a man obsessed with worldly success recognizes money as his true Lord (in which case we use a religious term metaphorically to point to the absolute and demonic power which the pursuit of money exerts over its devotees). This is what we mean by the "multi-stage pointings-beyond-themselves" of certain words.

At this point it is necessary to introduce the term "myth" into our discussion. Since it is used in a bewildering variety of senses by various writers, we want to stipulate that we shall use it almost interchangeably with the term "metaphor" in religious contexts. Wherever a metaphor is elaborated in the form of a coherent story we shall feel free to call it a myth. It indicates that the story, although couched in terms of concrete empirical happenings, is metaphorical and refers to the Divine reality which by its ineffable nature cannot be described in direct first-order language.

Metaphors function in two different ways: they *explain* and they *enlarge* our experience. Explanation usually involves making the strange "plain" or by use of the more familiar. Molecules or atoms are strange entities to most of us; picturing them as miniature billiard balls and "explaining" their behavior in terms of analogous movements and collisions supplies an acceptable elucidation (until the analogy breaks down and another theory has to be developed).

The functions of explaining and enlarging our experience by means of metaphors or models overlap frequently. To describe the behavior of gases in a container we use the model of billiard balls moving around in random fashion at various speeds ("faster" corresponding to higher, and "slower" to lower, temperatures). By extrapolating from this model we can arrive at Boyle's Law which enables us to predict the pressure and volume of the gas corresponding to changes in temperature. Thus the metaphor enlarges our knowledge by letting us predict behavior which we could not possibly expect without the help of the model.

Using the model of the organism to describe the various individuals and groups that make up society not only helps us to understand their mutual interdependence, but also adds a new dimension to life by helping us experience our role in society as that of an organic part that stands in a dynamic and intimate relationship to all the others. In order to see this we have only to observe people who do not experience their relationship to society in this manner; the rebel, the anarchist, or the hippie who looks upon "Them" or "the Establishment" as enemies, exploiters or tools of a "conspiracy." As a result he acts and feels differently, although he is aware of the same "facts" as the person who has a sense of "belonging" to the community.

By accepting a metaphor we may not add new facts to our experience, but we see the old disjointed facts in a new and meaningful way. "It is possible to have before one's eyes all the items of a pattern and still to miss the pattern."[10]

One risk in using metaphors is that of deploying our model (or analogue) too far, for the model is never completely isomorphic with the domain that is to be interpreted. Thus the model of light as travelling in straight lines (the principle of the rectilinear propagation of light) has made possible certain advances in geometrical optics. The metaphor "travelling" can be used, for instance, to ask the question: At what speed does light travel?—and the answer: at 300,000 kilometers per second, is an important piece of scientific information. But if we stretch the metaphor and ask: Does light "travel" by road, by rail or by rocket? we have overextended its range and have fallen into absurdity. The Torah uses the "travelling" and "light" metaphor of God:

The Lord came from Sinai;
He shone upon them from Seir;

> He appeared from Mount Paran,
> And approached from Ribeboth-kodesh . . . (Deut. 33:2)

Here, however, we can neither inquire about the Lord's speed nor His mode of transportation.

It is in these last two examples (light shining forth, and God shining forth) that a fundamental difference emerges between religious and other kinds of metaphor. In science and poetry, metaphor illuminates one domain of finite reality through another domain of finite reality. In discourse about God (myth) we use metaphors taken from an area of finite experience to illuminate the Infinite Source of all reality, which by its very nature cannot be reduced to categories of human knowledge. Since all our models and metaphors are taken from ordinary experience we are always in danger of either distorting the Divine by representing it in anthropomorphic or physicomorphic ways, or of abandoning all efforts to speak about God—except in negations—and thus isolating ourselves from any relationship with Him.

It is against this twofold danger of reducing God to human scale or resigning ourselves to utter ignorance, that we must understand the biblical approach. It tells us in the form of myth and metaphor something significant and true about God, but warns us at the same time that the myth and metaphor are not literal or scientific descriptions of the ultimate truth.

Since metaphors are not literally true, but allusive and evocative, we might think that we do not have to employ them with unchanging rigidity. Mixed metaphors make for poor style, but they do not necessarily frustrate the communication of the intended meaning. The British Lion who roams the Canadian mountains and African jungles and who will never pull in his horns or withdraw into his shell may be an odd creature; but nevertheless, we get the message! In the Song of Songs the girl is called a mare, a rose, a dove, a sister and a palm tree, but there is no danger that we misunderstand the poet's intention.

It might seem, therefore, that although we cannot do without *some* metaphor where literal descriptions fail us, it does not matter *which* particular metaphor we use. God and His relationship to the world cannot be described in empirical terms, but does it really matter whether we allude to Him as the Begetter, the Engineer, the Arranger or the Creator of the Universe? This view, however, is erroneous, and so fraught with dangerous consequences that we have to expose it decisively. The *raison d'être* for teaching the story of Genesis, and not Babylonian or modern "scientific" myths, as fundamental truth lies at the foundation of Jewish thought and conduct. We shall not be able to teach the Creation story as an important doctrine of our faith unless we have clarified the question of the metaphorical conception of God.

The relationship between God and the world is of crucial importance to one's way of thinking and acting. The way we conceive of the Ultimate and its connection with the here-and-now—nature and mankind—must inevitably influence our views about the potentialities and purposes of life. Our metaphors about particular domains of reality, such as the nature of society, determine our modes of conduct and the quality of our interpersonal experiences. Now, the more comprehensive the scope of a metaphor, the more pervasive is its influence on the lives of those who accept it.

A root metaphor extracted from an area of common-sense fact is extended into a "world hypothesis" or a philosophical system.[11] A root metaphor embedded in a religious myth gives rise to a system of values and a way of life. We shall briefly discuss three root metaphors used to describe the relationship of God to the world: God as the Begetter, God as the Stranger, and God as the Creator.

◻ Three Types of Cosmogony

The account of the beginning—discourse about the origin of our world—is not merely a report of how the Universe came into being. It is also an explanation why things are as we find them, and a clue to the latent potentialities that emerge into actuality as the story of the world unfolds. Since myths of origin tell us what went into the making of the world, they also reveal what kind of a world it is and what we can expect in it. What was at the beginning determines what may be at the end.

The root metaphor of much pagan thought about origins is the idea of *sexual procreation*. Now in sexual generation the begetter begets something like himself. Dogs have puppies, human parents have human children, and if the gods generated the universe it must itself be something divine or godlike. In such a scheme the gods, however elevated, are still basically like things of the world, and the things of the world, however less powerful, are still basically like the gods. This metaphor was influential not only in Greek popular religion, but even in some of the philosophical systems. The world was conceived as animate, divine, moved by an inner principle, its soul. "The cosmos is a god; the stars are gods; the earth is a god. . . ." Although Greek religion contained a strong tendency to emphasize the gulf between man and the gods, there was the drive toward apotheosis, the divinization of man. Empedocles greeted his fellow townsmen with the cry: "All hail! I go about among you an immortal god, no longer a mortal!"

Belief in the divinity of the world and man can lead to a pantheism which sees everything as holy. A vivid feeling of cosmic piety enhances all experience, and every tree reminds one of the god. But since everything is somehow divine there is hardly a criterion by which to judge right from wrong. The lion and the lamb are both embodiments of divinity. In such a world-view, religion cannot be a genuine source of ethics. There is no voice which speaks from beyond earthly reality and judges it. Thus it is no accident that pantheistic world-views have failed to develop ethical systems for improving or changing the status quo, that they have not developed sciences and technologies which aim at re-making reality by dominating and controlling its forces.

Around the beginning of the Christian era a religious movement flowering in numerous sects and infiltrating early Christian groups stirred the consciousness of the Hellenistic world. Known by the name of *Gnosticism*,[12] it was a dualistic transmundane religion of salvation, regarding the world as incurably evil and promising to its adherents release from earthly existence by a saving knowledge of the true God.

Gnosticism as a world hypothesis affirms the radical opposition between God and the universe. Its root metaphor for God is that of the *Stranger*, its root metaphor for the universe that of the *Prison* or *Tomb*.

> The cardinal feature of gnostic thought is the radical dualism that governs the relationship of God and the world, and correspondingly that of man and the world. The deity is absolutely transmundane, its nature alien to that of the universe, which it neither created nor governs and to which it is the complete antithesis: to the divine realm of light, self-contained and remote, the cosmos is opposed as the realm of darkness. The world is the work of powers which though they may mediately be descended from Him do not know the true God and obstruct the knowledge of Him in the cosmos over which they rule....[13]

Against the pagan idea of the Divine as the Begetter of the world, the gnostic idea of the Alien God removes not only all divinity from the world but makes this earth and all its creatures vile and valueless. Man has within him a spark of the true God, but this trace of the divine is encased in the garment of the earthly body and thus remains in perpetual exile.

The gnostic world-view raises a question and poses a problem: "How did this world come into being if it is not the work of the highest God?" and "What can man do to attain salvation from the bonds of his prison house?" The answers differ slightly in the various gnostic systems. Most of them tell of a cosmic Fall, a rebellion by spiritual beings who were originally loyal to the highest God and who in demonic disobedience created the physical world into which they lowered the human soul spark. In some versions the demonic Archon (ruler) who is responsible for the scandal of the world's creation is the God of the Jewish Bible. Marcion (second century), son of a Christian bishop in Asia Minor, distinguished between the God of creation or generation, the craftsman (demiurge), and the hidden, unknown Supreme God of salvation. The Jewish God is evil; He creates, legislates and punishes. The Supreme Unknown God is good and gracious; He sent His own son Jesus to break through the cosmic curtain to liberate men from the clutches of the Jewish God of justice.

If the world is the antithesis of God, man's task must be liberation and release from his prison. In some gnostic systems this is attained through esoteric knowledge which enables the soul to return to the divine source; in Marcionite Christianity salvation is attained by faith in Jesus who saves the elect from the God of the Jews.

It is clear that Gnosticism produces an attitude which renders futile all attempts to improve society, to develop civilization and to realize values. In the realm of morality it led either to extreme asceticism or libertinism. Some sects tried to reject the world and its ruler by abstaining from material functions. Thus Marcion decreed abstemiousness in matters of food and prohibited matrimony and procreation; Mani advocated poverty and counselled against building a house. On the other hand contempt of the world resulted in licentiousness: Since only the "spiritual" part (*pneuma*) matters, and since the laws of morality were devised to perpetuate and preserve the world and society, it becomes a positive good to undermine morality and to throw off all restraints. The true destiny of the elect lies beyond good and evil.

In the Bible, God is described as the Creator of the world.[14] He is represented under the root metaphors of the *Artisan* and the *Ruler*.[15] Let us deal briefly with the meaning and implications of each of these ideas.

The words most frequently used about God's creative activities are originally technical terms used by artisans and referring to mechanical fashioning: God forms or molds (*yotzer*) like a potter; He makes (*'oseh*) heaven and earth; He spreads out (*noteh*) the sky like a tentmaker; He lays the foundation (*yosed*) of the earth like a builder. Now the metaphor of the artisan or craftsman excludes two views which we associated with the metaphors of God as Begetter and God as Stranger—the divinization, and the devaluation of the world. Whereas the Procreator begets offspring of his own species, the Artisan produces something different from his own self. Whereas the gnostic Alien God is wholly other and has no positive relationship to the things of this world, the model of the Artisan and his handiwork points to a relationship in which something of the wisdom, the purpose and the character of the Maker is expressed and realized in His creation.

Let us pursue our metaphor by applying it to the realm of human artistic creation: There is no danger that one might mistake Rembrandt's paintings for their creator (as there is danger of mistaking a king's son for his father and paying the former the honor due the latter!). But it would be absurd to deny that a great deal of Rembrandt's genius, his purpose and his message to men are embodied in his paintings and can be seen and interpreted by sensitive viewers. In fact we might go further and say that since we cannot interview Rembrandt himself, our only way of understanding him is through his creations. Yet no one would maintain that all of Rembrandt is exhaustively revealed in his works.

The analogy to God as the Artisan is obvious: the world as His handiwork reflects His wisdom and purpose and must be accepted as "very good." But at the same time the earth is not our Mother as the Greeks thought and as Santayana seemed to think when he exclaimed: "Great is this organism of mud and fire, terrible this vast, painful experiment. Why should we not look on the universe with piety?" Biblical metaphor leads us to value but not to worship nature. And since—unlike Rembrandt or any finite artist—God is always active, one must never presume to judge Him on the basis of His past works and to assume that all the evidence is in and that He has spoken the last word.

The metaphor of God as the Supreme Artisan has its drawbacks. In the first place it still conjures up physical limitations; but, more importantly, the craftsman does not have a reciprocal relationship to the products of his art. He brings them into being, but he is not concerned with them for their own sakes. Moreover, he need not maintain a continuing relationship with his handiwork once it is completed. The Bible, however, is not a handbook on origins seeking to satisfy scientific curiosity; it describes the world as the scene of life and history and seeks to understand man in his continuous relationship with God. The more comprehensive and suggestive root metaphor of God as *King* or *Ruler* shows the Creator not only as the source of power, will and skill, but also as the source of care and concern for His creatures.

The ideal king combines the attributes of power *over* his subjects with care and concern *for* them. He uses his strength not to crush them but to benefit them. Although they can be forced to obey, he will try to gain their loyalty through freely-given consent. He will not act the tyrant but will establish his relationship through an agreement in which he gives each party rights as well as duties. This involves the delegation of power, the allocation of tasks, the instruction of the subjects and the possibility of acceptance or rejection of the Ruler with alternative consequences. The root metaphor of God the King illumines the role allotted to man vis-à-vis God, nature and his fellow man. It introduces the idea of the *Covenant (berit)*. It involves the concepts of law, sin, history and the ideal end of the historical process which, in biblical language, is called "the end of days" (*aharit hayamim*)[16] and, in rabbinic language, (not surprisingly) the "Kingdom of God" (*malkhut shamayim*).

It is our opinion that this root metaphor of God as King is behind the Creation story in the first chapter of Genesis and numerous other biblical passages, although it is often combined with locutions taken from the picture of the Divine Artisan. The idea of Creation by *fiat* in Genesis 1 expresses the sovereignty of the Divine King and in addition points to the absence of all physical effort in His formation of the universe. The narrative in Genesis 1:1 to 2:4a makes much better sense when viewed against the archetypal pattern of the Ruler who first establishes his city and after furnishing it with all necessities, populates it and establishes its governance. Man, the last of God's works, is given a special rank and function. Created in the divine image and likeness he is capable of responsible conduct and intelligent action. God appoints him as His Vassal, to rule on His behalf on earth, with rights and duties befitting his intermediate position as God's servant and His vice-regent over all living things.

The Zohar, using the analogy of God as the Ruler, offers a clear understanding of man's role in the Divine plan:

> Why was man created in the image of God, as it is said: "And God created man in His image" (Gen. 1:27). Like a king who ruled over the state and erected castles and installations for the city, and all the townspeople were subject to him. One day he called all the townspeople and appointed an officer of his over

them. He said: Until now I have troubled myself with all the city's needs, constructing towers and castles. From now on this one is like me. In that respect it says about man: "God created man in His image." And he said to him: I built this city and all that is in it, and as I ruled over it and built it according to my will, so now you shall build and do the world's work.[17]

The metaphor of God as Ruler is so deeply embedded in the Creation story that its corollary idea—that of the *Covenant* (*berit*)—is even mentioned in connection with the formation of the physical universe. Jeremiah speaks of God as having established His covenant with day and night and the ordinances of heaven and earth (Jer. 33:25).

It should be noted that the first narrative in Genesis, culminating in the creation of man, contains the first in a series of arrangements into which God enters with those whom He elects to responsible partnership. In Genesis 1:28–29 newly created man is blessed and endowed with dominion over the earth; in chapter nine a covenant with Noahide mankind is established; in chapter seventeen there is a covenant with Abraham and his descendants; and in Exodus (and Deuteronomy) the Sinaitic covenant is made with the Israelites liberated from Egypt.

Creation culminating in the formation and investiture of man and later formalized in the Sabbath as the covenantal sign (*ot berit*, *cf.* Ex. 31: 12–18) is the first mighty act of the Divine King.[18] It is followed by Revelation and Redemption, basic categories of biblical religion in which the King, after having established His *polis*, promulgates His ordinances and saves His people.

Let us summarize the main conclusions of the preceding sections.[19] The biblical root metaphor for God is that of King or Ruler. It is so fundamental that in liturgical language "King of the world" (*melekh ha'olam*) became the standard appellative for God in benedictions. Its consistent use guards against the dangers of the deification of man and nature inherent in the metaphor of the Divine Procreator, and the devaluation and denial of the physical world inherent in the gnostic metaphor of the Alien God. It establishes a view of reality in which the goodness of nature as well as its incompleteness is accepted. Man as a finite being created in the image of God is capable of entering into a covenantal relationship with his Maker, reflecting his dependence and obligations as well as his dignity and inner worth.

The perceptive reader may have noticed that this paper is pleading for two approaches which may pull the Bible teacher in opposite directions: On the one hand we have advocated the use of modern scholarship and the findings of comparative religion; on the other hand, we have tried to make a case for accepting with all seriousness the root metaphors and "myths" found in the biblical text. It is our conviction that these two tendencies, though they may at times generate tensions, are not opposed, but complement each other.

The reason ought to be fairly clear: If we believe that God's message is to be found in Scripture, we can expect that the basic motifs, metaphors and paradigmatic tales contain guidance ("Torah") for all ages, and it becomes our duty to delve into their implications with reverence and seriousness. On the same assumption, however, the timeless message can never be read through the spectacles of our great-grandparents. It becomes our duty and challenge to do what previous generations have done: to focus upon the sacred text the fullest light of knowledge at *our* disposal.

To study the Bible as if we lived in 1100 or 1750 may give some people the satisfaction of accepting "eternal truth" instead of modern error. But to mistake yesterday's dated interpretation for timeless truth is not the traditional method of Jewish scholarship. Rabbi Samuel ben Meir, grandson of Rashi, tells us that he often debated issues of interpretation with his grandfather: "He admitted to me that if he had more time he would consider it necessary to rewrite his commentaries in the light of the ordinary meanings being disclosed every day."[20] "New *peshatot*" are still being discovered every day and we cannot afford to ignore them any more than Rashi and his followers did in medieval France.

But while the methods and findings of scholarship change, the condition of man in quest of meaning, and the basic options open to him (expressed in the past in theological doctrines and root metaphors) remain identical. These options tend to appear in our secular age in non-theological formulations, but that does not change their import. The secularized type of pantheism in which all is divine can be seen in contemporary culture as the doctrine that all natural impulses are to be accepted and deified, and that the good life consists in everyone doing whatever he feels impelled to do, because nothing natural can be wrong. The gnostic doctrine of the Alien God is reflected in the literature of the absurd. Some of the most sensitive and articulate novelists and playwrights have given up hope in the possibility of a meaningful life and have proclaimed the utter absurdity and emptiness of human existence.

The archetypal myths and metaphors continue to give vision to our life and direction to our conduct. The better we understand the ancient tales in terms of the most up-to-date knowledge the better we can hope to preserve and strengthen the vision and direction of those whom we teach.

The scandal of religious metaphor is the use of finite human categories for the infinite Divine reality; but the necessity for religious metaphor is man's inability to apprehend the infinite except through such human and finite categories. The revelatory power of the Bible is its ability to achieve this paradoxical task:

> "You turn things upside down! Shall the potter be regarded as the clay?" (Is. 29:16). They liken the creature to its Creator, the plant to its planter![21]
>
> Said Rabbi Yudan: "Great is the power of the prophets that they liken the creature to its Creator."[22]

NOTES

1. Rashi (1040–1105), for example, who was not acquainted with all the research of grammarians using Arabic philology could not utilize knowledge which was readily available to Abraham Ibn Ezra. Moderrn recovery of Mesopotamian languages and literatures has given contemporary scholars knowledge of the Bible that was unavailable to the Babylonian rabbis who lived in Mesopotamia fifteen hundred years ago.

2. *Mekhilta de-rabbi Ishmael,* Yitro ch. 7; Lauterbach ed., Vol. II pp. 255f.

3. *Ruth Rabba,* 2, para. 22.

4. Leo Strauss, (Introductory Essay," *The Guide of the Perplexed,* tr. Shlomo Pines, Chicago, 1963, p. xiv.

5. *Zohar, Tiqqune Zohar, Zohar Ḥadash* in the printed editions.

6. Quoted in G. Scholem, *Major Trends in Jewish Mysticism,* p. 158.

7. *Zohar* III, 152a.

8. *Moreh Nevukhim* I, ch. 23.

9. Shimon Kasher, *Peshuto shel Mikra,* Vol. I, Jerusalem, 1963, p. 9.

10. John Wisdom, "Gods," *Logic and Language,* First Series, ed. A. G. N. Flew, Oxford, 1951, p. 191.

11. Cf. Stephen Pepper, *World Hypotheses,* Berkeley, 1942.

12. Greek: *gnosis* = knowledge; cf. the English term "diagnosis." The only surviving sect of Gnostics in our time is a small Aramaic speaking group in Iraq, known as Mandeans, from the Aramaic *manda'* = knowledge.

13. Hans Jonas, *The Gnostic Religion,* Boston, Beacon Press, 1958, p. 42.

14. The Hebrew *root* (*bara* = create) in the *qal* is used in the Bible exclusively with God as the subject.

15. The root metaphor of God as Artisan is generally accepted (e.g., H. A. Wolfson's lucid treatment of this topic in *The Philosophy of the Church Fathers,* Vol. 1, pp. 287ff.). The assertion that the root metaphor of Ruler or King is equally basic is the thesis of this paper. It ought to be remembered that the Bible uses a number of other metaphors with respect to God: Father, Husband, Lover, Rock, Refuge, etc. But these are not made the basis of so pervasive a cosmological and theological scheme as the root metaphors which are treated here.

16. The term *aḥarit* is, of course, the antonym of *reshit* (beginning).

17. *Zodar Ḥadash*, Ashlag edition, Vol. 9, p. 117.

18. The question of the relationship between universal Creation (Gen. 1) and its commemoration in the Sabbath covenant with Israel (Ex. 31:12–18) cannot be discussed fully in the framework of this essay.

19. The thesis that the analogy of the King is the root metaphor of much biblical material on Creation is presented in this paper. A separate study by the author endeavors to set out in a more detailed and systematic fashion his grounds for holding this view.

20. *Lefi hapeshatot hamitḥadshim bekhol yom. Rashbam al Hatorah*, ed. Rosin, p. 48 (on Gen. 37:1).

21. *Genesis Rabbah* 24, 1.

22. *Genesis Rabbah* 27, 1.

APPENDIX C

The Concept of God in Jewish Education

Fritz A. Rothschild

APPENDIX C

The Concept of God in Jewish Education

Fritz A. Rothschild

> To be religious is to seek God with all one's being; to be blessed is to find Him; to be theological is to make the search and its object evident in discourse.
> Paul Weiss

Discourse about God (*theo-logy*) is an ancient and honorable discipline, pursued since the days of Plato and Aristotle and acclaimed the queen of the sciences in the Middle Ages. At the present time a multitude of scholars lecture and write on systematic theology, philosophical theology, existentialist theology, historical theology and, *mirabile dictu,* even atheistic theology. The non-Jewish world seems to be undergoing a theological revival—perhaps even a theological renaissance.

It would seem, therefore, that no apology is needed for considering the concept of God in Jewish education and even for according it a central place in our curricula. But, as we know, the opposite is true: there is hesitancy (and even outright opposition) about dealing with the idea of God and the problem of God in a systematic manner. One must justify its legitimacy and centrality.

Opposition to the study of theology[1] in Jewish schools stems from various grounds. The aversion of some spokesmen of modern Orthodoxy to the treatment of the God-idea is based partly on the doctrinal view that *halakhah* is the sole fountainhead and embodiment of Judaism, and partly on the prudential wish to avoid the intellectual ferment, doubt and possible pluralism which may follow in the wake of theological and philosophical discussions.

Religious liberals (Conservative and Reform Jews) avoid theology for almost the opposite reason. Any attempt to make the God-idea central to Jewish studies would, they fear, lead inevitably to limitation of freedom of enquiry and attempts to circumscribe the area of "correct belief" (*orthedoxa*). Once we start discussing the concept of God we shall become involved, they fear, in the kind of doctrinal strife which is bound to end with the winning faction imposing its own brand of theology on the rest.

Jewish secularists and folk-culturists, in turn, fear that the idea of God may prove embarrassing, since it may be a divisive concept. From their standpoint it becomes meaningful to assert that "secularism is the will of God."

The view that *halakhah* is the sole fountainhead of Judaism is tantamount to saying that theology is somehow "un-Jewish." Yet the vast literature of *agadah* deals with questions of theology in numerous places. G. Scholem has shown that proto-Kabbalistic treatment of such topics as *ma'aseh bereshit* (the esoteric doctrine of creation) and *ma'aseh merkavah* (the esoteric doctrine of God) goes back to Mishnaic times, and A. J. Heschel has demonstrated that a great part of *agadah* can no longer be said to represent merely "opinions and views uttered on the spur of the moment" or "creations of popular fancy." They are expressions of consistent and profoundly thought-out theological doctrines, which in the case of Rabbis Akiva and Ishmael, for example, influenced decisions in the realm of *halakhah*.

It may be true that certain topics were not discussed by our ancient sages, but this would be no reason why we should abstain from dealing with them. Ideas which were accepted without question and formed part of the climate of opinion of many generations have become questionable in our time. We cannot evade our religious problems on the ground they were not problematical to our ancestors in Pumbeditha, Worms and Wilna, or to some of our contemporaries in Williamsburg.

The fear that discussion of the God-idea will arouse doctrinal strife and lead to new forms of dogmatism and heresy-hunting implies that unity in matters of religion is desirable even at the cost of evading basic issues. This is a snare and a delusion. If our ideas about God make no difference to our life and conduct, there is something radically wrong with our ideas, or ourselves, or both. If they do make a difference, then we cannot afford to present them to our students as being unimportant. The problem of doctrinal strife will be solved, not by avoiding the God-idea, but by dealing with it in a way that will produce neither cynical unconcern nor narrow-minded fanaticism.

A frank and continuing discussion of the God-idea among the various factions of contemporary Jewry might disclose that we have to face certain theological differences and live with them as mature and reasonable men. On the other hand, it is conceivable that as a result of such a continuing discussion we might discover an underlying consensus beneath the differences of emphasis and theological methods, thus restoring the idea of God as the core of our common faith and the source of our religious commitment. We do, after all, have differing views of the meaning of many rituals, and they do not necessarily lead to doctrinal strife.

Thus, to some Jews, the *seder* ritual means the fulfillment of a divine commandment from the God who slew the Egyptian firstborn and took our forefathers out of slavery to become an exclusive and chosen kingdom of priests. To the Israeli secularist it may be a symbol of Israel's declaration of political independence. To many Conservative and Reform synagogue members it signifies the triumph of freedom over tyranny. Similarly, mitzvot are observed as divine commandments, as historically conditioned cultural forms of expressing man's response to the Divine, as folkways maintaining the coherence of the Jewish people, or as customs adding color and excitement to the workday world and contributing dignity and structure to the *rites de passage*, from cradle to grave.

Pedagogical considerations are also cited as a reason for the exclusion of theology from the curriculum of Jewish schools. Two separate questions are raised by those who hesitate to teach about God in our schools.

The first question is: Should knowledge about the idea of God be taught?

The second question (which arises only when the first one has been answered in the affirmative) is: Should the idea of God be taught as a separate, special and distinct topic?

I have the impression that many teachers opposed to "teaching about God," really oppose introduction of the subject in a formal and scholastic manner reminiscent of Christian catechism lessons. They would be quite willing to deal with the topic in their regular classes wherever theological problems arise naturally out of the text and stories studied. This is as it should be. It is properly the teacher's decision where and when such matters should be taught. However, I am reasonably sure that they would agree it is desirable that the idea of God be a central aspect of Jewish education.

❐ A Common Purpose and a Common Faith

Apart from some institutions concerned with higher learning for its own sake, the conscious aim of all Jewish religious education is: (1) to convey knowledge of Jewish religious literature, culture and history; and (2) to inculcate commitment to Jewish observance, Jewish ideals (religious and moral) and the Jewish people ("the Community of Israel").

Neither of these goals can be achieved or even attempted competently, unless the idea of God is afforded a central place. The reason is clear. In the chief classic of our literature, the Bible, God plays a conspicuous and central role. Since He is also central in the prayer-book and the teaching of religious observances (*mitzvot*), we frequently pronounce His name. Unless we take *Him* seriously, we take His name in vain.

Addressing myself to the two-fold aims of Jewish education enumerated above, it seems to me that the following points are of the utmost importance. (1) Judaism is a theotropic religion; more precisely, a religion in which the central subject is not man in isolation, but God in His relationship with man. A clear and full exposition of this idea is a necessary condition for even an elementary understanding of Jewish literature, culture and history. (2) To inculcate *religious* commitment to Jewish observance and values means to understand life as lived in response to the divine demand.

I am fully aware that a wide range of opinions exists about how much is *divine* and how much is *human* in Jewish tradition. But all these opinions share the view that the Jewish religion is acted out not by men alone but with a divine partner, a partner to whom men react and whose commands and demands they try to understand and to heed. No matter how much faith or doubt, no matter how much pious acceptance or critical rejection a Jew brings to his heritage, if he considers himself to be within the *religious* tradition of Judaism, he accepts as a minimum commitment (1) the awareness that life is lived in the presence of Him who is the Ground and Creator of all reality; and (2) that our tradition embodies in some way the voice and demand of God, and not merely the projections of our needs, drives and aspirations.

The philosopher will complain that in all the above the key terms lack precision. His complaint is legitimate; it points to the dilemma which no theologian can hope to avoid. "He cannot define God in a way to satisfy the strict canons of logical proof, yet he *must* define God sufficiently to guide 'man's attempt to find his way in the world'."[2] And this problem is closely connected with a second one. God is controversial; the truth about Him cannot be demonstrated. It is even doubtful exactly what one means by "truth" in this field. As Whitehead has pointed out, what is unsettled and doubtful is usually unimportant, and we postpone decision and action in regard to it. But unlike some abstruse and unsettled topics the question of God is of the highest importance, and the answer one gives determines one's life and character. It cannot be evaded or postponed indefinitely. "Your character is developed according to your faith. This is the primarily religious truth from which no one can escape."[3]

Thus the modernist cannot be spared the "religious test" of accepting the minimum commitment, if he wants to be accepted as a *bona fide* member of *religious* Jewry. By a *bona fide* member I mean one who claims to represent the tradition, whose views, though not necessarily acceptable to all, are listened to as those of an "insider"—a member of the convenantal circle. Thus, *bona fide* membership is not restricted to the traditionalist, and the latter is warned not to reject the "good faith" (*bonam fidem*) of those who accept as divine less of the tradition than he does. After all, there is hardly anyone who does not exercise his right to distinguish between the eternal and the temporal, the divine and its embodiments conditioned by human records of its reception and appropriation. He who is committed to faith in God and a life lived in response to His demands, and who finds the *locus* of these demands in the classical sources of Judaism and the historic experiences of Jewry, draws his religious substance from the basic roots of our faith and cannot be said to be *kofer ba'ikkar*.

Because Judaism is conviction which affects attitudes and actions, the circle of its authentic representatives must exclude those who do not share this conviction. Yet, since no one can lay down precise specifications as to what this conviction implies and what it excludes, we cannot presume to draw the circle of membership in such a way that only those who stand with us are within it. And because no single discourse can adequately define or even evoke the inexhaustible reality of Judaism, we cannot hope to arrive at a definite *theo-logy*.

It follows that teaching about God in Jewish education must draw on the *variety* of formulations and approaches which have emerged in the history of Israel's religion.

Even an exhaustive treatment of Judaism's teachings on the nature of God will avail us little, unless we become aware of the questions which these teachings are attempting to answer. The author of Genesis, for example, assumed that the reader has entertained some such questions as: How did the world come into being? Was it always the way it is now? If not, what was it like in the beginning, and who made or generated it? Is the world the outcome of accidental happenings, of cosmic conflicts among gods and monsters, or was it planned and intended for a purpose?

The statements about God in Jewish documents must be seen as answers to questions, as solutions to problems. "The primary task of religious thinking is to rediscover the questions to which religion is an answer, to develop a degree of sensitivity to the ultimate questions which its ideas and acts are trying to answer."[4] It follows that religion and the knowledge of God are not the result of man's flight or withdrawal from the world, but of a more discriminating attention to reality, and an openness toward certain aspects of experience which are commonly overlooked or taken for granted.

The facts of life and death, of ideals achieved and hopes disappointed, generate the problems of religion. These experiences pose the questions and point to possible answers. They do not, however, *determine* these answers in a definite way. It is important to insist on this distinction, since it touches upon a basic issue in religious thought, the issue of *natural* versus *revelational* theology.

☐ God's Work and God's Word

The adherents of *natural* theology maintain that man can attain knowledge of God through the ordinary experiences of life, especially through the contemplation of the visible processes of nature: "If you want to know Him through whose word the Universe came into being, observe His works."

The proponents of *revelational* theology have insisted that man can never attain knowledge of God's being or of His demands except through divine self-disclosure in revelation. The way to God cannot be discovered through His Works, but must be disclosed through His Word.

Both these views present difficulties which make them unacceptable to us.

The claim of *natural* theology that God can be adequately known through the contemplation of reality is refuted by the fact that such experience has led people to a bewildering variety of contradictory religious, irreligious and agnostic views. The variegated facts of nature do not supply unambiguous answers to the questions which they raise. Nature has been described as morally neutral by those who have pointed to examples of exquisite adaptation of means to ends as well as of colossal waste. Depending on the context and the principle of selection, nature can be seen as indifferent to man and his interests, or as the nurse and fostermother of the race. Facts no more teach a definitive theology, than tools teach their own use. "The heavens declare the glory of God; and the firmament sheweth His handiwork" only to the Psalmist who believes that "the *Torah* of the Lord is perfect."

The exclusive claim of *revelational* theology encounters equally formidable obstacles. It asserts a radical split between the divine and human, and denies that ordinary experience is conducive to the understanding of God. But surely such a sundering of the two elements makes revelation impossible or ineffectual. God's message may be eternal, but its reception requires that it address itself to the questions and problems of human existence. Thus man's experience and the knowledge of God cannot be totally disparate. Revelation which is unrelated to human concerns and modes of understanding is neither meaningful nor illuminating for men. A world and a humanity which do not reflect the divine or intimate it in some way can hardly be said to represent God's creation and His image. If human existence is utterly irrelevant to the awareness of God, then a supernatural revelation of God must be irrelevant to man.

An adequate view of God must combine the insights of natural and revelational theology while avoiding their individual shortcomings. This can be achieved by the *method of correlation*[5] in which the questions originate in human existence, but the answers must be drawn not only from existence but also from divine revelation and sacred tradition. This is the case because the questions do not concern the facts of existence, but their meaning and value as directions to life. The answers require an act of personal commitment and faith, which need not be "blind," since it may or may not prove relevant to the basic problems of human existence. Neither it is "rational" in the sense that it can be deduced from the empirical facts which it imbues with meaning and direction. It follows that every man, except the cynic, the skeptic or the person who goes along with the values and directions of his environment without having any convictions of his own, has (implicitly or explicitly) a *theology* of sorts.

If we seek to avoid both the fallacy of confusing God with the conditions that instigate our quest for Him, and the absurdity of adding to God's glory by proclaiming the radical irrelevance and worthlessness of His creation, two important consequences follow for Jewish educational theory and practices. The nature of God must be taught by posing relevant questions; and Jewish theology must stress the characteristic affirmations of Jewish experience.

One cannot teach about God and religion through indoctrination, where the answers of the tradition are presented and advocated by the teacher. Since answers can only make sense in terms of the questions to which they are addressed, such teaching would be putting the cart before the horse. Religious education has to present the facts of human existence (which the pupil studies in secular schools and experiences in his personal life) in a new manner. The role of the teacher is to draw attention to aspects of ordinary reality which the student is likely to overlook or which he does not take seriously, in order to show him which tensions, problems and evocations of the transcendent challenge us and point to the Divine.

The phenomenon of *change* is known to everyone, although few of us realize its import. An awareness that each blade of grass, each human being and each situation, although conforming to the general laws of nature, is unprecedented and in some respect unique, points up the marvel and miracle of "continuous creation" and the preciousness of each being. Internalization of such awareness enhances the quality of man's life and opens his soul to consider the question of the source of all creativity.

Religious education should also develop a keen awareness that man is not self-sufficient and independent but the product and meeting place of forces beyond his control. Paradoxically, even our power of self-assertion, our refusal to accept our dependence on a higher power, are *dependent* on something beyond ourselves. Such awareness makes one receptive to the answer of Judaism which sees man as a creature of God the Creator.

And only when the pupil has been shown that *responsibility*, being answerable for one's actions, is a pervasive facet of human existence, can he understand the moral dimension of reality which points to the obligatoriness of life as an objective pre-condition of humanity. It will then make sense to teach the biblical message that there is One to whom we are responsible and that God's question to Adam, "Where art thou?" is not an ancient fable but an ever-present reality.

In addition to these universal aspects of existence, common to all civilized and moral people, Jewish theology must stress the basic affirmations unique to Judaism, as expressed in the classics of the Jewish faith. Thus, for example, it should be made clear to the student that the exodus from Egypt and its after math are *not* depicted in the Bible as just another struggle for national survival, freedom and independence by a downtrodden minority (though they were that too, of course!), but as the consecration of a people to the service of God and obedience to His commandments.

The shared and the unique aspects of Jewish faith cannot be separated, although they must be clearly distinguished by the teacher. The more skillfully their mutual relationship can be established, the more meaningful will our religious teaching be. To show that Bible, *halakhah* and *agadah* are relevant and are addressed to universal and ever-present challenges in the lives of men, will do more in the long run to create the necessary motivation for Jewish studies than superficial attempts to "modernize" the classical texts by transposing them into the current idioms of the latest literary or social fads.

◘ The Experimental Matrix of Religion

It has been said that "religion is for simple people, and so must itself be simple."[6] If that were true it would be easy for us to locate its sources in human experience. But unfortunately, seemingly simple things turn out to be complicated on closer analysis. One such deceptively simple fact is that religious consciousness is always characterized by a *profound dissatisfaction with reality as immediately given*. If man were but an ingenious robot photographing the visible and recording the audible aspects of his environment he would not develop religious problems. It is the unexpectedness of reality, the frequent failure of things to conform to our expectations, which is at the bottom of the quest for the Divine. Although we know ourselves to be *finite* we refuse to accept anything short of the Ultimate as *de-finite*. Man is a self-transcending being. In the cognitive realm perceptions refuse to stay isolated and drive us to more comprehensive knowledge, where general statements, laws and theories include and surpass single facts. In the realm of moral conduct, partially glimpsed values with competing claims impel us to search for ultimate meaning and purpose. The religious man "accepts" reality, but he never accepts it at *face value*.

Five fundamental experiences basic to the religious understanding of life are change, dependence, order, value and imperfection.[7]

(1) The fact of *change*, although sometimes neglected because that which is "real" is taken to be permanent and enduring, is ubiquitous. But change means something much more radical than difference, it means creation and destruction. Through memory and discrimination we can compare past and present experiences, and become aware of the appearance of the new and the disappearance of the old. The daily appearance of novelty confronts us with the problem of primordial Creation in an acute form. Anything that *begins* to exist confronts us with three alternatives: (a) We can dismiss the problem of where it came from as scientifically meaningless and limit ourselves to acceptance of change and attempts to discover the laws which describe and predict it. (b) We can accept God as the source of reality,

whose creative activity is manifested in the origin and the sustenance of the world. The religious attitudes engendered by the awareness of change include a sense of mystery in the face of the inexhaustible character of reality, an expectancy based on the possibilities of the truly new and surprising, and the humility which comes with awareness of our limitations in the face of the mystery.

(2) The consciousness of *dependence* is the awareness that our life and our resources for growth and development are not of our own creation, but a gift. This points to the causal factor in existence and, more generally, to the relatedness of all beings. It poses the basic question: What are the sources of being? The unearned gift of life is seen in Jewish faith as a sign of God's goodness and mercy. Man's stubborn assertion of his individual or group self-sufficiency is seen by biblical faith as the root of idolatry and arrogance. The sense of dependence leads to thankfulness, generosity, confidence and humility, as well as fear and awe. The realization that "He is God, He has made us, and not we ourselves"[8] assures us that "to Him we belong," of being accountable to God and of being sheltered and protected in His loving care.

(3) The experience of *order* reflects the fact that reality is not chaotic, but exhibits pattern, regularity and determinate structure. Order circumscribes the realm of the possible; even the new and unexpected happens within a framework of pattern and regularity. In biblical wisdom literature, the determinate structure and regularity of nature is a confirmation of God's beneficence and wisdom. The regularity of nature is closely related to this design and purpose.[9] In Rabbinic literature the pre-existent Torah, which is equated with wisdom, serves as the blueprint for the orderly structure of the world to be created. (*Gen. R., Proem.*)

The experience of order not only underlies the theological concept of divine wisdom but is closely connected with the structure and the consequences of human conduct as realized in the moral order. Law, whether ritual or moral, establishes modes of behavior, and by limiting possibilities creates a pattern which can be handed down, learned and imitated, thus preserving values and living up to expectations.

The relationship between order and pattern on the one hand and novelty and spontaneity on the other is of fundamental importance for analysis of reality, for Jewish theology, religious life and observance.[10] The experience of order in natural phenomena gives rise to the confident expectation of the intelligibility of future events in terms of observed precedents. The order of man's duties toward God and fellow man is disclosed in the *mitzvot*, gives the Jew the assurance that, no matter how fallible and incomplete man's acts are, his efforts to fulfill God's will are not left entirely to his whims or intuitions, but can be discerned through the pattern of halakhic precepts and principles.

(4) Many people tend to denigrate *value* experiences as "subjective" and hence not valid, since they depend on the relativities of time, culture and society. Yet in morals and in science and art, values are pervasive not merely as personal decision but as reflections of objective structures and qualities that affect the valuer. Man does not invent values but finds or discovers them. In science, the "truth-value" of an idea depends on its congruence with the established body of science. In art, the esthetic value of a work is a function of many factors among which subject-matter, form and substance merge in a dynamic vision of the artist's encounter with the world. In human conduct, "moral value" represents a congruence between the potentialities of the agent, the lure of the overarching aims issuing from the divine source of meanings, and the adaptation of means to ends in the given situation.

Values do not, of course, "prove" God any more than facts do. But seen from the standpoint of Jewish faith, they affirm the goodness and justice of God and the obligatory character of divine guidance for the achievement of the good. Creation, Revelation and Redemption—the three great concepts of our faith—speak meaningfully to the religious consciousness since they address themselves to universal experiences of value. The biblical account of Creation has as its refrain the words "And God saw that it was good," and its climax in the statement that it was *very good*. The central message of Revelation is expressed in the law of love (Deut. 6:5) and the exhortation of *imitatio Dei* (Lev. 19:2). The relevance of this injunction for the grounding of ethics in the divine identity was singled out by the Rabbis, who found it indicated in Deut. 32:4 that "all His ways are justice."[11] The ideal of Redemption is anticipated whenever men join together to give praise and thanks in common song: "O give thanks to the Lord, for *He is good*, for His steadfast love endures forever."[12]

The religious attitudes engendered by the experience of value include a sense of loyalty, a vivid apprehension of aims worth striving for, and a sensitivity to the potentialities of life.

(5) The sense of *imperfection* begins in the general recognition that things are almost always less than what they might be.

Confronted with any state of affairs we can (and often do) envisage a better, more perfect one. Janus-like, imperfection points in two directions. It reflects the omnipresence of limitation, finiteness and partial failure in every situation, and it gazes equally at improvement, progress, evolution and a still unrealized perfection. If man were a godlike being he would not be imperfect; if he were an animal like all the others he would not be *aware* of his shortcomings. The sense of imperfection, then, is a manifestation of man's place as a rope stretched between the realm of "perfect" repetitive processes and the far shore of ever new, more ideal achievements and adventures. It is in the sense of imperfection that the possibility of scientific progress and social and moral advance are grounded.

Within the religious consciousness of Israel the sense of imperfection points to two aspects of reality. The inexhaustibility of existence, the ever-stirring surplus and richness of being, beyond any of its apprehended embodiments, prepares the Jew to accept God as the inexhaustible source of all which infinitely transcends His manifestations and works. It is in the awareness of imperfection that man is awakened to his kinship to the divine. The lure of higher values, aims and perfections prepares the Jew to accept God as an ever-active demand to surpass oneself and to reshape reality in the light of absolute standards of truth, goodness, beauty and justice which, though never finally attained or even clearly perceived, make possible whatever achievements fall to one's lot. Prophetic criticism in the name of the eternal God challenges every limited claim at final validity and drives man beyond all possible situations in the light of the divine and unconditional demand.

❐ A Program for Instruction in Theology

Teaching about God in a full and well-planned Jewish educational system must avoid the strait jacket of catechistic simplicity on the one hand, and the noncommittal looseness of a historical tour (where chronological succession is substituted for true tracing of the history of ideas) on the other.

As pointed out previously, the varied approaches of different periods and minds must be presented in all their richness, lest the student be led to believe that any one approach or doctrine "covers" the topic and that he can now label God in a final and satisfactory manner. And only by extracting from the underlying terms and categories the various "theologies" will the student acquire the conceptual tools to sort out, clarify—and thus to understand—the discipline of theology.

But before these complex and ambitious goals can be attempted in religious schools, a solid groundwork of teaching will have to be laid.

We can begin teaching about God by making use of two kinds of material. We can cull passages from world literature dealing with God, and we can start with passages from our own tradition. Each method presents unique opportunities and drawbacks. Our aim at this stage is not to present theologically formulated statements about God and His nature, but rather to present the experience of sensible and sensitive people who have testified to the presence and reality of God in their lives.

The advantages of drawing on a wide range of world literature are obvious; religious experience is not presented as the possession of the narrow specialist, but as something that belongs to mankind. The poets of the ages, the playwrights and novelists, the biographers and story-tellers can contribute to a broadening of experience, a deepening of sensitivity and the dislocation of normal consciousness, which enables us to perceive new things as well as to see old and familiar ones in a new perspective.

Yet the danger of this method is real. Even the most lyrical expression of direct and universal experience is usually framed in terms which reflect the theological convictions of its author T. S. Eliot's *Choruses from the Rock* (especially sec. III) echo Ezekiel's accents as faithfully as Bialik, but the teacher who selects these pieces must also be attuned to the underlying Christian doctrines which are often inextricably commingled with the universal message.

A scholar who combines literary taste, deep Jewish commitment, and a nose for "strange" theologies, should prepare an anthology of this kind. The anthology need not shun expressions of view which differ from Judaism, *as long as they are clearly recognizable as such*. What is to be avoided is unrecognized smuggling in of strange *teraphim* under the cover of a harmless looking camel-saddle.

Wordsworth's quasi-pantheistic poems ought to be required reading: they illuminate a way of sensing the presence of the Divine through nature, which is important, although in Judaism it is balanced and countered by the equally important experience of the transcendent voice of demand and command. Rilke's poem on beholding an archaic torso of Apollo may be more valuable than all the drivel served up as "poetry" in many American books for Jewish children. And Holderlin's inimitable lines

> *Nah ist*
> *Und schwer zu fassen der Gott.*
> *Wo aber Gefahr ist, wächst,*
> *Das Rettende auch,*

are too true and important to be withheld from mature students, although they are the opening lines of "Patmos"—a poem with a Christian theme.

This kind of reading can achieve something that was taken for granted in almost every culture prior to our technological age, but that can no longer be taken for granted as part of our normal consciousness. I shall indicate it by a quotation from Bradley who, incidentally, was not even a theist:

> All of us, I presume, more or less, are led beyond the region of ordinary facts. Some in one way and some in others, we seem to touch and have communion with what is beyond the visible world. In various manners we find something higher, which both supports and humbles, both chastens and transports us. And with certain persons, the intellectual effort to understand the universe is a principal way of experiencing the Deity. No one, probably, who has not felt this, however differently he might describe it, has ever cared much for metaphysics.[13]

☐ Jewish Material

A much more significant method of teaching theology is to present material to the student from Jewish classical sources—although I suspect that the initiation ought not be systematic. Rather, the younger pupil ought to encounter statements about God as they arise in his ordinary classes in Bible, prayer, holidays, etc. These chance encounters can then be used to generate discussion in which the idea of God is explored.

This approach prepares the way for a subsequent more systematic study of representative texts dealing with the God idea. Although the vastness of the material (and the inaccessibility of much of it to anyone but the specialist) makes it impossible to deal with more than a limited number of texts, I believe that a "reader" on the idea of God in Judaism, containing a judicious selection of texts exemplifying different insights, emphases, symbolisms and conceptual methods, should be developed.[14] Such an anthology would explore some of the contributions which each period of Jewish history has made to the understanding of God and His relation to man, and would introduce the student to mutually incompatible approaches to the concept of God, within the tradition of Jewish thought and faith.

The study of these representative texts will lead to the clarification of basic concepts and categories. Sometimes these basic terms can be extracted from the text itself; at other times modern conceptual tools will have to be used. When they are, we must be sure that connotations which do not apply to the original meaning of the text are not surreptitiously introduced (e.g., the Greek concept of perfection and changeless indifference, as applied to the anthropopathic God-idea of the Bible).

The God of the Bible who is passionately concerned with His creatures, who acts as Creator, Revealer of the Torah, and Redeemer of His people will be understood (not just "known"), as the drama of the divine-human encounter is made the basis for an elucidation of biblical theology.[15]

The thought-world of Talmud and Midrash will have to be analyzed in terms of the polarities of *halakhah* and *agadah*, by an examination of the epithets applied to God and His attributes (*midat ha-rahamim, midat ha-din,* etc.) as shown in Dr. Max Kadushin's works. Abraham Heschel's studies of the consistently developed theological systems of Rabbi Akiva and Rabbi Yishmael will have a revolutionary impact on our understanding of Rabbinic theology.

The empiricist *fideism* of Judah Ha-levi and the intellectualism of Maimonides' *Guide* will have to be represented as well as the kabbalistic doctrines of the *Zohar*, Lurianic mysticism and Hasidism. And study of such representative modern Jewish thinkers as Buber, Rosenzweig, Kaplan and Heschel will enable the student to understand the God-concepts of these men as their answer to the challenges of modern times, as well as their contribution toward achievement of a more adequate understanding of the traditional God-idea through the conceptual tools of modern philosophy.

☐ Analysis and Classification

Important as it is to examine a representative selection of texts, to extract their basic terms and to understand their propositions, it is not enough. It is necessary also to compare and juxtapose the different theologies, to find out their logical and existential compatibilities and incompatibilities, the differences in their thought and their way of saying things.

Such a dialectical examination of each system would include attempts to translate the propositions and postulates of one system into the philosophical key of the other, and "experiments" to test whether partial truths or truth-claims of one approach can be made compatible or complementary to partial truths of another.

Despite the difficulty of such dialectical examination, some idea of the character of different theologies and of what they can achieve is necessary in the curriculum. Otherwise the student is left with a hodge-podge of alternative doctrines, rather than a sense of the inevitably ongoing character of the divine science.

We can also impose a certain order upon the variety of God-ideas, a typology, such as the one I shall briefly indicate now. (The scheme used here makes no claim to exclusive validity or eminence. It is merely presented as an example in classification.) The various approaches to God can be classified as belonging to one of three types, of which the extremes are the *ontological* and the *moral* type of faith.[16]

In the *ontological, sacramental* or *cosmological* type of faith, the Holy is felt as present. God, the source of holiness, manifests Himself in reality and hence the world, its structures and all beings reflect and manifest the divine. In biblical terminology we can say that *kevod hashem* (the glory of the Lord) stands for this manifestation. Thus, what *is* conveys the sacred provenance of its source. Holiness is here and now; God manifests Himself in nature and history. This type of faith tends to be *conservative* and accepting of things as they are, since reality reflects the divine.

In the *moral* or *utopian* type of faith, the Holy is not experienced as that which *is*, but rather as that which *ought to be*. God is manifested in the demand, the command, the call to change reality and to hallow it, or in biblical terminology, *devar hashem* (the word of the Lord). This results in God summoning the prophets to convey His demands, and in His revelation of the Torah through whose commandments reality is perfected. This type of faith tends to be *revolutionary*, and critical of the status quo.

Every theological statement in the religious literature of Israel and of all other religions (and secularized pseudo-religions) can be related to one of these two types of faith. We face reality with reverence and feel piety toward the sources of our being, acknowledging the sacred ground of all that exists; or we look for holiness and the divine beyond the here and now, in the fulfillment of the divine promise and the partnership of God and Israel in making the Kingdom a reality by responding to the divine command.

Although no actual religion ever displays either of these two types in a pure form, we can generally state which tendency is dominant in any theological system. In secularized versions of theology (nationalism or socialism), sacramental faith glorifies the status quo and justifies existing injustices and inequalities, while utopian faith condemns all existing institutions and exists only in expectation of the coming revolution which will bring the secular equivalent of the messianic age.[17]

The third type of theology combines elements of the other two types in a polar tension. For lack of a better name I shall call it the *quasi-mystical* type.[18]

As man looks within his own depths, he becomes aware that he is rooted in something greater than his own individual self. Although we are part of this greater reality, we also experience ourselves as free and responsible agents. Although we *are* like all other creatures, we are aware that we *ought* to be different. Man is the only being who is aware of what he is and at the same time knows that he faces the demand to change and make himself over in the light of divine demands and ethical norms. We realize that in our own soul *that which is* and *that which ought to be* meet and merge. We can sense the holiness of God as manifested in reality, yet we are driven to be dissatisfied with that which is, because we also feel the holiness of that which ought to be, but is not yet.

The quasi-mystical tension between our own independence and our rootedness in God is always in danger of moving toward one of two poles. (1) The man who experiences only the divine reality and loses his individuality, succumbs to the complete mysticism of Hindu faith in which the self is negated and dissolved in the Godhead. (2) The man who experiences only his individuality makes himself divine, because he thinks that what is called God is only embodied in man. As Feuerbach put it: *theology* (discourse about God) becomes *anthropology* (discourse about man).

The quasi-mystical approach of Judaism tries to avoid both these extremes. It is difficult to maintain a balance between sensing the goodness of reality, and judging it by the ideals of the eternal demand. In the words of R. Simhah Bunam of Przysucha, a hasidic master, every man should have two pockets, in each of which he ought to carry a slip of paper to be taken out and reread as the need arises. One was to contain the biblical verse: "I am but dust and ashes" (Gen. 18:27); the other was to bear the affirmation from the Mishnah: "For my sake was the world created" (*Sanhedrin* 4.5).

❒ Implications for Education

In discussing the concept of God one may tend to forget that if God were nothing but a concept He would hardly deserve to be discussed. The religious person is acutely aware of the distinction between our changing ideas and fluctuating formulations of God, and the object of faith (which from the standpoint of the believer is the *Subject* of reality) whom our ideas can never adequately define or describe. Hence religious education cannot be limited to the conveying of theological information. Swimming instruction which provided only theory without actually getting the student to swim in water would be useless. Ethical education which turned out pupils who "knew" ethics but did not develop an instinct for decent conduct, would be a failure. Similarly, religious education must culminate in religious action and experience.

The relationship between theology and action, between religious knowledge and practice is one of mutual interdependence. Knowledge of God stimulates man to do His will; and only by actively doing His will can the knowledge of God be gained. In religion, knowledge cannot be acquired by study alone. Some of the central statements of faith do not disclose their meanings to the student who tries to analyze them objectively. It is only by acting out the pattern of practices prescribed by religion that one can slowly grasp what was meant by those statements. By *doing* we gain insight and intellectual illumination and through study our actions gain meaning and relevance. The Rabbis thought that the words "We shall do and we shall hear" (Ex. 24:7) revealed the "angelic" insight that only through doing can understanding be obtained.[19]

Acting religiously, fulfilling *mitzvot,* has a two-fold function in terms of man's relationship to God: (1) The religious act may represent one's attempt to approach God, to present oneself before Him and to gain an awareness of His reality. (2) Religious observance—whether "ceremonial" or "moral"—represents one's reaction or response to the experience of God's reality. For it is of the essence of God-awareness that it evokes a sense of *responsibility.* He who has been addressed, he who has heard the demand, cannot but respond.

These two functions of observance are not mutually exclusive. Very often they reinforce one another. A person prays to attain a sense of God's presence out of the despair of emptiness and the absence of the Divine. And the same person will pray again, once the despair and emptiness are gone.

The implications of these observations for the theory and practice of Jewish education are clear. If study and observance are mutually complementary, then we cannot plan them in isolation. We shall have to explore how *mitzvot* can be made more meaningful to students at different age levels. And we shall have to investigate how differences in the teaching about God affect the students' attitudes toward other aspects of life and their over behavior pattern.[20]

If we accept that religious actions are either human attempts to approach God or human responses to the experience of the Divine, some important consequences for education result. We will have to conclude that mere study or action without the accompaniment of the appropriate feelings will not evoke the sense of the divine-human confrontation which is at the basis of all genuine faith.

Judaism can not be reduced to a form of knowledge conveyed through doctrines and symbols, nor is it solely an emotional experience or a system of ethical behavior. It is a total relationship between man and God, in which neither intellect nor action nor emotion are thwarted. The god of the philosophers is a necessary condition of reality; the God of religion is a transforming agent. The sense of humility and courage, the vivid experience of divine judgment and love, and the sense of the reality of the spirit, are qualities which may reward those who heed the call: "Seek you My face!" (Ps. 27:8).

NOTES

1. The term "theology" is commonly applied to the broad subject of religious doctrines dealing with "God and related matters." In this essay it is employed in the more limited sense of discourse dealing with the idea of God.
2. E. A. Aubrey, "Naturalism and Religious Thought," *Journal of Philosophy*, Vol. 48, No. 3, p. 76.
3. A. N. Whitehead, *Religion in the Making*, p. 15.
4. A. J. Heschel, *Between God and Man*, p. 35.
5. Quoted in the name of R. Meir in *Teshuvot haRambam*, ed. Freimann, p. 312.
6. The term was coined by Paul Tillich, *Systematic Theology*, Vol. I, pp. 59–66; Vol. II, pp. 13–16; *The Protestant Era*, Ch. VI. Cf. Heschel, *God in Search of Man*, Ch. I.
7. H. J. Paton, *The Modern Predicament*, New York: Collier Books, 1962, p. 70.
8. See Philip H. Phenix, *Intelligible Religion*, New York, 1954, pp. 29–92.
9. Psalm 100:3.
10. Cf. Ps. 104:24, Job 28:25, Ps. 148:15, Jer. 31:34, 35.
11. For the centrality of these polar concepts in Abraham Heschel's philosophy of religion, see my introductory essay in *Between God and Man*, Free Press-Macmillan paperback edition.
12. See also, Deut. 8:6, 10:12, 11:22, 19:9, 26:17, 28:9, 30:16.
13. The intepretation of "good" as a key word of Creation and Redemption is found in Franz Rosenzweig, *Der Stern der Erlösung*, II, pp. 82–87, 185–186.
14. F. H. Bradley, *Appearance and Reality*, 1893, p. 5.

15. A first step toward such a source book is the collection of texts (in Hebrew) on God as Creator in Jewish thought, which I have compiled for the use of my students.

16. For simplicity's sake I have assumed the existence of an entity called "biblical theology," although the biblical scholar may well object and point out differences in various parts of biblical literature.

17. In the initial bifurcation of types, I follow Tillich. Cf. his *Dynamics of Faith*, where a full and lucid presentation of this typology is given in chapter 4.

18. Cf. K. Mannheim, *Ideology and Utopia*, translated by L. Wirth and E. Shils, London and New York, 1952.

19. Cf. my remarks in *Between God and Man*, p. 16.

20. Cf. T.B. *Shabbat* 88a, Leviticus Rabbah 1:1. See also Heschel's views on the "leap of action" in *Between God and Man*, Ch. 12.

21. Henry Cohen's article, "The Idea of God in Jewish Education," *Judaism*, Vol. 12, No. 2 (Spring 1963), is an excellent contribution to this subject.